Making the Table

VEGETARIAN RECIPES TO NOURISH COMMUNITY

Noah Rubin-Blose

Durham, NC
2021

Printed in the so-called United States of America on occupied Indigenous land

Illustrations by Assata Goff
Front cover illustration by Saif Wideman
Cover design and book design by Saif Wideman

Making the Table: Vegetarian Recipes to Nourish Community
www.makingthetable.com

Library of Congress Control Number: 2021904699

Dedicated to beloved community
working towards collective liberation.
May you be nourished, my people.

Happy Cooking!
Noah

Table of Contents

CHAPTER TWO:
SALADS &
VEGGIE SIDES

CHAPTER THREE:
SOUPS

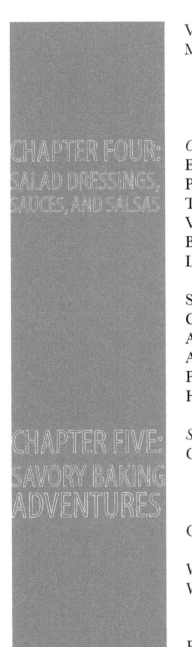

CHAPTER FOUR: SALAD DRESSINGS, SAUCES, AND SALSAS

CHAPTER FIVE: SAVORY BAKING ADVENTURES

Making the Table
SOME THOUGHTS ON NOURISHMENT

"Seeking a now that can breed
futures
like bread in our children's mouths
so their dreams will not reflect
the death of ours"
-AUDRE LORDE, "A Litany for Survival"[1]

Every recipe carries stories. Perhaps someone passed the recipe into our hands, or we remember how and why we first cooked and shared the dish. The food itself holds the story of how its ingredients came to be on this continent, and why our ancestors prepared these foods. Sometimes, these histories have to be uncovered. Often, the full-body experience of cooking also carries these memories—the smells and sounds of a bubbling soup, the sizzling of a stir-fry in the pan, the crackling of roasted nuts just after you take them out of the oven, the sweet aroma of baking bread. The sensory joys of preparing the dishes I love brings me a feeling of home, comfort, and connection.

When we share these dishes, we are sharing pieces of who we are. We literally take this food with its stories into ourselves, and together, the food and the stories nourish our bodies and our spirits. We honor where we come from and share that with other people. In my fifteen years of planning and cooking meals for groups of people as a chef and caterer, I would ask myself, *How do I nourish these human beings in a way that honors who they are, where they come from, and what home is for them; and that honors who I am, where I come from, and what home is for me? How do I cook in a way that honors the healing magic of plants, what they have to offer, and all that has gone into them getting to my kitchen so that I can toss them into a pot, filling the air with their pungency?* Whether I am baking up loaves of bread to share at a march on the North Carolina legislature or serving a meal for a youth organizing program, carrying these questions inside me makes cooking into an expansive practice of love.

Cooking has much to teach us about the liberated future that we are seeking, and how to care for each other as we build it. Food is a gathering place for people, and a reminder that we need each other. One of my favorite things over the years has been cooking for groups on retreat. It is always an honor to nourish people, supporting them over the course of several days as they celebrate an important moment, strategize and plan towards freedom, engage in meditation and insight-building, learn how to be youth leaders, or create an audio piece. Participants often come into the kitchen to relax into its sounds and smells, take a break from their work, and chat about their lives.

We build relationships through food: both the acts of cooking and eating together are places we can encounter and learn from each other. When we are putting love into the food and being present with the stories carried by the steam rising from the pot, we create a sacred space in which our communities can be nourished.

In the kitchen, we are facilitating nourishment. Facilitation is a spiritual practice of being present: Black feminist poet Alexis Pauline Gumbs talks about facilitation as being present to your own brilliance, the people in the room, the purpose that brings you together, and ancestors present and trying to come through.[2] Cooking is an opportunity to be present to the reality of the interdependence that makes the food possible. I can be present to the Divine spark of creativity moving through me; the women and other people who made it possible for me to be here cooking this particular dish; the patterns of migration, slavery, oppression, and resistance that moved seeds with people across continents; the sacredness that makes plants grow from earth, water, and sunlight—and the hard work put in by so many to grow them, often in unjust conditions. And I am present to the purpose and work of the people I am feeding, the work that the food will nourish them to do. The kitchen can be a lab where we learn how to be present to this multiplicity, and carry the lessons out into the whole world with us.

Food is art that is made to be impermanent. Cooking builds our capacity for change, teaching us to appreciate sensory details without holding on. After all, even the most gorgeous food is intended to be eaten, and it must be released into the world in order to nourish. The joy of the moment of generosity, sharing a fresh-baked tray of cookies and watching them disappear, is worth all the work that went into it. In our movements, we say that the role of teachers and organizers is always to "work ourselves out of a job." This is a letting go—we do the work, and it was never only for us, so we pass it along down the line. Time in the kitchen can help us practice the same.

Food is a reminder to feel satisfied and unsatisfied at the same time. Cooking and creating ritual around food can help us to practice being grateful for the simple flavors of a fresh carrot, beans cooked with onions, or a loaf of bread. This is radical within a society where capitalism, colonialism, and white supremacy teach us never to be satisfied, to always consume more and more. But Torah instructs us, "V'achalta, v'savata, u'verachta," you shall eat, you shall be satisfied, and you shall bless.[3] It is because of this text that, in Jewish tradition, some say the Birkat HaMazon after a meal is complete. Whether or not we say this extended blessing, we are invited to appreciate how miraculous food is, and the sensations of satisfaction moving through our bodies as the food digests.

And yet, we are often fundamentally unsatisfied. For those of us who long for a world where everyone can have access to daily bread and food of celebration, the bread we may have on our own table is not enough. We can express gratitude for what we have, while simultaneously remaining committed and steadfast in our work towards collective liberation. We want every morsel to be like Audre Lorde's "bread in our children's mouths," nourishing us in the work of creating a just future for all. May this very meal be the sort of "now" that will make the future we dream of possible for all of us—and we will be satisfied with nothing less than liberation in our lifetime.

The kitchen is a place to learn how to collaborate and share power. In movements for racial and economic justice, an often-quoted saying is, "If you're not at the table, you're on the menu."[4] If we aren't allowed to make decisions about our lives, they'll be decided for us, by those in power who, too often, do not wish us well. We want a seat at the table to make those decisions, yet we usually show up to the table and find the agenda already set. What if we actually made the table together?

Sometimes, it is necessary and transformative to start from scratch in the kitchen, decide what we are going to make, experiment, and cook together before we set the table. Outside of the kitchen, I helped build Demilitarize! Durham2Palestine, a large coalition in Durham, NC organizing against state violence.[5] Coming together as coalition partners to discuss common ground and decide whether and how to collaborate was a powerful experience: by starting from scratch together, we could honor the gifts and wisdom that each coalition partner brought to the table and find ways to deeply support each other's ongoing work. The kitchen can be a place to practice the kind of deep collaboration that we need more of in the world.

Food carries stories, and one of the challenges of writing this book has been to honor the full lineage of these recipes—often so expansive that each one could fill many pages. Some recipes were given to me from a specific person; others were inspired by another recipe or even just the photograph of a dish, sparked by a conversation or a story, or adapted to accommodate a friend's food allergies. Many were a combination of several of these lineages, and their roots go beyond the individual recipe itself. They have been shaped by structures of oppression and histories of resilience. Each recipe here has been touched by so many ancestors who are and are not my own. And all of these recipes are possible only because of the bounty of the living land, air, sky, and water.

I hope that, in sharing these recipes with you, we can both honor all that makes this food possible. I hope that these recipes will take on new lives of nourishment in your kitchen, in your heart, and in the bellies of your loved ones. These recipes are for everyone—from the vegan to the vegetarian-curious. They are for you to make magic and gather people at your kitchen table or on a summer porch at twilight. They are for you to adapt and make your own, experiment with, or combine with your own ancestral recipes. They are for you to enjoy and share. Relax and put love into it.

Love,

Noah

July 2020 / Tammuz 5780
Homelands of the Occaneechi Band of the Saponi Nation, also known as Durham, NC

How this Book is Organized

This book is an on-paper chronicle of how I move through kitchens. It is a collection of recipes interspersed with tips, stories, and reflections.

Recipes

The recipes are organized into chapters based on the type of dish:

MAIN DISHES has hearty meals for dinner, lunch, and breakfast.

SALADS & VEGGIE SIDES includes one-vegetable dishes, tasty cold salads, and other seasonal favorites.

SOUPS includes both hot and cold soups.

SALAD DRESSINGS, SAUCES, & SALSAS has condiments you might serve as appetizers or use as ingredients for other recipes in the book.

SAVORY BAKING ADVENTURES includes favorite yeasted breads, biscuits, and more.

DESSERTS is an assortment of cakes, pies, cookies, and bars.

BEVERAGES includes a handful of simple teas and other refreshing drinks.

Each recipe includes a headnote, with suggestions about other dishes to make alongside that particular recipe, what to expect when you make it, and sometimes notes about its origin story.

For the most part, quantities of ingredients are given by volume, such as in cups. In some cases, both weight and volume are given. For recipes that originated in Bread Uprising Bakery—the cooperative credited in many of the baked goods recipes here—both weight and volume are given. Weight is the most accurate measurement for baking, so I have retained the original Bread Uprising measurements for those who wish to use a kitchen scale. Since many home cooks do not have a kitchen scale, I've also converted the recipes to volume.

Serving sizes given are an approximation: Main dish serving sizes account for a large portion anchoring a meal, usually paired with at least one side. Many of the sides could also work as main dishes, but you'll want to up the portion size if you're using them that way, and vice versa.

Stories

Each chapter begins with a short reflection inspired by the recipe that immediately follows it. These stories, musings, and lessons give meaning and life to the food, allowing me to share living recipes with you on the written page.

Allergy-Friendly Icons accompany each recipe to indicate recipes that are already accessible to people with a variety of food needs; and to indicate recipes that include alternative instructions to make the dish free from dairy, eggs, gluten, or nuts.

 Vegan: contains no eggs, dairy, or honey

 Gluten-free: contains no wheat or other glutenous grains

 Nut-free: contains no peanuts or tree nuts

 Can be made vegan

 Can be made gluten-free

 Can be made nut-free

Lazy Baker Method

This note provides an approximation of how I cook most of the time, and includes suggested modifications to reduce the number of bowls you have to wash, the number of times you have to change oven temperature, and so forth. The lazy baker notes are intended for cooks who are relatively comfortable in the kitchen. If you are the type of person who needs to follow a recipe exactly to make sure you don't leave anything out, or someone who often burns things in the kitchen, this section is for your entertainment only. You can read it and imagine me throwing vegetables into a bowl with reckless abandon, and then you can return to the main instructions and enjoy carefully measuring them out into a measuring cup.

Notes

The short sidebars included with many recipes contain modifications, additional serving suggestions, and advice about working with particular ingredients. Longer sidebars, included with a handful of the recipes and also noted in the table of contents, may outline an extra recipe that goes with the dish—like frosting for a cake—or give extended advice on a particular theme to help you in the kitchen—like how to cook in large quantities.

Assata Goff's beautiful illustrations decorate these pages both to demonstrate how to carry out particular methods and simply to impart the joy and beauty of the food.

Finally, a few appendices contain additional information. I've given Bread Uprising Bakery its own section (page 228) for those who would like to learn more about this transformative project. I close with appreciation for the many, many people who made this book possible (page 230).

In My Kitchen
TOOLS, INGREDIENTS, & TIPS

INGREDIENTS & SUBSTITUTIONS

Herbs & Pantry

Veggie broth cubes—I like to use these rather than liquid broth because they're cheaper, easier to store, and you can control how much liquid you add to the recipe. I find Rapunzel's low-sodium variety to be the tastiest. If you use one that's high in salt, be sure to reduce the salt in the recipe. My secret to using broth cubes is to chop them up before adding them to any dish—it helps them dissolve quickly and evenly. You can also substitute broth paste in a jar (1 cube = 2 teaspoons paste) or liquid broth (1 cube = 2 cups liquid broth; make sure to reduce the amount of water in the recipe by 2 cups).

Smoked paprika—This magical spice gives an amazing smoky flavor to food. I used to use bottled liquid smoke, which works fine, but smoked paprika is much tastier. Be careful not to buy the spicy kind, unless you like heat.

Ancho chili flakes—At some point, I stopped buying the chili powder blend available at supermarkets and started making my own chili powder from mild ancho chile peppers. It's infinitely more delicious. There are instructions for making ancho chili flakes on page 97. You can always substitute store-bought chili powder in place of the ancho chili flakes in these recipes, it just won't be as flavorful.

Fresh herbs—These are a staple in my kitchen. I feel strongly that parsley, cilantro, and dill have to be fresh: the dried versions just don't cut it. Basil is best fresh, but in recipes where it is going to be cooked, dry basil can easily replace it. Oregano is great either dry or fresh. To make sure that I have fresh dill around, when it's available in the summer I wash and dry a couple of bunches, and freeze them whole in a reusable, freezer-safe bag. When ready to use, make sure to chop the dill up while it is still frozen, and then return the rest of the bunch to the freezer to use later.

Fresh veggies—I almost always prefer fresh veggies to frozen or canned. The exception is in the winter, when it can be wonderful to eat veggies that were preserved at the peak of freshness in the summertime. All recipes in this book call for fresh vegetables unless otherwise specified, and I give substitutions when possible.

Ginger—Fresh and dried ginger root have different flavors, so it's best not to substitute one for the other. Store fresh ginger in the freezer in an airtight container. It's actually easier to slice when it's frozen. To use frozen ginger, remove it from the freezer five minutes before using it, then slice or grate. I rarely peel fresh ginger, but many people prefer to do so.

Golden flaxseed meal—Flaxseed meal is a great binder for vegan cooking and baking, and is often used as an egg replacer. When mixed with warm or hot water, it turns into a slimy goo that holds burgers or brownies together. I prefer golden flax because it has a milder flavor and color than brown flax meal. Store it in the freezer to preserve freshness.

Nutritional yeast—Used sparingly, these magic vegan flakes give a cheesy flavor to almost any food they touch. Used in excess, their own flavor—and the fact that they are indeed not cheese—will come through. I love nutritional yeast for vegan cooking, and for putting on popcorn! Unlike baking yeast, nutritional yeast is no longer active, so it is safe to eat raw. It's also not the same as brewer's yeast, which has a different, stronger flavor. Nutritional yeast is high in protein, and is usually fortified with B vitamins, which are otherwise hard to come by in a vegan diet. Red Star and Bragg are the most common brands. Nutritional yeast is available in the bulk or packaged dry goods section at natural food stores and some supermarkets.

Onion—The recipes in this cookbook call for yellow onion unless otherwise specified, but in most cases you'd do fine with using white or red onion if you prefer them. White onion tends to be milder than yellow, and red onion is sweeter than both. I usually use yellow onion for cooking, and when I'm using raw onion in a recipe, it's almost always a white or red one. In any color, choose onions that are firm and smell mild when the peel is on, which indicates freshness. If the onion smells earthy or sour, or if any strong odor wafts through its skin, it may be rotting.

Garlic—I always use fresh garlic, not garlic paste or chopped garlic preserved in a jar—these have lost a lot of their fresh flavor. To save time, I often buy peeled garlic, available in many grocery stores refrigerated near the produce section. Latin American and Asian supermarkets usually have the best quality peeled garlic.

Eggs—Eggs in the recipes in this book are large, though eggs from pastured chickens will vary slightly in size. If the recipe calls for more than one egg and you have eggs of different sizes, pair a smaller egg with a larger one for balance.

Egg substitutes—Eggs play many different roles: they leaven, bind, create a custard, or do a combination of all of these. Depending on the role the egg is playing in a specific recipe, different substitutions are required. Bean water, or aquafaba (page 189), can do all of these things but is challenging to work with. Extra baking powder can be a great leavener. Flax and chia seed meals work great as binders, but yield dense baked goods. Potato, corn, and tapioca starch can create a custard and work as a binder as well. Chickpea flour and almond flour can sometimes work as excellent binders, too. Many vegan recipes in this book include one or more of these egg substitutes, which I chose by experimenting until I found the best option for that particular recipe.

Vegan "Meat" Products

Tofu and tempeh—Usually made from soy, these vegan staples are delicious and readily available in many grocery stores. Sometimes they work as a meat substitute. They are ideal if you are seeking a vegan protein that does not resemble meat.

•••

Soy patties— Found in the freezer section in plastic packaging in natural foods stores, soy patties tend to be made by local companies and distributed regionally. Delight Foods in Morrisville, NC makes the very best soy patties. Often made from a combination of soy and wheat, these patties are incredibly flavorful with a just-chewy-enough texture that holds up well in any recipe. This brand may not be available depending on where you live, so check your local co-op or Asian supermarket for a similar product.

•••

Chick'n or mock chicken—Sometimes sold refrigerated and sometimes frozen, there are a variety of brands that make mock chicken, and some are significantly better than others. For the recipes in this book that call for mock chicken or soy patties, any that is minimally seasoned and not breaded should work. Tofurky's "lightly seasoned" Slow Roasted Chick'n works well; it is sold as large shreds and tastes a bit like a veggie hotdog.

•••

Textured vegetable protein (TVP)—Also called carne de soya, these soy-based crumbles are affordable and versatile as a beef or chicken substitute. Rehydrate TVP in hot water before adding it to a dish. TVP doesn't have a strong flavor, so it needs to be used in a recipe where it will be well seasoned. Because TVP comes broken up into small pieces, it must be used in dishes where that is an acceptable texture. It's sold in natural food stores and at many Latin American markets.

•••

Mock ground beef—Any brand will do for most recipes. Mock ground beef usually contains both soy and wheat. Note that while it works great as an ingredient, it will not hold together as a hamburger. TVP is a cheaper alternative with less flavor but a similar texture, so you can often substitute TVP for mock ground beef.

•••

Seitan—Made from vital wheat gluten, seitan works well as a beef substitute. It is usually expensive and can have a tough texture, so I don't use it often. But, for a fun cooking project, try making your own!

Oils & Shortenings

Extra-virgin (unrefined) olive oil—Mild, yet flavorful and versatile, this is my oil of choice for cooking. I don't usually use it for baking because of its olive-y flavor. It is liquid at room temperature, but will turn slushy in the fridge—for salad dressings made with olive oil, it helps to bring the dressing to room temperature before serving so it will pour easily.

•••

Canola oil—Works great in many cakes. You can substitute soybean, sunflower, or another mild oil for canola oil. Note that the product labeled "vegetable oil" in stores is usually soybean oil.

Palm shortening—Solid at room temperature, refined white palm shortening works wonders in vegan frostings because it is fairly flavorless. Crisco, made from a blend of oils, also works as a substitute, but is usually hydrogenated. The palm oil industry is incredibly destructive, so you may want to avoid palm shortening.

Vegan butter—Earth Balance is a great vegan option as a spread for bread. I find that the original and soy-free varieties work wonderfully in vegan baking, but ocassionally impart an unpleasant flavor. If you can find it in sticks rather than in a tub, that can help greatly with accurate measuring. If you are using whipped Earth Balance and measuring by volume, you'll want to add a little extra to make up for the air that is taking up space in the butter. Other brands of vegan butter are less widely available, but should work just fine.

Coconut oil—Solid in the winter and liquid in the summer, virgin unrefined coconut oil is tasty and full of medicinal properties. I use it as a butter substitute in select recipes where I have found that it is tastier than vegan butter. But coconut oil does have different properties than butter, so substitutions won't always work. I also use it when I want to give a dish its distinctive nutty, creamy flavor.

Cooking oil spray—This is a convenience, not a necessity. It is helpful for quickly coating the top of muffin pans to make sure vegan muffin tops don't stick to the pan, and for spraying over vegan patties like crab cakes or burgers to coat them with oil with minimal effort. If you don't want to use spray-on oil, just put some canola oil in a little bowl and gently brush it on with a pastry brush.

A Note About Salt

If you are used to a low-sodium diet or just prefer less salt in your food, you'll want to reduce the salt by a half-teaspoon in most recipes. Additionally, the amount of salt a recipe needs depends on the size of the salt granules you are using. I prefer to cook with fine sea salt, which is just slightly coarser than table salt. You can use the same quantity of sea or table salt in these recipes with no problem. If you are using a large flaked salt like kosher salt, you may want to add in a little extra.

COOKING DRY BEANS

Buying dry beans and cooking them yourself requires more time and planning than opening a can, but it's much cheaper! I like to cook up a big pot of beans, then store the beans in the freezer in 2- or 4-cup containers to pull out later for easy use in recipes. If a recipe calls for beans cooked with lots of flavor (white beans with roasted tomatoes, page 40, or black beans with cumin and poblanos, page 46), it's ideal to start with dry beans so the flavors can absorb during the cooking process. For most other recipes, it's really just a matter of preference whether you use dry or canned beans.

To cook dry beans, place them in a large pot and cover generously with water. Soak overnight, or for at least 8 hours.

Drain soaked beans in a colander, and rinse until the water runs clear. Place drained beans back in the pot, and cover with 3 times the volume of water as the quantity of beans you originally soaked. That is, if you soaked 2 cups of dry chickpeas, cover with 6 cups of water. If it doesn't seem like enough water, you can always add more—it generally won't affect the recipe. Add salt to taste—about 1 tsp of salt per 2 cups of dry beans will yield tasty, low-sodium beans. Bring beans to a boil on medium high, then turn heat to low and simmer until soft, about 1 to 1 ½ hours. Acidic foods like lemon juice or tomatoes slow the cooking time of beans, so avoid adding any of these flavorings until the beans are close to fully cooked.

EQUIPMENT

Dough scraper—This tiny little tool is amazing! Also called a bowl scraper, it is a thin, hard piece of plastic 3-5 inches wide that will work wonders for scraping bread or biscuit dough out of bowls and off of countertops. It also works great to cut dough into pieces, and to clean encrusted food off the bottom of burnt pots.

Immersion blender—I love this hand-held blender for blending soups right in the pot. Review "The Immersion Blender is Your Friend" (page 115) for tips and safety information.

Blender—This old favorite is especially helpful for making salad dressings and sauces. In most cases, you can use either a food processor or an immersion blender for these things, but a blender works better than any other blending device for liquids.

Food processor—A simple food processor will chop veggies or herbs into fine pieces in seconds. Fancier ones will grate for you, saving lots of time if you're making a big cabbage and carrot slaw (page 109). It's indispensable for making thick purées like cashew cheese (page 21) or hummus (page 82). I recommend at least an 8-cup food processor if you want to use it to purée; if you only have a smaller one, you can purée in batches.

Spice grinder—The same as an electric coffee grinder, but without the lingering flavor of coffee. This works best for grinding small, dry things. In many cases, if you prefer to go analog, you can use a mortar and pestle instead. But, I love an electric spice grinder for its quick and smooth performance.

Knife sharpener—Dull knives are much more likely to slip unexpectedly in the kitchen, cutting you instead of the tomato whose skin they bounced off of. If you are a knife-sharpening novice, I recommend finding, and using regularly, a two-stage knife sharpener—either mechanical or electric—rather than trying to use a sharpening stone. This can easily be shared between friends!

Rolling pin—So helpful for rolling cookie dough, biscuits, and more. As someone who used an empty glass bottle as a rolling pin for years, I can say that having an actual pin makes a big difference. But a bottle will do in a pinch!

Pastry brush—I recommend having and using this to brush baking pans with oil, and brush the surface of baked goods. If you don't have one, you can use two fingers or a piece of folded-up paper towel.

Pastry blender—It is possible to use two butter knives to cut vegan butter into biscuit dough, but I much prefer a pastry blender, as it's quicker, easier, and yields a more even dough. Any variety will do.

Sheet pan—Also called a baking sheet, this large pan is great for for baking cookies, roasting veggies, or pretty much anything else you might want to cook in the oven. Sheet pans come in standard sizes for restaurant kitchens, but can be purchased for use at home, too. I prefer a sheet pan rather than a cookie sheet because it has sides that keep whatever I'm cooking from falling off the pan—but really, any type of baking pan will work for most recipes.

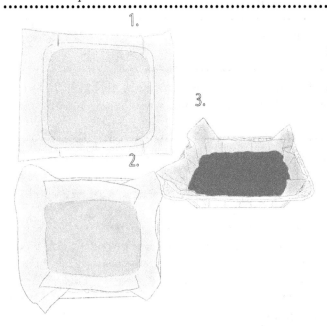

Parchment paper—I never used to use this, but now I live by it for lining almost any pan. It makes cleanup a breeze, and allows you to pull baked goods out of a pan without breaking them apart. This is especially important for vegan baking, where baked goods are more likely to stick and crumble. To line a cake pan, cut a circle of parchment to fit the bottom and place it in the bottom of the pan. Then oil the sides of the pan. The circle of paper will help the cake pop out easily. To line a rectangular pan, as for brownies, cut one slit in each corner of the paper perpendicular to the paper's edge, and fold (refer to illustration). Silicone baking mats work great in place of parchment paper, but you cannot substitute wax paper or deli paper. If you don't have parchment paper, you can either oil (for cookies) or oil and lightly flour (for cakes and bars) a pan, and hope for the best!

Stand mixer—These are quite expensive, but if you are going to make a lot of frosting or whip a lot of aquafaba (page 189), it might be worth it. We got through five years of Bread Uprising using simple hand-held electric mixers, but I also developed chronic pain in my forearms. When I've been lucky enough to be in a space that has a stand mixer, it's so helpful. Many stand mixers have several attachments, allowing you to mix up cookie dough, whip frosting, and even knead bread dough.

From my kitchen to yours, I share these tips in hopes that they can help you to be more confident in the kitchen. The most important thing is to develop and use your intuition in the kitchen. Cooking is art, so trust that you can move through the creative chaos. Let's get into it!

NOTE ON USING THE OVEN: Some of the recipes in this book say to preheat the oven to one temperature and then immediately turn it down, because a lot of heat is lost by opening the oven door. If you want a 400°F degree oven, heating the oven to 425°F will ensure that it is actually at 400°F after you open it to put your batter or roast in to bake. I have found that this also prevents the oven from having to come on quite so much during baking, which makes for a more even bake. Whether or not a recipe calls for immediately turning down the oven, try not to let the oven door hang open excessively, letting all of that heat out. Just find a friend to open it for you so you can pop that pan into it right away.

NOTE ON CHOPPING VEGETABLES: As a lazy baker, I usually chop up vegetables regardless of the specific way a recipe says to chop them. But, sometimes it's nice to chop different ingredients into particular shapes and sizes, giving a lovely texture and appearance to your finished dish. It's also really helpful to chop all of one ingredient into same-sized pieces for uniform cooking.

Chapter One:
MAIN DISHES

Ancestors in the Kitchen
PARSLEY MAKES FOOD SWEET

"A life in the struggle has taught me to trust in the wisdom of those who came before me; to honor the recipes that have been handed down."

-BETSY RAASCH-GILMAN[6]

When my grandmother died a few years ago, I inherited the bright orange, floral-patterned pot that she always used to cook vegetarian chili. She'd make it the day we were coming into town and have it on the stove ready to offer to my parents, my brother, and me the minute we got out of the car from our long drive.

She started making the chili after I became a vegetarian at age ten. Every kind of meat was a staple in her cooking, so she must have searched her files to find a recipe for me; this was an act of love and care. The recipe was clipped from a magazine, and included V8 as a key ingredient. The first time I made chili, in college, I tried to re-create her recipe without having a copy of it. I whipped up a big pot based on the familiar flavors, and a friend who tried it exclaimed, "This tastes like minestrone!" I realized then that who we are comes out in our food in ways we may not even know. My grandmother, known as Concetta Quagliarello, Connie Blose, and Aunt Tina, was born in Italy, and she had passed a lineage of minestrone-chili on to me without either of us realizing it.

When I was a child, we would drive up to visit my grandparents twice a year, spending close to a week at their house in central New Jersey. We came all the way from North Carolina, much farther than most of my aunts, uncles, and cousins had to travel, and it always felt like a special trip. Everyone else in the family came over for daytime visits while we were there, so we got to help grandma and grandpa prepare feasts for everyone.

Both my grandparents loved food, each in their own way. My grandpa, James Blose, grew up in a rural Pennsylvania Dutch family, and was a fantastic gardener. He grew lots of tomatoes, peppers, and herbs, which he would freeze and use to make a chunky tomato sauce in the middle of winter. He had his own space in the basement of their house, with a woodworking shop on one side and a door leading out to the garden on the other. In between was the washing machine, a big sink, and a pole that was probably holding up the whole house. I would sit on the washing machine, laundry hanging up around me and bare feet dangling down, and watch him prepare ingredients for tomato sauce in the utility sink.

Grandma took that sauce and made lasagna, and meatballs smothered in more sauce to go with it. She never skimped on the ricotta when we were around, always using whole-milk cheese, the not-so-secret ingredient to her rich and delicious lasagna. If I was lucky, I would come upstairs and get to help out with this, too. It was my dad's job to prepare the antipasto platter—slices of fresh bread, cheese, olives, and pepperoni to snack on before the meal.

When my cousins arrived, we would go back down to the basement and chase each other in circles around the pole. The concrete floor was painted with a thick layer of gray paint, and the feeling under my feet was cool, solid, and comfortably cratered. Then, we would run back upstairs to eat steaming plates full of home.

Food is a way we carry culture and pass it to each other. Writing about the multiple displacements that her Iraqi Jewish family experienced, Dr. Ella Shohat theorizes, "food, it seems to me, has become a kind of portable home, where the repetitive, almost ritualistic act of cooking the same old dishes becomes a way of maintaining a sense of stability in an unstable situation… an act of defiant survival in the face of a disappearing cultural geography."[7] While my grandmother's immigration story is not one of displacement fueled by colonialism, she also used food to create a sense of home and identity across time and space. After emigrating from Italy with her parents and sisters, she spent most of her childhood in Brooklyn, New York. Her mother was also an amazing cook, and my dad remembers homemade manicotti at family gatherings when he was a child. Grandma carried the family recipes forward with her own flair. She always used to remind me to add parsley to any dish, because it makes the food sweeter. In passing her kitchen wisdom to me, she has allowed me to connect with my heritage, towards a cultural survival beyond assimilation.

Grandma spent much of her life raising her five children. As a religious Catholic woman, she cared deeply about people and wanted to make things right in the world. She was so focused on caring for others that I sometimes wondered whether she was able to find joy for herself. Once, I took a solo trip to visit her after my grandfather's death. We looked through an old photo album, and she smiled wide at a handful of snapshots—a day at the beach with friends as a young woman. "I guess I really had a wild time," she said, a twinkle in her eye. She wouldn't elaborate, but the joy of the memory was contagious. When I make her recipes, I can feel that spark of joy coming through the food.

Grandma's Lasagna

These recipes are adapted from my grandmother's amazing lasagna, a staple of family get-togethers. She never added vegetables, but her lasagna was packed with parsley that gave it lovely flecks of green. Serve it with vegan meatballs, green beans, and garlic bread—or just with a salad. These recipes make a lot, enough for eight people if served with little else, or twelve if served with several side dishes.

> **NOTE:**
> Both these lasagne freeze well. I like to chill leftover lasagna in the refrigerator until it is firm, then cut it into neat slices and wrap them in foil or plastic. I freeze the slices to pack for lunches, reheating each leftover slice in the oven or microwave before eating. To freeze a whole lasagna, bake it first, then cool in the fridge, cover, and place the whole pan in the freezer. It can be thawed and then reheated whole or by the slice.

Traditional Lasagna

Makes: 8 large or 12 medium servings
Prep time: 45 minutes, including boiling the noodles
Bake time: 45-50 minutes
Rest time: 15 minutes

+

Grandma was born in Italy and raised in Brooklyn, NY, and always made her lasagna full of rich, whole-milk ricotta. While working under chef and baker Roberta Campani at La Gemma Fine Italian Pastries in Wilmington, NC, I learned that in Northern Italy, lasagna is not made with ricotta at all, but instead is usually filled with meat or veggies and a creamy béchamel sauce. While my grandma's version is probably closer to what most people in the United States are used to, there are actually many different types of lasagna. I've stayed true to the way I learned it, and share it with you in hopes that you will find it as comforting, filling, and delicious as I do.

For the filling:
2 pounds whole milk ricotta, softened for 30 minutes
4 eggs
¾ cup + 2 Tbsp grated parmesan cheese, divided
½ cup fresh parsely, chopped
1 ½ tsp salt
For assembly:
12 lasagna noodles (about ⅔ of a 1 pound box of noodles)
1 Tbsp canola oil
3 ½ cups tomato sauce (page 139)
¾ pound mozzarella, grated

1. Boil the noodles according to package directions, erring on the side of al dente (slightly chewy), and rinse. For no-boil instructions, review lazy baker method on page 19.

2. Mix up your filling: Place the ricotta in a bowl and mash it gently with a large wooden spoon to soften. Add the eggs one by one. I like to crack all 4 eggs into different corners of the bowl and then mix them in one at a time. Once it is well mixed, add ¾ cup of the parmesan, plus the chopped parsely and salt, and mix well.

3. Layer your lasagna: Preheat oven to 375° F. Have the sauce, noodles, mozzarella, and ricotta ready. Follow instructions for how to layer (below).

4. Bake the lasagna: Cover the lasagna in foil, tenting the foil slightly so that it does not touch the top of the lasagna. Place in the upper half of the oven and bake for 45-50 minutes, uncovering after 30 minutes. When you uncover the lasagna, sprinkle the reserved mozzarella and the 2 Tbsp parmesan cheese over the top, then return it to the oven. It's done when it doesn't jiggle when you gently shake the pan back and forth — this means the ricotta egg custard has set.

5. Remove from oven and let sit at room temperature for 10-15 minutes to allow the custard to firm up so it will slice more cleanly. Then cut and serve.

HOW TO LAYER

The beauty of lasagna is its distinct layers of noodles, ricotta or cashew cheese, sauce, and melty cheese. Layering the ingredients in that exact order works best, because spreading sauce over ricotta is much easier than spreading ricotta over sauce. Follow these steps to success:

1. Coat the bottom of a 9x13 pan with 1 Tbsp canola oil, and then with ½ cup tomato sauce.

2. Lay down the first layer of 4 noodles. If the noodles are boiled, they will overlap slightly. There may be some space on either end of the pan.

3. Gently spread ½ of the ricotta or cashew mixture over the noodles. It's helpful to place the mixture in 5 or 6 dollops around the pan and then spread it out with a spoon or spatula.

4. Spread ⅓ of the remaining tomato sauce (about 1 cup) in a thin layer on top of the ricotta mixture.

5. Sprinkle ⅓ of the mozzarella evenly over the tomato sauce (omit for vegan version).

6. Add a second layer of 4 noodles, repeating steps 2-5 to add another layer of ricotta or cashew mixture, sauce, and mozzarella.

7. Add a third layer of noodles and the remaining sauce. Reserve the remaining mozzarella and the 2 Tbsp of dairy or vegan parmesan/cheddar to add partway through baking.

Vegan Lasagna with Cashew & Tofu "Ricotta"

The combination of cashews and crumbled tofu makes for a delightful ricotta texture with a creamy and nutty flavor. I'm proud of how much this vegan recipe reminds me of my grandma's original, and it's always a hit. Make sure to allow enough time to soak and prepare the cashew cheese (page 21).

Makes: 8 large or 12 medium servings
Press time for tofu: 30 minutes
Prep time: 45 minutes, including boiling the noodles
Bake time: 45-50 minutes

For the filling:
1 recipe cashew cheese (page 21)
1 pound firm or extra firm tofu
½ cup fresh parsley, chopped
1 Tbsp nutritional yeast
½ tsp salt

For assembly:
12 lasagna noodles (about ⅔ of a 1-pound box of noodles)
1 Tbsp canola oil
3 ½ cups tomato sauce (page 139)
½ cup shredded vegan cheese (Follow Your Heart vegan parmesan or Daiya vegan cheddar, optional)

1. Prepare cashew cheese (page 21).

2. Drain, rinse, and press the tofu. To press, place tofu between two cutting boards and place a 2-pound object on top, such as a couple of metal cans (don't use a breakable object!). Let press for about 30 minutes. You can also set a towel underneath to absorb the water that will drain out of the tofu.

3. Boil the noodles according to package directions, erring on the side of al dente (slightly chewy). Drain and rinse. For no-boil instructions, review lazy baker method below.

4. Mix up your filling: Place the cashew cheese in a large bowl. Take the tofu and crumble it into the bowl, smooshing it between your fingers. Sprinkle chopped parsley over the tofu mixture. Add the nutritional yeast and salt to the bowl, and mix it all up.

5. Layer your lasagna: Preheat oven to 375°F. Have the sauce, noodles, vegan shredded cheese (if using), and cashew-tofu ricotta ready. Follow instructions for how to layer (page 17).

6. Bake the lasagna: Place in the upper half of the oven for 45-50 minutes. After 30 minutes, sprinkle the grated vegan cheese over the top of the lasagna, then return to oven to continue baking.

7. Serve immediately, or let rest for 5-10 minutes before cutting.

LAZY BAKER METHOD

Boiling noodles means an extra 20 minutes, an extra dirty pot, and the risk of either burnt fingers or ripped noodles when you try to pry them apart; on the other hand, it allows you a little less bake time, and makes spreading the ricotta or cashew mixture a little easier. To make a no-boil lasagna, use plenty of sauce, especially on the bottom and top of the lasagna. Noodles marketed as no-boil have been pre-cooked and then dehydrated so they'll cook nicely in the oven. They are also more expensive than regular noodles, and come in smaller packages. I have had good luck baking many regular lasagna noodles without boiling them, just adding extra sauce so they have plenty of moisture to absorb in the oven. Here are modifications for the above recipes using the no-boil method:

1. Use a total of 4 ½ cups sauce in the recipe, rather than 3 ½ cups. Use 1 cup sauce on the bottom of the pan instead of ½ cup. Use 1 ½ cup sauce on top of the lasagna, to make sure the top of the lasagna is completely smothered in sauce, with not a bit of noodle showing.

2. Press each layer of noodles gently into the layer of sauce below it to ensure the entire bottom of the noodle is in contact with the sauce.

3. Cover and bake for 1 full hour. Cover with foil for the first 50 minutes, until the noodles are soft, then bake uncovered for the remaining 10 minutes. Sprinkle the last bit of cheese over the lasagna when you uncover it—this ensures that the cheese will stick to the lasagna, not to the foil.

Vegan Meatballs

Growing up, my grandma's Italian meatballs were a treat at family gatherings. The recipe was one of the first I ever had in my childhood recipe box, written out on an index card. For years I worked to come up with a vegan version. Here it is, meant to be lovingly smothered in tomato sauce (page 139) and served alongside lasagna (pages 16 or 18), with spaghetti, or on some nice crusty bread as a meatball sub.

Makes: About 24 meatballs, 6-8 servings
Prep time: 15 minutes
Cook time: 35 minutes

1 cup cooked kidney beans
1 pound extra firm tofu
¼ packed cup fresh parsley
2 Tbsp tamari or soy sauce
2 Tbsp olive oil, divided
¼ cup tomato paste
2 Tbsp nutritional yeast
1 ½ tsp dried oregano
1 ½ tsp garlic powder
½ tsp salt
½ tsp ground black pepper
1 cup vital wheat gluten
¼ tsp baking soda
½ tsp lemon juice
1 recipe tomato sauce (page 139)

1. Preheat oven to 425°F.

2. Drain the kidney beans and place in a large bowl. Use a wooden spoon to mash them up a little bit.

3. Rinse the tofu and pat dry with a towel. Crumble it into the bowl on top of the beans by smooshing it between your fingers. Aim for fairly small pieces, no larger than a pea.

4. Finely chop the parsley, and add it to the tofu mixture along with the soy sauce, 1 Tbsp of the olive oil, and the tomato paste. Sprinkle with nutritional yeast, oregano, garlic powder, salt, and pepper. Stir until well mixed, making sure to break up any clumps of tomato paste.

5. Spread the mixture out in the bowl. Sprinkle the vital wheat gluten over it, then the baking soda. Mix well. A dough should start to form that is soft and clings together in large clumps.

6. Grease a large sheet pan with the remaining 1 Tbsp olive oil.

7. Sprinkle lemon juice over the meatball mixture and mix well. Knead the mixture in the bowl about 10 times—it should still be soft, but come together into one mass of dough. Break off walnut-sized pieces, roll into balls, and place them on the sheet pan about 1 inch apart from each other.

8. Place pan in the oven, and immediately turn oven down to 400°F. Bake for about 35 minutes, until the outsides of the meatballs are reddish brown and the insides have cooked through.

9. To serve as a main or side dish, place in a bowl or casserole dish and smother with tomato sauce. Serve hot.

NOTE: To make ahead, or to store leftover meatballs in the fridge, store them separate from the tomato sauce and add the sauce just before serving. This will ensure that the meatballs hold their shape, as they can break down if submerged in sauce overnight.

NOTE: Vital wheat gluten is the portion of the wheat grain that makes bread hold together, because it is stretchy and high in protein. Too much of it will make a dish very tough, but just the right amount will help it hold its shape and give a nice, spongy texture. Vital wheat gluten can be found at most natural food stores.

VARIATION: To make this recipe as a vegan burger, form the dough into patties ¼ to ½ inch thick. These are best cooked on the stovetop in an oiled skillet. Cook on medium-low heat for about 5 minutes on each side, until browned and crispy on the outside. Alternatively, bake burgers in a 400°F oven for 25 minutes. Before baking, be sure to coat them generously with oil by spraying the tops with cooking oil spray or by placing each patty on the oiled pan and then flipping it over. Serve on whole wheat rolls (page 162) with your favorite condiments and a side of spiced sweet potatoes (page 96).

CASHEW CHEESE

I love to use this as the main ingredient in vegan lasagna or as a pizza topping. It also works as a dip for raw veggies or crackers!

Makes: About 2 cups
Soak time: 2 hours or overnight
Prep time: 10 minutes

2 cups raw cashew pieces
1 medium clove garlic
2 Tbsp olive oil
1 tsp lemon juice
½ tsp salt
½ tsp pepper
¼ cup nutritional yeast

1. Soak the cashews: Place cashews in a large measuring cup or small bowl and cover with warm tap water. Let soak for at least 2 hours. If soaking overnight, use cold water instead of warm.

2. Drain the cashews, reserving ½ cup of the liquid and discarding the rest. Place the cashews and the reserved ½ cup liquid in a food processor with the garlic, olive oil, lemon juice, salt, and pepper. Process on high for about 5 minutes, pausing halfway through to scrape down the sides of the food processor to ensure it all gets well blended. It should be a smooth, thick paste—if not, continue to blend on high until smooth.

3. Add the nutritional yeast and blend until well mixed.

4. Use immediately, or store in the refrigerator in a tightly closed container for up to 4 days.

VEGANIZING FAMILY RECIPES

One of the beautiful things about family recipes—whether they are from your family of origin, a mentor, or a dear friend—is that they are yours. You are in the lineage of this recipe, and it belongs to a "we" that you are part of.[8] This is really my definition of what makes a family recipe: a recipe that moves in you and is of you, in a collective way.

I became vegetarian and then vegan, because eating animals gave me a deep sense of spiritual injustice. So, for the most part, I didn't miss meat and cheese. But there were certain recipes that I longed for, because of the feeling of home and the sense of memory, comfort, and belonging they gave me. For dishes like these, I have taken great care to create a vegan version that can bring that sense of "we" with it.

When I veganize a recipe, I like to replicate the smell, taste, and texture of the original dish as much as possible. Smell is a sense that I most acutely associate with memory, so I especially want to match the smells of the dish. My grandma's meatball recipe smells like beef, tomato, and parsley, and what I love the most is its tangy, earthy sweetness. I don't want my version to smell like beef, but I do want it to have that tangy sweetness to remind me of my grandmother's kitchen.

Adapting a recipe usually takes multiple tries, and I don't like to make the same dish over and over again—it is often a special dish that I want to be able to make for a particular time of year. I will experiment over a period of many months, making sure to keep clear notes about what I did each time. Before I begin, I like to make sure I have a copy of the recipe I'm going to try on a piece of paper—either printed out or handwritten. Depending on how much I get into the zone of cooking, I'll make notes as I'm going, or once the dish is in the oven. Then, I'll add a few more notes after I've tasted it, including ideas about what to try for next time.

Depending on how the recipe was passed down, it might just be a list of the ingredients. If that's the case and it's a recipe I'm unfamiliar with, it can help to talk to someone who has made this type of dish before. If that's not possible, I might research several recipes for the same dish, making a few notes on the different methods used and deciding what I want to try out.

If you are modifying several different aspects of a recipe, you can research different options for meat, egg, and dairy substitutes—you may need to try different combinations to find one that feels right for that particular dish. If you're trying recipe modification for the first time and your first version doesn't work out, try changing just one thing at a time. That way, you'll be able to witness the impact (or not) that each particular change has on the final dish. If you are experimenting, it's a good idea to make a half-recipe so that you don't waste ingredients—just in case the test dish doesn't quite work out the way you had hoped.

Allow the essence of the recipe to find its way into the dish. These recipes are ours and they have always adapted while moving through generations: they do not have to be unchanging in order to feel authentic.

When I inherited my grandmother's cooking pot, along with it, I got the spoon my great-grandmother used to make her tomato sauce. I can feel the magic in that spoon, the edges worn down from so much stirring, the hands of these women working their craft to nourish their families. But my grandmother herself used the sauce my grandpa made from his garden-grown veggies more often than she made her mother's recipe. She honored recipes passed down to her while honoring her present life and love, the home she was making with her garden-growing, rural Pennsylvania-born husband. I, too, do this within my lineage. When I work on a recipe and think of my grandmother—matching memory to smell, to love, and to my own life and commitments—I am walking in her footsteps. When I create a vegan version of a recipe with these intentions, I feel her presence as I cook, eat, and share it.

VEGAN ANTIPASTO

Antipasto, meaning "before the pasta" in Italian, is an appetizer platter. It typically includes several kinds of preserved meats, cheeses, marinated vegetables, and bread. In my grandparents' house, this was usually pepperoni, purchased as a whole sausage and cut into chunks; mozzarella cheese; green olives; roasted red peppers; and a sliced loaf of Italian bread, a soft, crusty white bread much like a baguette. We prepared antipasto and set it out on the table the day all my aunts, uncles, and cousins came over, so everyone could snack before the main meal. I love the flavors in antipasto, and since I became vegetarian at age ten and vegan at age sixteen, I didn't get to fully enjoy it. Here are some suggestions for putting together a great vegan antipasto platter:

Veggie sausage—I like to use either Field Roast or Tofurky vegan Italian sausage. Take one sausage and slice it diagonally into about 12 ovals. Heat a few tablespoons of olive oil in a cast iron pan, and cook the sausage pieces for about 10 minutes, flipping them over halfway through. They should have a light brown crispiness on both sides. I prefer veggie sausage over pre-sliced vegan pepperoni because you can serve it in thick chunks rather than thin slices.

Marinated vegetables—I like to include olives, either a nice country mix or a combination of Kalamata and green olives. Sometimes I include artichoke hearts or quick-pickled carrots and onion (page 69).

Roasted red peppers—You can purchase these in a jar from most supermarkets. They should be either whole or in large pieces, and you can cut them into large strips for the platter. Or, place a whole pepper on a pan in a 400°F oven for about 30 minutes, turning it once halfway through. Once out of the oven, place it in a paper or plastic bag to steam for 10 minutes. Then, the skin should peel off easily.

Cut the pepper open, remove the seeds and stem, and slice the remaining roasted red pepper into about 10 pieces for your antipasto platter.

Vegan cheese—I've found Miyoko's Creamery fresh mozzarella to be especially tasty. For a less traditional but homemade option, make some cashew cheese (page 21) and place it in a small bowl on your platter for dipping with bread.

Bread—I like to use a white bread with a nice crust, like a sliced baguette. If purchasing a baguette from a supermarket, place it in a 350°F oven for 5-10 minutes before slicing, to give it a nice crispy crust and soft, warm insides. For a softer crust, you can bake white rolls (page 164), slice into several pieces, and serve.

Arrange the antipasto items in small bowls or artful piles on a platter, and garnish with fresh parsley.

This hearty antipasto serves about 6 people.

Almond-Crusted Tofu Cutlets

These cutlets are flavorful and delightfully nutty. I love to make this recipe at home, alternately with tofu or tempeh. With tofu, the effect is a bit like a fish stick, and with tempeh, more like a chicken nugget. If you don't like this comparison, you'll probably still like these tasty morsels. This recipe is inspired by a very non-vegan recipe in Esalen Cookbook.[9]

Makes: 4 servings of 3 cutlets each
Press time for tofu: 30 minutes
Prep time: 30 minutes
Cook time: 25-30 minutes

For the marinade:
1 pound extra firm tofu
½ cup lemon juice
¼ cup olive oil
1 tsp ground cumin seed
½ tsp garlic powder
½ tsp salt
½ tsp ground black pepper

For the breading:
1 cup raw almonds
½ tsp whole fennel seed
1 cup cornmeal
1 Tbsp dried oregano
1 Tbsp dried sage
1 Tbsp paprika
1 tsp dried basil
1 tsp dried thyme
1 tsp garlic powder
1 tsp salt
1 tsp ground black pepper
½ cup nutritional yeast

To cook:
1 tsp olive oil

1. Drain, rinse, and press the tofu. To press, place tofu between two cutting boards and place a 2-pound object on top, such as a couple of metal cans (don't use a breakable object!). Let press for about 30 minutes. You can also set a towel underneath to absorb the water that will drain out of the tofu. Pressing the tofu will help it absorb the flavors from the marinade, and will help the breading stick.

2. Prepare the marinade: Place all ingredients in a wide, shallow dish and whisk together. Slice the block of tofu crossways into 12 large cutlets, each about ¼ inch thick. Add them to the marinade, turning each piece to coat. Let marinate for about 20 minutes.

3. Meanwhile, prepare the breading: In a food processor, pulse the almonds and fennel seeds about 15 times until finely chopped. Add the cornmeal and all remaining breading ingredients. Run the food processor until you have an even breading without noticeable chunks of almond, about 2 minutes depending on the food processor. If you don't have a food processor, you can crush the nuts by placing them inside a bag and rolling over it with a rolling pin. Then mix everything up in a bowl—or, use almond meal and ground fennel seed so nothing needs to be crushed.

4. Preheat oven to 400°F. Coat a sheet pan with the 1 tsp olive oil. Place the breading mix in a wide, shallow bowl.

5. Dredge the marinated tofu cutlets in the breading mix: With one hand, pick up a single piece of tofu, dipping it into the marinade to make sure it is coated on both sides. Then place the piece of tofu in the breading mix. Use your dry hand to coat the cutlet in breading mix and then place it on the pan. Using one hand for the wet and one hand for the dry will help keep your hands significantly cleaner and avoid wasting ingredients. Repeat this process until all the cutlets are breaded.

6. Place in the upper half of the oven and bake for 15-20 minutes, then use a spatula to flip the cutlets over. Bake for 10 minutes more. There should be some light browning on all sides of the cutlets.

VARIATION:

To make tempeh cutlets, use 1 pound of tempeh (usually two 8-ounce packages) in place of the tofu. Cut each block crossways into 3 almost-square pieces. Then, turn each piece on its side and slice in half to create thin filets (refer to illustration on page 27). There is no need to press the tempeh—just marinate as directed in step 2.

NOTE:

You should have a little bit of breading left over. It keeps well for months in an airtight container in the freezer, and also works great as a topping for baked mac and cheese (page 52).

LAZY BAKER METHOD:

Place marinade ingredients in a gallon freezer bag, seal, and slosh around to mix. Gently add the cutlets, reseal, and marinate them right in the bag. Be careful not to break the pieces of tofu.

Honey Tempeh with Peaches

This has become a staple in my summer kitchen, because NC peaches are just so sumptuous. The honey combined with the juices from the fruit give the tempeh a sweet golden glaze, and the thyme and basil add tasty flavor.

Makes: 4 large servings or 6 small ones
Prep time: 10 minutes
Marinate time: 30 minutes
Cook time: 35 minutes

For the tempeh:
1 pound tempeh (two 8-ounce packages)
3 medium cloves garlic
½ medium onion
1 ½ pounds fresh peaches (about 4 medium-large)

For the marinade:
¼ cup olive oil
¼ cup honey (can substitute agave nectar)
¼ cup lemon juice
1 tsp dried thyme leaves
1 tsp dried basil leaves
1 tsp salt
½ tsp garlic powder
½ tsp ground black pepper

To cook and serve:
1 Tbsp olive oil
10 large fresh basil leaves

1. Slice the tempeh into thin, large cutlets: each 8-ounce block of tempeh should yield 6 cutlets. Cut each block crossways into 3 almost-square pieces. You can cut through the packaging, then easily pop each piece out of the plastic. Turn each piece on its side and slice in half to create thin filets (refer to illustration on next page). Place cutlets in a gallon freezer bag.

2. Finely mince the garlic and slice the onion into thin ribbons. Wash the peaches, cut into halves and quarters, and remove the pits. You can leave the skins on, as they'll soften while baking. Set aside.

3. Mix up the marinade: place all marinade ingredients in a measuring cup or jar. Whisk or shake until well combined. Pour marinade into bag with tempeh, and agitate gently to ensure all tempeh pieces are well-coated. Add garlic, onion, and peaches to bag, and let all marinate for at least 30 minutes.

4. Preheat oven to 375°F. Oil a large sheet pan with the 1 Tbsp olive oil. Place marinated tempeh in a single layer on the pan, with the marinated onions, garlic, and peaches on top. Reserve any excess marinade for the next step.

5. Bake the tempeh for 20 minutes. Move the tempeh from the oven and use a spatula to flip the pieces over. Remove peaches and onions to one side of the pan. Spoon excess marinade over each tempeh cutlet. Return pan to oven and bake for another 15 minutes, or until tempeh is browned on top.

6. Tear fresh basil leaves into a few pieces each. Remove tempeh and peaches from oven and toss with basil leaves. Serve warm.

HOW TO CUT THE TEMPEH:

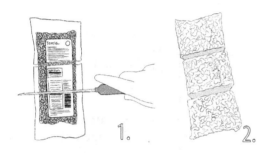

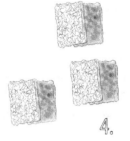

1. 2. 3. 4.

VARIATION:

When fresh peaches are not plentiful, I like to make this dish with fresh or frozen mangoes. Mangoes tend to be larger than peaches, so measure them by weight. Fresh mangoes will need to be peeled and cut into large slices.

NOTE:

This recipe is tastiest with ripe peaches that are sweet, a little juicy, and easy to slice into. If your peaches are crisp under-ripe, add a little extra honey for sweetness. If over-ripe, be aware that it may be difficult to cut them into neat pieces. They will be delicious, but you may not want to serve them to someone who you are trying to impress with your fancy plating preparation.

Jerk-Seasoned Tempeh

This is a recipe that evolved through collaboration. I first started making jerk chicken for groups at The Stone House *retreat center, inspired by a recipe in* The Sugar Reef Caribbean Cookbook.[10] *Then, I stopped making it, but my co-worker Miriam Biber started using the marinade to season black beans. I picked it back up as a marinade for tempeh. I love the depth of flavor that the combination of pepper, allspice, and thyme creates, and the long marination time is worth it! Jerk seasoning is typically very spicy, and this recipe offers options for different spice levels.*

Makes: 4 servings of 3 pieces each
Prep time: 15 minutes
Marinate time: 2 hours
Cook time: 20-25 minutes

For the marinade:
2 habanero peppers, ½ jalapeño pepper, or 3 ají dulce peppers (refer to note)
½ medium onion
2 cloves garlic
1 Tbsp tamari or soy sauce
2 Tbsp honey or brown sugar
¼ cup olive oil
¼ cup white vinegar
¼ cup lime juice
2 tsp ground allspice
2 tsp dried thyme leaves
1 tsp dried sage
½ tsp salt
½ tsp ground black pepper
¼ tsp ground nutmeg

For the tempeh:
1 pound tempeh (two 8-ounce packages)
1 Tbsp olive oil

1. Mixing up the marinade is easiest in a blender. Remove the seeds and stem from the pepper(s)and discard. Place pepper(s) in a blender. Peel the half onion and cut into quarters, and add to the blender. Peel the garlic cloves and add them whole along with all the remaining marinade ingredients. Blend on high for about 30 seconds, until all ingredients are puréed into a smooth sauce. (If you don't have a blender or food processor, finely mince the peppers, onion, and garlic. Then, place all marinade ingredients in a tightly-lidded mason jar and shake well.)

2. Slice the tempeh into thin, large cutlets: each 8-ounce block of tempeh should yield 6 cutlets. Cut each block crossways into 3 almost-square pieces. You can cut through the packaging, then easily pop each piece out of the plastic. Turn each piece on its side and slice in half to create thin filets (refer to illustration on page 27).

3. Marinate the tempeh: Place marinade in a narrow pan or heavy-duty gallon freezer bag. Arrange tempeh in the bag so that all pieces are submerged.

4. Let the tempeh marinate for at least 2 hours. If all the pieces won't completely submerge in the marinade, rotate them after 1 hour for even coverage. Two hours is plenty of time, but if you prefer, you can let it marinate overnight in the fridge.

5. Preheat oven to 400°F. Oil a sheet pan with the 1 Tbsp olive oil. Remove tempeh from marinade and place it in a single layer on the pan, leaving as much spices and sauce on top of each piece of tempeh as possible, without it being soupy and drippy. I like to place each piece on the pan, then use a butter knife or my fingers to spread a little marinade on top of each piece. Reserve any extra marinade for the next step.

6. Bake for 15 minutes. Use a spatula to flip the pieces over—they may stick to the pan a little— and spread a little more of the leftover marinade over the pieces. Bake for 5-10 minutes more, then remove them from the pan. The cutlets should be dark but not burnt, with crispy edges.

7. Serve warm. Jerk-seasoned tempeh is great served over cilantro rice (page 50) with peach tomato salsa (page 148), or with a simple garnish of diced fresh tomatoes and scallions.

NOTE:

You can choose your preferred heat level for the marinade. Jerk seasoning is usually made very hot, with handfuls of habanero peppers. Habaneros are incredibly spicy and also carry a unique flavor. Using 2 habaneros will make a marinade that is hot, but not overwhelming. For a very mild version, I love to use ají dulce peppers, which look and taste like a habanero pepper, without any heat. In NC, it's usually possible to find these beauties fresh at a farmers market in the summertime, or in the produce aisle at a Latin American supermarket. For a medium spice level and a slightly different flavor, use a jalapeño or your favorite variety of chile. If using habaneros, I suggest wearing gloves when removing the seeds, because they can burn your skin.

BBQ Tofu

The barbecue sauce for this dish is sweet, tangy, and tomato-y, all at the same time. With all respect to the long-standing feud between Eastern NC vinegar-based and Piedmont tomato-based BBQ, this sauce is really more of a Kansas City-style sauce. In any case, it's great for a summertime dinner! The tofu cutlets are delicious on a sandwich, or served as a meal with potato salad (page 99) and cabbage and carrot slaw (page 109)—and you can use any extra sauce as a condiment.

Makes: 4 servings of 3 pieces each
Press time for tofu: 30 minutes
Prep time: 10 minutes
Marinate time: 30 minutes
Cook time: 30-35 minutes

For the tofu:
1 pound extra firm tofu
½ medium onion
1 Tbsp olive oil

For the sauce:
⅓ cup tomato paste (about half of a 6-ounce can)
¼ cup apple cider vinegar
¼ cup molasses
¼ cup honey (can substitute agave nectar or maple syrup)
2 Tbsp olive oil
2 Tbsp tamari or soy sauce
2 tsp smoked paprika
1 tsp garlic powder
1 tsp ground mustard
½ tsp ancho chili flakes (page 97, or substitute chili powder blend)
½ tsp ground black pepper
½ tsp salt (optional, to taste)

1. Drain, rinse, and press the tofu. To press, place tofu between two cutting boards and place a 2-pound object on top, such as a couple of metal cans (don't use a breakable object!). Let press for about 30 minutes. You can also set a towel underneath to absorb the water that will drain out of the tofu.

2. Meanwhile, place all sauce ingredients in a small bowl and whisk until smooth.

3. Dice the onion into small, ¼ inch pieces, and add to the sauce.

4. When the tofu has pressed, slice the block of tofu crossways into 12 large cutlets, each about ¼ inch thick.

5. Place half of the sauce in a narrow pan—an 8x8 baking pan works well. Dip each cutlet into the sauce, arrange so all pieces are generously coated, and cover with the rest of the sauce. Allow cutlets to marinate for at least 30 minutes.

6. Preheat oven to 375°F and oil a sheet pan with the 1 Tbsp olive oil. Place cutlets on the pan in a single layer, ensuring each is generously coated with sauce and onions.

7. Bake for 15 minutes. Use a spatula to flip the cutlets over and bake for 15 minutes more. The edges of the cutlets will begin to brown. Some burnt spots on the pan may appear where excess sauce has caramelized, but the tofu itself should not be burnt.

8. While the cutlets are baking, place the remaining sauce in the oven and bake for 15 minutes—you can use the same 8x8 inch baking pan in which the tofu marinated. Baking the sauce will cook the onions and you'll have a nice, thick sauce you can spoon over the tofu to serve.

9. Remove tofu from the pan and place on a serving platter. Spoon a little of the extra sauce over it, and serve hot.

NOTE:

Find ground mustard and smoked paprika in the spice aisle of well-stocked supermarkets. You can also substitute 1 Tbsp bottled mustard (Dijon or spicy brown) in place of the 1 tsp ground mustard, and 2 tsp liquid smoke plus 1 tsp sweet paprika in place of the smoked paprika.

LAZY BAKER METHOD:

Mix up the sauce in a blender, rather than whisking it.

Vegan Crab Cakes

I've always been skeptical of vegan seafood, because it's hard to get the texture right. The combination of shredded hearts of palm and crumbled tofu works well in these crab cakes, and the seaweed flakes give the cakes a nice ocean-y flavor. I developed this recipe several years ago for a community ceremony held by two dear friends.

Makes: About 15 patties (serves 6)
Prep time: 30 minutes
Chill time: 20 minutes
Cook time: 20-25 minutes

1 medium onion
2 large stalks celery
6 medium cloves garlic
2 Tbsp olive oil
2 14-ounce cans hearts of palm
8 ounces firm or extra firm tofu (half of a 1 pound block)
2 Tbsp fresh parsley
¼ cup vegan mayo
2 tsp bottled mustard (Dijon or spicy brown)
1 tsp apple cider vinegar
2 Tbsp Old Bay seasoning
1 Tbsp golden flaxseed meal
1 Tbsp dulse seaweed flakes (review note)
1 tsp sweet paprika
a few dashes ground black pepper
1 ½ cup panko (bread crumbs)
1 Tbsp canola oil (for pan)

1. Chop the onion and celery into a fine ¼ inch dice. Finely mince the garlic.

2. Heat the olive oil in a large pan on medium heat. Sauté the onion, celery, and garlic for about 5 minutes, until they begin to brown on the edges.

3. Meanwhile, drain the cans of hearts of palm, discarding the liquid. Take each piece of palm heart and separate the outer, fibrous part from the inner, softer portion. If the center portion of any of the hearts is so soft that it squishes easily between your fingers, break it up into pieces and place in a large bowl. Place the more fibrous parts in a food processor and pulse about 10 times, just until they break into strips that are about ½ to 1-inch long. Add these pieces to the bowl.

4. Drain and rinse the tofu, and crumble it into the bowl on top of the hearts of palm. Add the onion-celery-garlic mixture.

5. Finely chop the parsley and add it to the bowl.

6. Add the vegan mayo, mustard, vinegar, Old Bay seasoning, flaxseed meal, seaweed flakes, paprika, and black pepper. Mix well. The mixture should come together in a crumbly, textured dough.

7. Cover and chill in the refrigerator for 20 minutes.

8. Preheat oven to 400°F. Place ½ cup of the panko on a large plate. Oil a large sheet pan with the canola oil.

9. Scoop ¼ cup portions of the heart of palm mixture into your hands, rolling each into a ball and flattening into a patty about ½ inch thick and 3 inches in diameter. Lay out several patties on top of the panko, and sprinkle more panko on top. Pick up each patty and ensure each is generously coated in bread crumbs before placing it on the sheet pan. Repeat until you have formed all of the patties.

10. Bake at 400°F for 12 minutes. Use a spatula to carefully flip the patties over—they will be fragile—and cook for 10-12 minutes more. They should be golden brown and crispy on the outside.

11. Remove patties from oven and allow to cool on the pan for 10 minutes before serving. They should firm up as they cool.

12. Serve just a bit warm, with dipping sauce (below).

NOTE:

Dulse is a type of seaweed, so it gives these cakes their necessary ocean-y flavor. Find dulse seaweed flakes in the international section of your local food co-op or supermarket. While most seaweeds are green, dulse is red-brown in color, which lends a nice color to the cakes. If you can't find it, you can substitute most dried, pulverized seaweeds. And if you can only find seaweed in a large sheet, you can grind it yourself with a spice grinder.

DIPPING SAUCE

½ cup vegan mayo
1 Tbsp fresh dill, finely chopped
1 tsp lemon juice
¼ tsp agave nectar
1 tsp Old Bay seasoning
½ tsp garlic powder
½ tsp ground black pepper
⅛ tsp salt

Place all ingredients in a small bowl and whisk with a fork. Serve cold, with warm crab cakes.

Thai Red Curry

This warming, coconut-based curry is definitely a comfort food for me. It takes a bit of work to make, as you have to fry the tofu separately from cooking the curry, but it is just so tasty. The curry works well with a variety of veggies, and the recipe here has my favorite combination. In order to make sure the veggies come out perfectly cooked—with just a little crunch—it is essential to add different veggies at the appropriate time intervals. Sweet potatoes and onions are added first, because they take the longest to cook. You'll want to add the broccoli when the sweet potato is just barely under-cooked—if you add it too soon, you'll have soggy broccoli and crunchy sweet potato, and if you add it too late, you'll have overcooked sweet potato that falls apart. It may take a couple of tries to get the timing right, and that is okay—make some notes and keep trying! If you want to try other veggies, be mindful of how long they take to cook and plan accordingly. For example, root vegetables, like carrots, should be added just after the sweet potato, while quick-cooking veggies like green beans or mushrooms should be added with the broccoli. Serving this curry over rice is tasty, and you'll want to prepare the rice alongside the curry—the veggies will continue to cook as they sit in the hot coconut sauce, so you should serve it immediately once it is ready.

Makes: 4-6 large servings
Press time for tofu: 30 minutes
Prep time: 20 minutes
Cook time: 25 minutes

For the tofu:
1 pound firm or extra firm tofu
2 cups canola oil
¼ cup corn starch

For the curry:
1 large onion
2 medium cloves garlic
1-inch piece fresh ginger root
1 medium sweet potato (about ½ pound)
1 large bell pepper (green or red)
1 pound broccoli crowns (2-3 crowns)
2 Tbsp olive or coconut oil
1 4-ounce jar or can red curry paste
  (refer to note)
1 ½ 13.5-ounce cans full-fat coconut
  milk (about 2 ¼ cups)
¾ cup water
1 tsp salt

To serve:
juice of ½ lime
a handful of fresh cilantro (optional)

Prepare the tofu:

1. Drain, rinse, and press the tofu. To press, place tofu between two cutting boards and place a 2-pound object on top, such as a couple of metal cans (don't use a breakable object!). Let press for about 30 minutes. You can also set a towel underneath to absorb the water that will drain out of the tofu.

2. Cut the tofu into large, oblong chunks about ½ inch by ½ inch by 2 inches. This shape is called a rectangular prism!

3. Heat 2 cups of canola oil in a medium pot to about 375°F. If you don't have a thermometer, heat for about 5 minutes on high heat, until there's some movement in the oil. You can drop one piece of tofu in to test: if the oil sizzles and bubbles a lot when a piece of tofu is added, you're good to go.

4. Place cornstarch in a shallow bowl and dredge the tofu pieces in it, lightly coating them on all sides. If it seems like all the tofu pieces won't fit in the oil at one time, dredge and fry them in 2 batches. It is important to dredge each batch just before frying, because if they sit in the corn starch, the wet surface of the tofu will just dissolve the starch.

5. Carefully drop the pieces of tofu into the hot oil and fry them for about 15 minutes, until they are a light golden brown color. Use a tongs or a slotted spoon to flip pieces over halfway through frying so they fry evenly.

6. Place a couple of paper towels on a plate for draining the fried tofu.

7. Use a strainer or slotted spoon to remove pieces of fried tofu from the oil and let them drain on the paper towels.

Make the curry:

1. This dish is especially nice when the veggies are cut into fairly large pieces. Cut the onion into large, 1-1 ½ inch chunks. Finely chop the garlic and grate the ginger. Cut the sweet potato in half lengthwise, then slice each half into thin, half-moon pieces, about ¼ inch thick. Place the sweet potato, garlic, and ginger in a small bowl, and set aside.

2. Remove seeds from the bell pepper and cut into large chunks the same size as the pieces of onion. Wash the broccoli and cut into evenly sized florets, discarding any excess stems. Keep the pepper and broccoli separate from each other.

3. In a large, wide pot, heat the olive or coconut oil on medium heat. Add the onions and sauté for 3-4 minutes. Add the sweet potato, garlic, ginger, and curry paste and sauté for 5 minutes, stirring frequently. The whole can of curry paste may seem like a lot, but it will give the dish a full flavor.

4. Add the coconut milk, water, and salt. Lower the heat, cover, and simmer for 5-10 minutes. A fork should go easily into the sweet potato, but it should still be a little too chewy for comfort.

5. Add the broccoli and stir to mix. Cook for about 3 minutes, until it darkens to a lush green color.

6. Add the peppers and cook for about 2 minutes.

7. Add the fried tofu and gently mix, ensuring that the tofu is coated in the curry sauce.

8. Squeeze lime juice over the pot, and garnish with fresh cilantro (if desired). Serve immediately, over rice.

> ## NOTE:
> My favorite curry paste is Maesri brand, available in a small can at many Asian markets. Thai Kitchen brand, available in a jar at many supermarkets, works just fine too.

Peanut Noodles with Tempeh and Veggies

When I'm cooking at home, I love one-bowl meals, and this is a favorite. It's good with almost any noodles, and lately I like to make it with gluten-free black soy bean pasta for a high-protein, low-carb meal. Carrots and bell peppers are my favorite veggie combination with the peanut sauce, but you can substitute most any veggies you have on hand—I also like it with zucchini, broccoli, peas, and sliced raw cherry tomatoes. It's delicious served warm or cold.

Makes: 4-6 servings
Prep time: 20 minutes
Cook time: 30 minutes

½ pound long, thin pasta (spaghetti, udon noodles, etc.)
1 recipe peanut sauce (page 138)

For the veggies:
1 medium onion
2-inch piece fresh ginger root
1 large carrot
1 bell pepper
3 small scallions
1 Tbsp olive oil
¼ tsp salt
⅛ tsp ground black pepper

For the tempeh:
8 ounces tempeh
¼ cup olive oil
½ tsp salt

To serve:
2 handfuls pea shoots or bean sprouts (about 2 ounces)
¾ cup fresh cilantro, optional
¼ cup fresh basil, optional

1. Cook pasta according to package directions. Prepare peanut sauce (page 138).

2. Prepare the veggies: Slice the onion in half, cut into thin ribbons, then cut each ribbon in half. Cut carrots and peppers into thin spears about ¼ inch wide and 2 inches long. Slice the ginger into small half-moons. Slice the scallions into rounds.

3. Heat 1 Tbsp olive oil in a large cast iron pan on medium heat. Add the onions and sauté for about 5 minutes, until they begin to soften. Add the ginger and carrots, cover, and sauté for 5 minutes, stirring once. Add the bell peppers and sauté about 5 minutes more, until the carrots are soft, not crunchy. Add the scallions, salt, and pepper. Stir, cover, and turn off the burner. Leave the pan covered for 5-10 minutes so the veggies continue to steam.

4. Meanwhile, cut the tempeh into thin, small matchsticks: Slice the block in half so you have 2 thin slabs. You can cut through the packaging, then easily pop each slab out of the plastic. Turn each slab on its side and slice to create 4 thin filets. Cut each of these into strips about ¼ inch wide, and cut each strip in half so you have lots of little tempeh pieces that are about 1 ½ inches long (review illustration).

5. Cook the tempeh: Heat the ¼ cup olive oil in a large pan or skillet on medium-high heat. You'll want a pan big enough so the tempeh will fit in a single layer, or close to it. Test to make sure the oil is hot by adding one piece of tempeh to the pan—if it sizzles around the edges, the pan is ready. Add the tempeh and let it cook undisturbed for about 4 minutes, until the bottoms of the pieces brown. Use a spatula or fork to turn the pieces, then sprinkle with the ½ tsp salt. Continue to cook until all sides brown nicely, turning the tempeh every 3-4 minutes.

6. Prepare the garnishes: Rinse and dry the pea shoots and cut into pieces 2-3 inches long—if using bean sprouts, leave them whole. Wash, dry with a towel, and coarsely chop cilantro and basil, if using.

7. Assemble the dish: Place the pasta, tempeh, and veggies in a large bowl. Pour peanut sauce over them and toss to coat. Just before serving, add half the garnishes and stir. Add the remaining garnishes on top, and serve warm or cold.

HOW TO CUT THE TEMPEH:

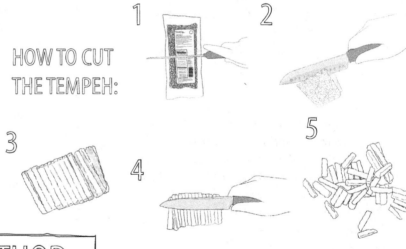

LAZY BAKER METHOD:

Preparing this dish generates a lot of dirty pots and pans. To cut down on the dishes, I often cook the tempeh first, then set it aside in the serving bowl and use the same pan to cook the veggies. Wait to mix up the peanut sauce until everything is cooking, rather than at the beginning, and you cut down on prep time too!

Awesome Vegetarian Chili

I love this chili—it is sweet and smoky, with a nice dark color. It makes a great one-bowl meal on a cold day, served with some cornbread or toast. I've been making this chili for years. The addition of the secret ingredients of cocoa powder and molasses comes from my dear friend Aiden Graham, who always used to make a chili and cornbread recipe from the cookbook La Dolce Vegan.[11]

Makes: 4-6 servings
Prep time: 20 minutes
Cook time: 30 minutes

1 medium onion
1 medium sweet potato (about ½ pound)
1 large bell pepper
½ cup dry texturized vegetable protein (TVP), or 1 12-ounce package mock ground beef
1 cup boiling water
3 Tbsp olive oil
1 Tbsp cocoa powder
2 Tbsp chili powder blend
2 tsp ground cumin
2 tsp garlic powder
1 ½ tsp salt
1 14.5-ounce can crushed tomatoes
1 14.5-ounce can diced tomatoes
4 cups cooked kidney beans (about 2 ½ 15.5-ounce cans)
2 Tbsp molasses

1. Chop the onion and sweet potato into a large ½ inch dice and set aside. Chop the bell pepper into a large ½ inch dice, keeping it separate from the other veggies. If using TVP, place it in a small bowl and cover with the boiling water to rehydrate it.

2. Place the olive oil in a large heavy-bottomed pot and heat on medium heat. Add the onion and sweet potato, cover, and sauté for 10 minutes, stirring occasionally, until the sweet potato begins to soften.

3. When the TVP has absorbed most of the water and is soft but still chewy, drain it and discard the excess water. Add the TVP to the pot along with the bell pepper. If using mock ground beef, add it here. Cover and cook for 10-15 minutes more, stirring occasionally, until the sweet potatoes and TVP are both completely soft, or the mock ground beef has browned slightly.

4. Add the cocoa powder, chili powder, cumin, garlic powder, and salt to the vegetables, and mix well. Add the crushed tomatoes, diced tomatoes, beans, and molasses, and mix well.

5. Reduce the heat to low and allow the chili to simmer for at least 15 minutes so the flavors can combine.

6. Serve hot, with avocado sauce (page 146) or sour cream, grated cheddar cheese, and chopped cilantro. The chili will be even more flavorful the next day, so this is a good one to make ahead of time. It also freezes well.

VARIATION:

I usually make this recipe with kidney beans, but it's also tasty with different combinations of pinto beans, chickpeas, black beans, or small red beans. You can soak 1 ½ cups of dry beans and cook them especially for your chili; use beans you've previously cooked and frozen; or use canned beans. Use 4 cups of cooked beans in all, and make sure to drain the liquid out of the beans before adding them to the chili.

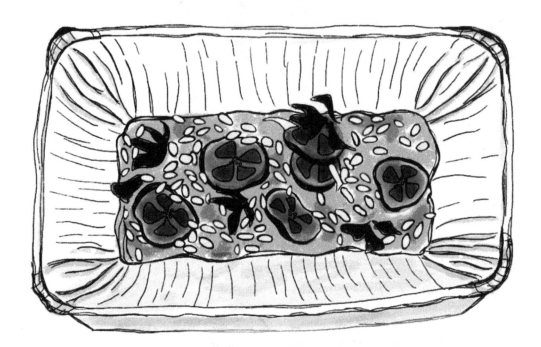

White Beans with Roasted Tomatoes

This recipe is a simple, tasty, and nutritious way to eat and share fresh tomatoes. The combination of large tomatoes, cherry tomatoes, and fresh basil is a beautiful, multi-sensory experience. It's inspired by a dish I found online many years ago, and quickly became a favorite during summer meals at the Center for Documentary Studies at Duke University. Many a student has commented that "beans and tomatoes" on the menu seemed uninspiring—but then they were wowed by the beauty and flavors of this dish. The finished dish is a bit like a bean stew, so it's ideal to serve with rolls or garlic bread for sopping up the caramelized-tomato-and-olive-oil juices from the plate.

Makes: 6-8 large servings
Soak time for beans: 8+ hours or overnight
Prep time: 15 minutes
Cook time: 1 ½ hours

For the beans:
2 cups dry cannellini or navy
  beans (about 1 pound)
6 cups water, plus more for
  soaking the beans
2 medium onions
2 tsp salt

For the tomatoes:
1 ½ pound slicing tomatoes
  (about 3-4, in varying colors if
  available)
1 pint cherry tomatoes
¼ cup olive oil
1 ½ tsp sugar
½ tsp salt

To serve:
3 sprigs of fresh basil (about 20
  leaves)

1. Soak the beans overnight, then drain and rinse.

2. Cook the beans: Place soaked beans in a large pot and cover with the 6 cups of water. Heat on high to boiling, then immediately turn down to a simmer and cook for about 30 minutes.

3. Roast the tomatoes: While the beans are cooking, preheat oven to 450°F. Core the slicing tomatoes and cut them in half crossways. Place the tomato halves in a 9x13 inch baking dish with the cherry tomatoes. Sprinkle with the olive oil, sugar, and ½ tsp salt. Toss to coat, then arrange tomato halves with cut sides up.

4. Roast tomatoes, uncovered, for about 50 minutes, until the large tomatoes are very tender and the cherry tomatoes are starting to fall apart.

5. Meanwhile, peel the onions and cut into large quarters. This dish is really nice with large chunks of onion in it.

6. After the beans have cooked for 30 minutes, add the onions and the 2 tsp salt to the bean pot. Stir to mix, then cover and continue to simmer on low heat for 45 minutes more, until the beans and onions are both very soft.

7. Just before serving, transfer beans and onions to a wide, shallow serving bowl or platter. Use a slotted spoon to strain the beans and onions, discarding as much liquid as possible so the beans can absorb the tomato juices instead.

8. Arrange tomatoes on top of the beans and pour all of the juices from the tomatoes evenly over the dish.

9. Cut basil leaves into several large pieces each—scissors work great for this. Sprinkle the dish with basil leaves and serve.

NOTE:

You can make this dish ahead of time and reheat it. Assemble the cooked beans and tomatoes in a wide, oven-safe baking dish, cover, and store in the refrigerator. Reheat in the oven, covered, at 350°F for about 30 minutes. Cut and add basil leaves just before serving: they will turn brown if heated, so leave them off until the very end.

Mock Chicken "Carnitas" with Roasted Onions and Peppers

To make these tasty morsels, slow cook mock chicken in a lime juice marinade until most of the liquid has evaporated and you're left with a tangy, flavorful sauce. I started making this as a taco or fajita filling, and it's also great served alongside warm tortillas or whole wheat rolls (page 162), over rice with tomato and onion (page 48), or as a filling in quesadillas. This recipe is spicy, so it's a good idea to serve it with creamy condiment like avocado sauce (page 146) or sour cream. Review note for milder options.

Makes: 4 medium servings
Prep time: 20 minutes
Cook time: 1 hour and 30 minutes

For the mock chicken:
½ cup lime juice
1 cup water
1 cube veggie broth, chopped
2 Tbsp olive oil
1 Tbsp honey (can substitute agave nectar or granulated sugar)
1 3.5-ounce can chipotle peppers in adobo sauce (about 5 peppers plus sauce)
3 medium cloves garlic
2 tsp ground cumin
1 tsp ground black pepper
1 10.5-ounce package Delight Foods soy patties or other mock chicken (for advice about varieties, visit "In My Kitchen" on page 9)
½ tsp salt (optional)

For the peppers:
2 large poblano peppers
1 large green bell pepper
1 large onion
1 Tbsp olive oil
1 tsp ground cumin
½ tsp salt
½ tsp ground black pepper

Prepare the mock chicken:

1. Place all ingredients except the mock chicken in a medium pot and stir. Bring to a boil on medium-high heat. Add mock chicken, and stir to coat.

2. Reduce heat to a simmer, and let cook uncovered for about 1 hour and 30 minutes, stirring 2 or 3 times, until most of the liquid has evaporated and you have soft patties coated in a thick red sauce.

3. If using large pieces of mock chicken such as soy patties, let cool slightly, then slice the patties into strips. Remove any large pieces of chipotle peppers and discard. Add the optional ½ tsp salt, to taste.

As soon as the mock chicken is cooking, prepare the onions and peppers:

1. Preheat oven to 375°F. Wash, core, and halve the peppers. Cut into strips ¼ inch wide and as long as the pepper. Peel the onion, cut in half, and cut into long, thin strips that are a similar size and shape to the pepper strips.

2. Place onions and peppers in an 8x8 inch baking pan. Sprinkle with the olive oil, cumin, salt, and pepper, and toss to coat. Cover pan tightly with foil.

3. Roast, covered, for 45 minutes.

4. Uncover, stir, and roast for another 30 minutes. Veggies should be very soft and lightly browned.

To serve: Mix the strips of soy patties and the sauce with the peppers and onions. Add any remaining sauce. Serve warm.

VARIATION:

The heat in this dish comes mainly from the chipotle peppers—it will be pretty spicy with a full can of them. For medium spice, use just the adobo sauce and one whole pepper from the can of chipotle peppers. For milder carnitas, leave out the chipotles entirely, replacing them with half a 6-ounce can of tomato paste and a teaspoon of mild chili powder. The poblano peppers also add a little bit of heat, so if you want a completely mild dish, replace the poblanos with 1-2 additional bell peppers.

Potato Enchiladas

I first developed this potato enchilada recipe for an event with youth and families from Student Action with Farmworkers. I have modified the recipe over the years, and find this version with coconut milk especially tasty. You can also serve the filling on its own as an extra-flavorful, cumin-y mashed potatoes. I like to serve these with black beans with cumin and poblanos (page 46), cilantro rice (page 50), and sour cream.

Makes: 16 enchiladas (serves 8)
Prep time: 45 minutes
Bake time: 20 minutes

For the potato filling:
4 cups water
1 tsp + ¾ tsp salt, divided
2 pounds gold, red, or white potatoes
½ medium onion
2 medium cloves garlic
2 Tbsp olive oil
1 ½ tsp ground cumin
½ cup full-fat canned coconut milk
1 tsp ancho chili flakes (page 97), or substitute chili powder blend
½ tsp ground black pepper

For the enchiladas:
1 tsp canola or olive oil
16 6-inch corn tortillas
1 recipe enchilada sauce (page 137)
4 ounces shredded vegan or dairy cheddar cheese (about 1 cup, grated)

To serve:
a handful of fresh cilantro

Make the filling:

1. Place water and 1 tsp of the salt in a medium pot on high heat and bring to a boil.

2. Meanwhile, prepare the potatoes. Wash them and remove any bruised spots. I usually leave the skin on, but if you prefer no-skin mashed potatoes, you can peel them. Rough chop into large 1-1 ½ inch cubes.

3. When the water boils, add potatoes and cook for 15-20 minutes, until potatoes are soft when poked with a fork.

4. Meanwhile, dice the onion into small, ¼ inch pieces and mince the garlic. Place the 2 Tbsp olive oil in a pan and heat on medium heat. Add onions and garlic, cover, and sauté for about 10 minutes until soft and golden brown. Add the cumin to the pan, mix, and turn off heat. Allow the mixture to sit in the hot pan for a couple of minutes to infuse the cumin.

5. Drain cooked potatoes well and place in a large bowl. Add the onion mixture, coconut milk, ancho chili flakes, pepper, and remaining ¾ tsp salt.

6. Mash the potatoes, mixing them with the seasonings until smooth and fluffy. A metal potato/bean masher is best for getting a smooth texture, but a wooden spoon will work too, if you don't mind a few lumps.

Assemble the enchiladas:

1. Preheat oven to 375°F. Spread the 1 tsp oil evenly over the surface of a large sheet pan, or two 9x13 inch baking dishes.

2. Heat the tortillas to soften them and help them hold up when dipped in the sauce. You can do this in two ways:

Heat a comal, skillet, or cast iron pan until hot and then heat the tortillas, one at a time, about 30 seconds on each side, **OR**
Heat them in the oven: Lightly coat each tortilla with oil by placing each on the surface of the oiled baking pan, then flipping each over. Once all tortillas are coated and spread out in the pan—it is fine if they overlap a little—bake in the oven for 4-5 minutes, until they are warm and flexible.

3. Set up your enchilada-making station: Pour the enchilada sauce into a shallow bowl wide enough to comfortably hold several tortillas. Set out one plate for the tortillas and a second plate to use for rolling the enchiladas. Spread ¼ cup enchilada sauce evenly over the surface of the baking pan.

4. Dip each heated tortilla into the bowl of sauce, generously coating it on both sides. One by one, lay each tortilla flat on the enchilada-rolling plate. Place a dollop of ¼ to ⅓ cup potato filling in the center of each tortilla, depending on how big you want your enchiladas. Spread the filling out into a line right in the center of the tortilla. Fold over first one side of the tortilla, then the other. Flip the enchilada over and place it, seam side down, in the pan. Repeat until all the enchiladas are made. If possible, arrange them on the pan so that you leave about ½ inch between each enchilada: they'll be easier to remove from the pan and won't stick together once baked.

5. Once all the enchiladas are in the pan, fully coat the tops with a bit more sauce. Evenly sprinkle the cheese over them. Some sauce and filling may be left over.

Bake and serve:

1. Bake for 20 minutes, until the cheese melts and the enchiladas are heated through. Do not over bake, as the tortillas can become crunchy.

2. Meanwhile, wash, dry, de-stem, and gently chop the cilantro.

3. Remove enchiladas from oven and sprinkle cilantro on top as a garnish. Serve hot.

LAZY BAKER METHOD: You can actually roll 6 enchiladas at once directly in the pan. This takes less time than dipping and rolling each enchilada individually, and you also have one less plate to wash. It just requires a little geometric ingenuity! Dip 6 tortillas into the sauce and lay them out in the pan—they may overlap slightly. Then, fill and roll all 6 in one batch, and arrange them all on one side of the pan. To roll the second round of 6, lay out the sauce-coated tortillas in the pan again, laying some of them on top of the prepared enchiladas. Fill and roll, then proceed as above.

Black Beans with Cumin and Poblanos

In my kitchen, beans and rice are staple dishes whether I'm cooking for myself or for others. This simple recipe is full of flavor. If you make it with dry beans as suggested, you'll have a lot of down time while the beans cook, which you can use to make potato enchiladas (page 44) and cilantro rice (page 50), or to read your favorite book. Soaking the beans overnight and rinsing them well before cooking helps make them more easily digestible. For a quicker version, review the note about using canned beans.

Makes: About 6 cups, 6-8 large servings
Soak time for beans: 8+ hours or overnight
Prep time: 10 minutes
Cook time: 1 ½ hours

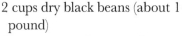

2 cups dry black beans (about 1 pound)
6 cups water, plus more for soaking beans
1 tsp + ½ tsp salt, divided
1 whole dried ancho chile pepper
1 bay leaf
1 medium onion
1 large fresh poblano pepper
¼ cup fresh cilantro
2 Tbsp olive oil
2 tsp ground cumin
1 tsp garlic powder
½ tsp ground black pepper

1. Soak the beans overnight, then drain and rinse.

2. Place beans in a medium pot and cover with the 6 cups of water. Add 1 tsp of the salt, the ancho chile, and bay leaf. Cover the pot and heat on medium high until it simmers, then immediately turn down to low and simmer for about 1 hour, until beans are comfortably soft.

3. Meanwhile, slice the onion and poblano pepper into long, thin strips, and set aside. Wash, shake dry, and coarsely chop the cilantro, and place in a separate bowl.

4. When beans are soft, add the olive oil, cumin, garlic powder, black pepper, and remaining ½ tsp salt on top of the beans. Add the sliced onion and pepper to the pot. Mix well, and gently simmer on low heat for 20-30 minutes. Peppers and onion should both be soft, and the ancho chile should have broken into pieces and mixed with the beans.

5. Add the chopped cilantro to the beans, cover, and let sit for 10 minutes before serving. Serve hot, over rice. The flavors deepen over time, so these beans are even better reheated the next day.

NOTE:

To make this dish with canned black beans, use 3 15.5-ounce cans. Heat the beans with their juices and just a little water in a pot with 2 tsp ancho chili flakes in place of the whole ancho chile. Then follow the recipe starting with step 3. Canned beans come in varying degrees of saltiness—rather than using the full 1 ½ tsp salt here, make sure to taste your beans just before adding the cilantro and add salt to taste.

Rice with Tomato and Onion

This tomato-y, onion-y, full-of-flavor recipe is great with black beans with cumin and poblanos (page 46). It has been a staple in my kitchen since I adapted the recipe from a dish on Elise Bauer's website Simply Recipes *over a decade ago.[12] Depending on the type of rice you use, it may require a little extra water and cooking time.*

Makes 4-6 servings
Prep time: 10 minutes
Cook time: 35 minutes

1 medium onion
2 medium cloves garlic
¼ cup olive oil
1 ½ cups long grain white rice
3 cups water
1 14.5-ounce can diced tomatoes
½ cube veggie broth, chopped
1 tsp oregano
1 ½ tsp salt

1. Dice the onion into small ¼ inch pieces, and finely mince the garlic.

2. In a large, heavy-bottomed pot, heat the olive oil on medium-low heat. Add the onion, garlic, and rice, and stir to coat. Toast the rice with the onions, stirring frequently, for about 15 minutes, until the onions begin to soften and the rice has toasted to a golden brown. Make sure to scrape the bottom of the pot when stirring so the rice doesn't stick.

3. Meanwhile, place the water, diced tomatoes, veggie broth, oregano, and salt in a small pot. Cover and heat on medium high to bring these ingredients to a simmer. Turn off heat and let cool for about 5 minutes.

4. Once the rice is toasted, remove from heat. Pour the broth into the pot with the rice—it will bubble vigorously, so be careful! Letting the broth cool slightly before pouring it over the rice will decrease the chances of it bubbling up and burning your arms.

5. Place the rice pot back on low heat, cover, and simmer for about 20 minutes until rice is soft and has absorbed all the liquid. Check the pot after 15 minutes; if the liquid is absorbed but the rice is still slightly crunchy, add an additional ¼ cup of water and continue to cook. If, after 20 minutes, the rice has absorbed the liquid but is just a tiny bit chewy, turn off the pot, cover, and let sit for 10 minutes: the rice will continue to steam as it sits in the pot.

6. Fluff rice gently with a fork or wooden paddle. Serve hot, with beans, red cabbage and carrot slaw (page 109) and potato enchiladas (page 44).

LAZY BAKER METHOD:

If you don't want to dirty another pot to cook up the broth, just boil the water in a kettle. When the rice has toasted and the water is hot, add the hot water to the rice pot and then add the diced tomatoes, veggie broth cube, oregano, and salt. Stir to mix, then proceed with step 5.

Cilantro Rice

I started making this rice because I got tired of always serving rice with tomato and onion (page 48) with beans. Sometimes I like to mix things up, and the cilantro rice became a huge hit with many of my catering clients. The trick is making a sort of cilantro pesto that you mix into the rice right after it's cooked—the fresh cilantro gives the dish a bright green color and a distinctive flavor.

Makes: 4-6 servings
Prep time: 15 minutes
Cook time: 25 minutes

1 medium onion
2 medium cloves garlic
1 Tbsp + 2 Tbsp olive oil, divided
3 cups hot water, plus more if needed (review note)
1 ½ cups long-grain white rice
1 cube veggie broth, chopped
1 tsp salt
1 packed cup fresh cilantro
1 tsp lime juice

1. Dice onion into small ¼ inch pieces. Finely mince the garlic.

2. Place 1 Tbsp of the olive oil in a heavy-bottomed pot over medium heat. Add the onions and garlic, and sauté for about 5 minutes, stirring frequently, until the onions just begin to brown.

3. Meanwhile, heat 3 cups of water in a kettle until it simmers.

4. When the onions begin to brown and the water is hot, add the rice, hot water, veggie broth, and salt to the onion mixture. Be careful when adding the water, as it tends to bubble vigorously and can splash hot liquid onto you. Mix well.

5. Cover with a tight-fitting lid and cook on low for 20 minutes, until rice is soft and has absorbed all the liquid. Check the pot after 15 minutes: if the liquid is absorbed but the rice is still slightly crunchy, add an additional ¼ cup of water continue to cook. If, after 20 minutes, the rice has absorbed the liquid but is just a tiny bit chewy, turn off the pot, cover, and let sit for 10 minutes: rice will continue to steam as it sits in the pot.

6. Meanwhile, prepare the cilantro: Wash and shake dry. Cut the ends off the stems and discard. Coarsely chop the cilantro leaves and stems, and place in a food processor.

7. Add the lime juice and remaining 2 Tbsp olive oil to the food processor. Blend or pulse until the cilantro is finely chopped and you have a pasty, pesto-like consistency. Scrape down the sides of the food processor to ensure all cilantro is finely chopped.

8. Once the rice is cooked, fluff it gently with a fork or wooden paddle. Scrape the cilantro mixture onto the rice. Mix gently, ensuring that the rice is evenly coated with the cilantro mixture and is a lovely, green color.

9. Serve hot.

VARIATIONS:

You can also make this recipe with brown rice—just add additional water and allow for extra cooking time.

If you are accustomed to using a rice cooker, sauté the onions and garlic in a pan, then add to the rice cooker with rice, broth cube, salt. and the appropriate amount of water. Once the rice is cooked, add the cilantro mixture as described in steps 6-8, above.

NOTE:

The key to this recipe is to use enough water to cook the rice well, without any extra moisture. The cilantro mixture added at the end will add some liquid, so the rice needs to be soft, but not mushy. Since different varieties of rice require different amounts of liquid, it's a good idea to check the quantity of water noted in the cooking directions on the package (if given). If you are unsure how much water to use, start with 3 cups and check the rice pot after 15 minutes as directed in step 5.

Mac and Cheese

I developed this recipe in 2015 for the cast and crew of When We Free, *a short film telling the story of a recently freed Black community's first camp meeting after emancipation.[13] Mac and cheese was one of the menu requests, and we shared it on the banks of the Eno River after a long day of filming. It's deliciously creamy, and the onions and sage add extra flavor. I always make this in large quantities, and the recipe scales up well for a potluck or family gathering.*

Makes: 5-6 servings
Prep time: 25 minutes
Bake time: 20 minutes

½ pound macaroni (8 ounces)
½ pound cheddar cheese,
   mixed yellow and white
½ small onion
2 Tbsp butter or olive oil
1 bay leaf
1 ½ tsp ground dry mustard
1 ½ tsp dried rubbed sage
½ tsp salt
¼ tsp ground black pepper
2 Tbsp all-purpose flour
1 ¼ cups whole milk, divided
¼ cup bread crumbs (optional)

1. Preheat oven to 350°F.

2. Cook macaroni according to package directions, erring on the side of al dente (slightly chewy). Drain and rinse.

3. Meanwhile, grate cheese and set aside.

4. Prepare the sauce: Dice the onion into small, ¼ inch pieces. Place butter or olive oil in a large saucepan, heat on medium-low heat, and add the onion and bay leaf. Cook for about 5 minutes, until the edges of the onion begin to brown.

5. Turn heat down to low. Add ground mustard, dried sage, salt, and pepper. Add flour and stir until evenly mixed and bubbly. You are making a roux that will thicken the sauce, so you want to make sure there are no lumps of flour—only little lumps of onion.

6. Add the milk in 3 batches, stirring with a whisk after each addition to ensure the milk mixes smoothly with the roux.

7. Continue cooking the sauce for about 5 minutes, stirring continuously, until it thickens. Add 1/3 of the grated cheese to the sauce and stir until it melts. Remove from heat.

8. Place the cooked noodles in a 9x13 inch baking dish, and mix in ⅓ of the cheese. Pour the cheesy sauce over the noodle mixture, ensuring it is well combined.

9. Sprinkle the remaining ⅓ of the cheese on top, along with bread crumbs, if using.

10. Bake uncovered for 20 minutes, until the center holds firm when you jostle the pan and the cheese on top is slightly crispy.

LAZY BAKER METHOD:

For a quicker, stove-top mac and cheese, make sure the macaroni is well-cooked. Return macaroni to its pot after draining it. Make the sauce, then add it directly to the pasta pot along with all the remaining grated cheese, omitting the bread crumbs. Serve!

Vegan Mac and Cheese

I love the squishy comfort of a good mac and cheese. I first learned to make vegan mac and cheese as a member of Fairchild Co-op at Oberlin College. The friend who taught me would always put in mustard powder as the secret ingredient, and that's still the magic ingredient I use to make this dish. Years ago, I created a cookbook zine to give to my family, including a version of this recipe which was delicious but had no quantities for anything. This new, improved version is baked, but you can also just eat it right out of the pot.

Makes: 3-5 servings
Prep time: 20 minutes
Bake time: 20 minutes

½ pound of your favorite pasta
 (macaroni, small shells, etc.)
¼ cup olive oil
3 medium cloves of garlic
½ tsp ground dry mustard
½ tsp ground black pepper
3 Tbsp all-purpose flour
1 ½ cups soy or almond milk
1 tsp soy sauce
¼ cup nutritional yeast
½ tsp salt
1 cup shredded vegan cheese
 (Follow Your Heart vegan
 parmesan or Daiya vegan
 cheddar, optional)

1. Preheat oven to 375°F.

2. Cook the pasta according to package directions, erring on the side of al dente (slightly chewy). Drain and rinse.

3. Meanwhile, make the sauce: Finely mince the garlic. Heat the olive oil in a small saucepan on medium heat, and add the garlic, mustard, and pepper. Cook just until the garlic is golden brown, about 3 minutes.

4. Reduce heat to low, add the flour, and use a whisk to stir until evenly mixed. You are making a roux that will thicken the sauce, so you want to make sure there are no lumps of flour. Add the soy or almond milk a little at a time, in 3 rounds, stirring to make sure it mixes with the roux with no floury lumps. Add the soy sauce. Let the sauce cook, stirring frequently, for about 5 minutes or until thickened.

5. Add the nutritional yeast and salt, and stir. Remove from heat.

6. Place the cooked pasta in a small casserole dish, and pour the sauce over it. This quantity will just barely pack into an 8x8 inch baking dish if the sides are tall, or will form a thin-ish layer in a 9x13 inch dish. If using shredded vegan cheese, mix ½ cup of it in with the pasta and then sprinkle the remainder on top.

7. Place the mac and cheese in the oven and bake for 20 minutes until cheese is bubbly and the top is slightly crispy.

LAZY BAKER METHOD:

For a no-bake mac and cheese, follow the recipe above with the following modifications. Do not preheat the oven. Drain the pasta and put it back into its cooking pot. Make the sauce as directed in steps 3-5. Pour the sauce directly into the pot with the pasta and stir to mix. It's ready to serve! I usually omit the vegan cheese if I'm not baking the mac. If you do want to use it here, be sure to mix it in well and then let the mac and cheese sit for a few minutes so that the cheese melts—most vegan cheeses are tastiest when allowed to melt completely.

Mesir Wat

I first tasted this delicious Ethiopian lentil stew at Blue Nile,[14] a restaurant in Durham's Lakewood Shopping Center when I was a teenager. The taste carries fond memories, and years ago I began making a version of the dish at home. Berbere, the blend of spices that is a key ingredient in this dish, is aromatic and delightful. Mesir wat, like the other Ethiopian dishes in this book, is traditionally served with injera, a spongy sourdough flat bread made with teff flour—review note on page 59 for some injera tips.

1 ½ cups split red lentils
1 large onion
5 medium cloves garlic
2 Tbsp olive oil
1 14.5-ounce can diced tomatoes, or 3 large fresh tomatoes
¼ cup berbere (recipe follows)
¼ cup paprika
2 tsp salt
4 cups water

Makes: 4-6 servings
Prep time: 15 minutes
Cook time: 1 hour

1. Rinse lentils until the water runs clear, and place in a medium bowl. Cover with cold tap water and let them soak for 15 minutes. Meanwhile, begin to prepare the rest of the dish.

2. Finely dice the onion and garlic.

3. Heat olive oil in a large pot on medium heat. Add the onion and garlic, cover, and cook for about 5 minutes, until the onion begins to soften and brown around the edges. Add tomatoes, then add berbere, paprika, and salt, and cook for about 5 minutes, stirring occasionally.

4. Drain lentils using a colander or large mesh strainer, and add to the pot. Cook for about 5 minutes without adding water, stirring often to prevent sticking.

5. Now add the water, cover, and bring to a boil. Reduce heat to low and simmer for about 45 minutes, stirring occassionally, until lentils are soft. You should have a thick, uniform paste.

6. Serve warm.

BERBERE

Berbere is usually very spicy. The version here is significantly milder, but extremely flavorful. If you want it spicier, add more chilies; if you want it even milder, use fewer. I adapted this recipe from the Dirty South Cookbook,[15] *a vegan cookbook I got as a teenager when I first went vegan. In addition to mesir wat and doro wat, you can use it in spicy tomato salad (page 106), sprinkle it over roasted vegetables, or put it on popcorn!*

4 tsp whole cumin seed
2 tsp whole cardamom seed or green cardamom pods
2 tsp whole fenugreek seed
2 tsp whole fennel seed
1 tsp whole coriander seed
1 tsp whole black peppercorns
1 tsp whole allspice berries (review note)
8 whole cloves
4 small dried red chilies, such as chile de árbol
1 tsp chopped fresh ginger root
¼ cup sweet paprika
2 tsp salt
½ tsp ground turmeric
¼ tsp ground cinnamon
¼ tsp ground cloves

In a small cast iron pan, toast the whole spices (cumin, cardamom, fenugreek, fennel, coriander, peppercorns, allspice, and whole cloves) for about 5 minutes on medium heat until they smell pungent and just begin to brown. Remove from heat and let cool until comfortable to the touch. Place in a spice grinder or mortar and pestle along with the chilies and ginger, and grind until smooth. Mix with the remaining spices (paprika, salt, turmeric, cinnamon, and ground cloves). Store in an airtight glass container for up to a month.

....

Note: Whole allspice can be difficult to find. As a substitute, add 1 tsp ground allspice when you add the turmeric, salt, and paprika.

Doro Wat

This Ethiopian stew, traditionally prepared with chicken and hard-boiled eggs, is made here with mock chicken and tofu. Its distinct flavor comes from slow-cooking the protein in a sweet onion sauce for several hours, so make sure to allow yourself plenty of time. This process infuses everything within reach with the scent of onions and spices—to the delight of my guests, my whole house continues to smell sweet and pungent for several days. Doro Wat ought to be served with injera, a delicious sourdough flat bread (review note), but you can also serve it with sliced bread or rice.

Makes: 6 servings
Prep time: 20 minutes
Cook time: 2 hours and 15 minutes

1 pound Delight Foods soy patties or other mock chicken (for advice about varieties, visit "In My Kitchen" on page 9)
Juice of 1 lemon
3 pounds onions
6 Tbsp niter kibbeh (recipe follows)
4 cups water
1 pound firm or extra firm tofu
1 Tbsp grated fresh ginger root
2 Tbsp berbere (page 57)
½ cup cooking wine or grape juice
1 cube veggie broth, chopped
½ tsp ground cardamom
½ tsp ground cloves

1. Place the vegan chicken in a bowl and coat evenly with the lemon juice. Let marinate while you cook the onions.

2. Finely dice the onions. A quick way to do this is to chop them in quarters, then place in a food processor and pulse until evenly and finely chopped. Heat a large, heavy-bottomed pot on medium-low heat. Add the onions and cook for about 20 minutes without oil, until they just begin to brown and the water begins to evaporate. Stir regularly to prevent burning

3. Measure out 6 Tbsp niter kibbeh in one container and 4 cups of water in another. Add 1 Tbsp of the niter kibbeh to the onions at a time in 10 minute intervals, allowing the onions to cook in between. If the onions begin to stick, add ½ to 1 cup of water at a time. Continue cooking for a full hour until you have a light brown, caramelized, sweet onion sauce about the consistency of puréed apple sauce.

4. While the onion sauce is cooking, drain, rinse, and press the tofu. To press, place tofu between two cutting boards and place a 2-pound object on top, such as a couple of metal cans (don't use a breakable object!). Let press for about 1 hour. You can also set a towel underneath to absorb the water that will drain out of the tofu.

5. Once the onion sauce is ready, add the ginger and berbere and let cook for about 2 minutes. Add the cooking wine or grape juice, any remaining water, and the chopped veggie broth cube. Cut the soy patties or vegan chicken into large pieces, add to the pot, and bring to a simmer.

6. Simmer on low heat for about 30 minutes, stirring when needed to make sure it doesn't burn.

7. Slice the tofu into thin squares, about 2 x 2 x ¼ inches. Add the cardamom and cloves to the pot, then the tofu, stirring gently to submerge the tofu without breaking the pieces. Allow to simmer for about 15 minutes more, or until tofu is cooked.

8. To serve over injera with mesir wat (page 56), slow-cooked collard greens (variation on page 89), and spicy tomato salad (page 106), cover a large round plate with a large piece of injera. Space out a portion of each dish directly on top of the injera, and use more injera to scoop up portions of the wats and eat them. The injera functions as a utensil and also soaks up the extra sauce from the wat. If you prefer, serve with bread or rice instead.

NOTE:

I've not yet had luck making injera, a spongy sourdough flatbread made with teff flour. In Durham, you can buy injera at Little India, a tiny grocery store that carries it fresh on weekends and frozen the rest of the week, made by a local baker. Check your local African or Indian market to see if they carry it. Injera becomes brittle when stored in a refrigerator or freezer—to reheat it, simply place the round pieces of injera on a sheet pan in a warm oven for about 5 minutes, or until soft.

NITER KIBBEH

Usually made with clarified butter, this vegan version uses coconut oil. Using virgin coconut oil will result in a distinct coconut flavor, while refined coconut oil will have less of that flavor. Both versions are tasty. This recipe makes a lot; you can use leftover niter kibbeh in place of butter or oil when sautéing or roasting vegetables.

1 pound coconut oil (about 2 packed cups)
½ medium onion
3 medium cloves garlic
2 Tbsp grated fresh ginger root
1 Tbsp fenugreek seeds
1 ½ tsp cardamom seeds
1 tsp dried basil leaves
1 2-inch piece cinnamon stick
½ tsp ground turmeric

Dice the onion into small ¼ inch pieces, finely mince the garlic, and roughly grate the ginger. Place coconut oil in a small pot on medium heat until it melts. Add the onion, garlic, and ginger to the pot, along with all the remaining spices. Reduce heat to as low as possible on your stove, and let cook, uncovered, for about 30 minutes, to allow the spices to infuse into the oil. The onions should be brown—if not, allow to cook until they are, making sure to remove from heat before they burn. Let cool until safe to handle, then strain, squeezing as much oil as you can through a fine sieve or cheesecloth. Discard the spices. Store the infused coconut oil in an airtight glass jar at room temperature for up to a month, or for several months in the refrigerator.

Rosemary Balsamic Tempeh Salad

This recipe was inspired by a chicken salad recipe from my former co-worker Miriam Biber. A summer staple for me, it is tangy, sweet, and nutty, and reminds me a bit of my favorite stuffing recipe because of the walnuts, celery, and parsley. Serve with whole wheat rolls (page 162), roasted seasonal veggie salad (page 102), and pasta salad with capers (page 72).

Makes: 6 large servings
Prep time: 10 minutes
Marinate time: 15 minutes
Cook time: 25 minutes
Chill time: 1 hour (optional)

For the dressing:
2 Tbsp fresh or 1 Tbsp dried rosemary
½ cup olive oil
½ cup balsamic vinegar
1 tsp salt
½ tsp ground black pepper

For the salad:
1 pound tempeh (2 8-ounce blocks)
¾ cup raw walnut pieces
½ cup celery
3 small scallions
¼ cup fresh parsley
½ cup dried cranberries
1 tsp agave nectar (optional)
2 tsp fresh or dried rosemary
¾ tsp salt

1. Preheat oven to 375°F.

2. Make the dressing: Finely mince the fresh rosemary, or crumble the dried rosemary. Place in a tightly-lidded mason jar with the olive oil, balsamic vinegar, salt, and pepper. Shake until well combined.

3. Marinate the tempeh: Slice the tempeh into thin, large cutlets: each 8-ounce block of tempeh should yield 6 cutlets. Cut each block crossways into 3 almost-square pieces. You can cut through the packaging, then easily pop each piece out of the plastic. Turn each piece on its side and slice in half to create thin filets (refer to illustration on page 27). Place tempeh in a bowl or shallow dish and toss with about half of the dressing, reserving the other half to toss with the finished salad. Let marinate for 15 minutes.

4. Bake the tempeh: Place marinated tempeh in a single layer on a large sheet pan and drizzle with any remaining marinade from the bowl. Bake for 15 minutes, then use a spatula to flip the tempeh pieces over. Bake for another 10 minutes, until tempeh is light brown and crispy.

5. Meanwhile, prepare the rest of the salad ingredients: Spread walnuts out on a sheet pan and toast for about 7 minutes in the oven until lightly browned. Let cool, then break or chop into small pieces. Thinly slice celery and scallions and place in a large bowl. Coarsely chop the parsley, and add to the bowl along with the cranberries and walnut pieces.

6. Assemble the salad: Cool the tempeh for about 5 minutes, until you can handle it easily. Cut it into ¼ to ½ inch cubes, and add to the salad bowl along with juice from the pan. Drizzle with agave nectar, if using. Toss with the rosemary, salt, and remaining dressing.

7. Serve warm, or chill in the refrigerator for at least 1 hour to serve cold. This salad will keep for several days in the refrigerator.

> ## NOTE:
> Balsamic vinegar lends a delicious, sweet grape-must flavor to this dish. If you're looking for a stronger grape-must flavor, you can add an extra tablespoon or two of balsamic vinegar when assembling the salad. If you happen to have balsamic reduction (page 141) in your kitchen, adding a tablespoon for extra flavor and sweetness is delicious. As a lazy baker, I wouldn't make the reduction just for this purpose, but it's quite a tasty addition when I already have it.

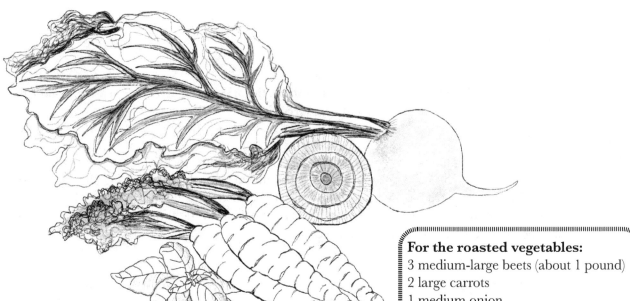

Roasted Beet and Lentil Salad

The fabulous Miriam Biber shared a version of this recipe with me. It is a favorite, even among people who don't like beets. Roasting the lentils helps enure they cook evenly, emerging from the oven tender yet firm, perfect for a salad. The combination of basil, mustard, sweet beets and carrots, and nutty lentils is really delicious.

Makes: 6-8 large servings
Prep time: 30 minutes
Cook time: 1 hour
Chill time: 2 hours (optional)

For the roasted vegetables:
3 medium-large beets (about 1 pound)
2 large carrots
1 medium onion
4 medium cloves garlic
¼ cup olive oil
1 Tbsp dry basil leaves
½ tsp salt
½ tsp ground black pepper
½ cup water

For the lentils:
2 cups French lentils (just under 1
    pound) (review note)
scant 3 cups water
1 cube veggie broth, chopped
½ tsp salt

For the salad:
½ cup olive oil
¼ cup bottled mustard (Dijon or spicy
    brown)
3 Tbsp apple cider vinegar
1 tsp salt
½ tsp ground black pepper
10 fresh basil leaves or 1 Tbsp dry basil
    leaves
2 Tbsp fresh parsley

1. Preheat oven to 450°F.

2. Roast the vegetables: Wash, trim, and peel the beets. Cut into 1-inch chunks. Wash and peel the carrots, slice in half lengthwise, then cut each crossways into large 1 ½ to 2-inch long pieces. Slice the onion in half lengthwise, then slice each half lengthwise into long, thin wedges. Finely chop the garlic.

3. Place beets, carrots, onion, and garlic in a 9x13 inch baking dish. Add the olive oil, basil, salt, and pepper, and mix well. Add the water, and cover tightly with foil. Bake for about 1 hour, until beets are soft. Halfway through baking, turn beets with a spatula, re-cover, and return to oven.

4. Roast the lentils: Place lentils in an 8x8 inch baking dish with the water. Sprinkle small pieces of chopped veggie broth cube over the lentils along with the salt. Cover tightly with foil and bake for 45-55 minutes, until the lentils have absorbed all the water and are tender. Stir lentils after 30 minutes, and check for doneness after 45 minutes.

5. Prepare the salad dressing: In a measuring cup or jar, pour in olive oil, mustard, apple cider vinegar, salt, and pepper. Stir or shake until well combined. Roughly chop fresh basil and parsley, and set aside.

6. Transfer lentils to a large bowl, and add the roasted veggies. Pour dressing over the hot lentil mixture and gently stir. Serve immediately, or chill in refrigerator for 2 hours. Mix in fresh parsley and basil just before serving.

NOTE:

French lentils are smaller than brown or green lentils. They're especially good for lentil salads since they hold their shape much better than their more common counterparts. You can find them at a natural foods store as French lentils, French green lentils, or lentilles du Puy. In a pinch, you can make this recipe with brown lentils, but they tend to fall apart once soft, so be careful not to overcook them. Roast brown lentils with just 2 ½ cups of water, adding more after 30 minutes if they have absorbed all the liquid and are not quite tender.

Chickpea and Fava Bean Salad

I love to make bean salad to have available as a quick lunch, served over a bed of mixed greens. This recipe is inspired by a favorite recipe from my childhood, the three-bean salad in the Moosewood Cookbook,[16] and by fava bean salads at Neomonde,[17] a Raleigh-based Lebanese restaurant. After much experimentation, I landed on this recipe, which is best in the summer when tomatoes are in season. You can purchase fava beans—dry or canned—at a local halal or Middle Eastern grocery store.

Makes: 4-6 large servings
Soak time for beans: 8+ hours or overnight
Cook time: 1 hour and 15 minutes
Prep time: 15 minutes
Marinate time: 2 hours or overnight

For the beans:
1 cup dry fava beans (about 2 ½ cups cooked)
1 cup dry chickpeas (about 2 ½ cups cooked)
12 cups water, divided
1 tsp salt, divided

For the dressing:
¼ cup lemon juice
¼ cup apple cider vinegar
¼ cup olive oil
1 ½ tsp salt
1 tsp dry oregano
½ tsp ground black pepper

For the salad:
½ small red onion
2 medium cloves garlic
½ pound tomatoes (about 2 small tomatoes)
1 bell pepper
½ cup fresh parsley
¼ cup fresh basil
½ cup Kalamata olives (optional)

1. Soak chickpeas and fava beans overnight in two separate containers. Soaking them separately helps the beans retain their distinct flavors, and ensures appropriate cooking time for both types of beans. Drain and rinse.

2. Place beans in two separate pots, cover each with 6 cups water, and add ½ tsp salt to each pot. Bring to a boil, then turn heat down to low, cover, and simmer for about 1 hour or until soft. The inside of the fava beans will soften before their tough outer skin does, so you may notice some of them breaking open while cooking.

3. Meanwhile, mix up the dressing. Place all dressing ingredients in a small bowl or large measuring cup and stir with a whisk to combine. Set aside.

4. Dice the red onion into small ¼ inch pieces. Finely mince the garlic. Combine and set aside.

5. Wash and chop the tomatoes and bell peppers into large 1-inch pieces. Wash, shake dry, and coarsely chop the parsley and basil. If using the Kalamata olives, slice them in half lengthwise.

6. Once beans are cooked, drain them. Place drained beans, still warm, in a large bowl. Add the red onion and garlic to the bowl and pour in the dressing. Mix well. Allow to cool until no longer steaming.

7. Add the tomatoes, bell pepper, parsley, basil, and olives (if using). Mix well.

8. Cover, place in refrigerator, and allow to marinate and chill for at least 2 hours, or overnight.

9. Serve cold.

NOTE:

If you prefer canned beans, use two 15.5-ounce cans of chickpeas and one 15.5-ounce can of fava beans.

LAZY BAKER METHOD:

Rather than mixing up the dressing in step 3, simply add each dressing ingredient directly to the bowl with the beans, just before adding the veggies, and mix well.

Lentil and Corn Salad

I started making this dish as a way to eat more fresh sweet corn in the summertime. The combination of lentils, chickpeas, corn, herbs and veggies is delightful in both taste and texture. This recipe is easily adaptable: you can make it with black beans instead of chickpeas, which brings out the flavor of the cilantro, or omit the cilantro and add feta cheese for a different flavor profile.

Makes: 4-6 large servings
Cook time: 50 minutes
Prep time: 10 minutes
Chill time: 1 hour

For the lentils:
1 ½ cups French or brown lentils
2 ½ cups water
1 cube veggie broth, chopped
½ tsp salt

For the corn:
3 ears fresh corn (to use frozen corn, refer to note)
1 cup water
½ tsp salt

For the salad:
1 ½-2 cups cooked chickpeas (1 15.5-ounce can, or ¾ cup dry, soaked overnight and cooked)
½ medium red onion
1 large bell pepper (any color)
½ pint cherry tomatoes
½ cup fresh parsley
½ cup fresh cilantro
1 cup blue cheese, crumbled (optional)

For the dressing:
1 clove fresh garlic
⅓ cup olive oil
⅓ cup lemon juice
¼ cup lime juice
¼ cup apple cider vinegar
1 tsp dried basil
1 tsp salt
1 tsp ground black pepper
½ tsp garlic powder

1. Cook the lentils: In a medium pot, pour in lentils, water, the chopped veggie broth cube, and salt. Mix well. Cover and heat on medium heat until it simmers. Turn down to low and simmer for 45 minutes. Check the lentils after 35 minutes to make sure there is still a little liquid in the pot—if not, add ¼ cup more water and continue cooking. Keep cooking, stirring occasionally, until lentils are tender.

2. Meanwhile, prepare the corn: If using fresh corn, clean the ears of corn, discarding husks and silk. Place the 1 cup water and ½ tsp salt in a small pot. Heat on high until it boils, then add the corn and cover. until it boils, add the de-husked ears of corn, and cover. Steam for about 4 minutes, just until the corn becomes brighter in color. Remove corn from pot and allow to cool until you can comfortably handle it, then cut the kernels off the cob. Place corn kernels in a large bowl. If using frozen corn, refer to note below.

3. Add cooked chickpeas to the bowl with the corn.

4. Finely chop the onion. Cut bell pepper into large 1-inch pieces. Slice cherry tomatoes in half. Wash, shake dry, and coarsely chop the parsley and cilantro. Place onion, bell pepper, tomatoes, parsley, and cilantro in a medium bowl.

5. Mix up the dressing: Finely mince the garlic. Place garlic and all remaining dressing ingredients in a large, tightly-lidded mason jar and shake until well mixed. Set aside.

6. When lentils are ready, drain, then add them to the large bowl with the corn and chickpeas. Pour dressing over them and toss to coat. Allow to cool for about 10 minutes, until the lentils are no longer steaming. Add the veggies, and gently toss until well mixed.

7. Cover, place in the refrigerator, and chill until cool, about 1 hour. Just before serving, add the cheese (if using).

> **NOTE:**
> To simplify your life, or if it's the middle of winter, replace the fresh corn with frozen corn. Use 10-12 ounces frozen corn, and cook according to package directions before draining and adding to the salad.

Summer Quinoa Salad

I developed this recipe while cooking for students in the summer continuing education program at the Center for Documentary Studies at Duke. I love to serve it as part of a summer lunch meal with lots of other hearty salads and a roll. When measuring the quinoa, you might think, "This tiny amount will never serve six people!" Be patient, and behold: the various veggies and herbs expand this salad bountifully.

Makes: 6 servings
Cook time: 25 minutes
Prep time: 15 minutes
Chill time: 1 hour

For the quinoa:
1 cup dry quinoa
2 cups water
½ cube veggie broth, chopped
½ tsp salt

For the salad:
½ cup raw walnut halves and pieces
1 large cucumber
½ cup black olives (half of a 6-ounce can)
¼ cup Kalamata olives
½ cup fresh parsley
½ cup fresh basil
½ cup quick pickled red onion (recipe follows) or ¼ cup raw red onion
2 Tbsp olive oil
1 Tbsp apple cider vinegar
½ tsp black pepper
½ cup lemon juice

1. Preheat oven to 350°F.

2. Cook the quinoa: Place the quinoa in a medium pot with the water, chopped veggie broth cube, and salt. Bring to a boil, then reduce heat to low and simmer 20-25 minutes, until quinoa is soft and has absorbed all the liquid. Check the quinoa after 15 minutes to make sure there is still a little water in the pot—if not, add ¼ cup more water and continue cooking.

3. Meanwhile, prepare the salad ingredients: Place walnuts on a small baking pan in oven and toast for 7 minutes, or until golden brown. Cool and chop into ¼ inch pieces. Place in a large bowl.

4. Peel the cucumber, slice lengthwise into 4 long spears, then cut each spear into lots of small chunks. Slice the black and Kalamata olives in half lengthwise. Wash, shake dry, and coarsely chop the parsley and basil. Place all of these veggies in the bowl with the walnuts. If using pickled red onion, drain and add the onion slices to the bowl. If using raw onion, dice it finely and add it to the bowl.

5. Once the quinoa is cooked, remove from heat and stir it with a wooden spoon or fork to fluff. While still hot, add the olive oil, vinegar, and pepper to the pot. Stir to mix.

6. Allow the seasoned quinoa to cool at room temperature until it stops steaming. Then, transfer it to the bowl with the veggies, add the lemon juice, and stir to combine. Add more salt and pepper to taste.

7. Cover and place in the refrigerator to chill for 1 hour, or until serving. Serve cold.

QUICK PICKLED ONIONS OR CARROTS

1 cup water
1 cup white distilled vinegar
1 Tbsp salt
1 medium red onion or 2 large carrots
1 bay leaf (optional)
1 medium clove garlic (optional)
½ tsp whole black peppercorns (optional)

Make the brine: In a small pot, heat the water and vinegar to boiling. Stir in the salt and turn off heat.

Meanwhile, prepare the vegetables: If using an onion, peel the onion and cut it in half lengthwise. Slice it crossways into long, ¼ inch wide ribbons.

If using carrots, wash, peel, and cut the ends off of the carrots. Slice each carrot into oversized matchsticks 2-3 inches long and about ¼ inch wide.

Place onion or carrot pieces in a quart mason jar. Add the bay leaf, garlic, and peppercorns, if using. I like a simple quick pickle, but you can also add other spices like fresh dill, dill seed, mustard seed, or chili peppers.

Pour ¼ cup of the hot brine into the jar and wait about 30 seconds for it to warm up the glass jar, so the jar won't crack when you pour in the rest of the hot liquid. Slowly pour in the rest of the brine. Put on the lid, and let rest in the refrigerator at least 4 hours, or overnight.

Your pickles are ready to use. Eat the carrots as a snack or include them in an antipasto platter (page 23), and add the onions to salads and sandwiches. They will keep for at least 2 weeks in the refrigerator. The onion will turn the brine a lovely shade of bright pink as it sits.

COOKING IN QUANTITY

When cooking for 15 or more people and multiplying recipes, strange and magical things can happen. Time seems to speed up, veggies take longer to chop, chilled dishes take longer to cool, soups take longer to cook, and cakes take longer to bake. I love the space of the kitchen where food itself seems to determine time, independent of the outside world. This can be intimidating if you want to prepare food for a family gathering or community event and are not used to this relationship to time. Make sure to allow yourself plenty of time, and get support in the kitchen as well.

When prepping and chopping veggies for a raw salad or as an ingredient in a cooked dish, remember that the more veggies you have to prepare, the longer it will take to wash, peel, and chop them. Having a sharp knife is a big plus. You can cut down on extra time if you have plenty of bowls that are large enough to hold the entire quantity of whatever you are chopping, as this reduces the number of times you have to move about the kitchen. Get creative and use a large baking pan or food storage bag as a prep bowl if you don't have a large mixing bowl. Of course, the best way to cook in quantity is with lots of friends, family, and support. If you are preparing food for a big event, invite people over to chop the veggies the day before, and store the prepped veggies, tightly covered, in the refrigerator.

If multiplying hearty salads that are cooked and then chilled, give yourself plenty of time for that pasta salad, pilaf, bean salad, or roasted veggie salad to cool down. Speed up the cooling process by stirring gently, being careful not to mash up your dish. The quinoa salad on the previous page, for example, cools quickly because as you add the dressing you stir the quinoa, which helps steam to escape. In a larger quantity, it takes longer to cool because it's harder to expose all the little grains to the cool air.

When I make this recipe times five, I take it out of the fridge and stir it every 30 minutes or so—mixing the cooled quinoa on the surface of the bowl with the warm quinoa in the center helps the salad cool faster. It takes about two and a half hours to cool completely.

If making large amounts of soup or stew, water will take longer to heat up and the veggies will take longer to cook, so plan to double the time you'd usually need if you were making a smaller quantity. Exactly how much longer it will take depends on how much more you're making, the shape of the pot, and the heat source. Regularly check the veggies in the soup for doneness. If the soup calls for water, speed things up by heating water in a kettle while the veggies are sautéing. Then, add hot water instead of cold tap water.

Baking times are the same for cookies or other single-serve items, and longer for a cake or brownies baked in a thick, wide pan. Check cakes and brownies for doneness by sight and with a toothpick once their regular baking time has passed. But, try not to open the oven door too much, as this lowers the temperature and will affect both baking time and quality. Additionally, when baking in large quantities (tripled or quadrupled), reduce the amount of baking powder, baking soda, and salt to about ¾, to make sure the recipe doesn't taste too salty or soda-y.

Quadrupling recipes often leaves you with lots of leftovers. Most recipes make a little extra, which, when multiplied, will turn into a lot extra. When serving a meal with multiple side dishes, people typically eat less of each dish, which also leads to more leftovers than expected. For summer quinoa salad, I will typically multiply it by five for 35 people (rather than by six). Gauging this can be tricky, and requires that you guess whether you are serving a group of big eaters. It's never good to run out of food, so you may want to err on the side of abundance and keep containers on hand for people to take home leftovers.

Lima Beans with Carrots and Dill

Lima beans are such a comfort food to me, and I love how flavorful these creamy little morsels get when cooked in this veggie and herb broth. Dill adds an extra zing to this summer favorite, which is delicious served with vegan biscuits (page 172), collard greens (page 87), and almond-crusted tofu cutlets (page 24).

Makes: 4 servings as a main dish, or 6 servings as a side
Prep time: 10 minutes
Cook time: 35-40 minutes

1 medium onion
1 medium carrot
3 medium cloves garlic
1 Tbsp + ¼ cup fresh parsley, divided
2 Tbsp olive oil
1 bay leaf
½ tsp dried oregano, or 1 tsp fresh
½ tsp salt
¼ tsp pepper
1 cube veggie broth, chopped
2 ½ cups water
1 pound frozen lima beans (regular size or baby limas both work well)
1 Tbsp dill, fresh or frozen

1. Dice the onion into small ¼ inch pieces. Peel the carrot and either dice into ¼ inch pieces or roughly grate it. Mince the garlic. Finely chop all of the parsley and set aside.

2. Heat the olive oil in a medium pot, and sauté the onions on medium heat until they begin to soften, about 5 minutes. Add the carrot, garlic, and bay leaf. Cover and cook 5 minutes more, stirring once or twice.

3. Add 1 Tbsp of the chopped parsley, plus the oregano, salt, pepper, and chopped veggie broth cube. Stir to mix. Add the water, cover, turn heat to medium high, and bring to a boil. Add the lima beans, cover, and bring to a boil again. Immediately reduce heat and simmer for 20 minutes, until the lima beans are tender but still light green in color.

4. Chop the dill and stir it into the pot along with the remaining ¼ cup parsley. Turn off heat, cover, and let sit for about 10 minutes to allow the herbs to infuse into the dish. Serve with a slotted spoon. You can make this dish a day or so ahead; the herbs will continue to infuse overnight, making the beans even more flavorful the next day.

Pasta Salad with Capers

I started making this dish in search of a pasta salad that would be neither too mayo-y nor boring. This recipe is packed with flavor, and contains just enough pesto and vegan mayo, which—along with the vinegar, capers, and parsley—make it a tangy summer treat.

Makes: 6-8 large servings
Prep time: 20 minutes
Cook time: 15 minutes
Chill time: 1 hour

For the pasta:
1 pound pasta like fusilli (spiral), farfalle (bow ties), or conchigliette (little shells)
2 quarts water
1 tsp salt
1 Tbsp olive oil

For the dressing:
¼ cup vegan pesto (page 140)
¼ cup vegan mayo, such as Veganaise or Nayonaise
3 Tbsp apple cider vinegar
1 Tbsp nutritional yeast
1 tsp salt
½ tsp ground black pepper
¼ tsp dried oregano

For the salad:
¼ cup fresh parsley
⅓ cup red onion, finely chopped
1 cup cherry tomatoes (half of a pint container)
1 cup artichoke hearts (about 3 whole hearts)
⅔ cup black olives (about half of a 6-ounce can)
¼ cup capers

1. Make the pasta: Bring 2 quarts of water to boil in a large pot with 1 tsp salt and 1 Tbsp olive oil. Add the pasta and cook according to package directions. Place in a colander, drain, and rinse with cold water. Cool the pasta enough so that it is no longer steaming, and make sure it's dry enough that no water drips from the colander. Stir to make sure there's not heat or water hiding in the middle of the pasta.

2. Meanwhile, prepare the dressing: Combine all dressing ingredients in a small bowl and whisk with a fork until well combined.

3. Prepare the veggies for the salad, placing them into a large bowl as you chop them. Wash, shake dry, and chop the parsley. Finely chop the red onion. Wash the cherry tomatoes and slice in half lengthwise. Dice the artichoke hearts. Drain the olives and slice in half lengthwise. Drain the capers.

4. Once the pasta is dry and relatively cool, place it in the bowl on top of the veggies. Add the dressing, and mix it all up.

5. Chill in the fridge for about 1 hour until cool. Serve cold.

VARIATION:

Use this dressing as a base over the pasta, and add any veggies you'd like (such as chopped bell peppers, steamed broccoli, or green peas) to the pasta salad.

VARIATION:

To make this recipe gluten-free, rice-based pasta works well, but it can get a bit tough if refrigerated for 24 hours or more. If you're using gluten-free pasta and this happens with your leftovers, try heating the salad for 20-30 seconds in a microwave to soften it back up.

LAZY BAKER METHOD:

If you don't want to get so many bowls dirty, set a timer and go do something else while the pasta cooks! After draining the pasta, place it in a large bowl. Measure each of the dressing ingredients and add them directly to the pasta rather than mixing the dressing in a separate bowl. Then, chop the veggies, place them directly into the bowl on top of the pasta, and mix again.

Scrambled Tofu

I don't remember who first taught me to make scrambled tofu, but it has been a brunch and breakfast-for-dinner favorite since I became vegan in high school. I once cooked up a giant batch of this simple, tasty recipe for 200 people when helping Chapel Hill chef Vimala Rajendran cater for a conference in Chicago.

Makes: 3-4 servings
Prep time: 10 minutes
Cook time: 25 minutes

1 pound firm or extra firm tofu
1 medium onion
2 medium cloves garlic
1 large carrot
½ large bell pepper (any color)
3-4 Tbsp olive oil
1 tsp ground cumin
½ tsp ground coriander
½ tsp ground turmeric
½ tsp dried oregano
½ tsp salt
½ tsp ground black pepper
2 Tbsp nutritional yeast
2 tsp bottled mustard

1. Drain and rinse the tofu, pat dry with a towel, and set aside.

2. Dice the onion into ½ inch pieces, and finely mince the garlic. Dice the carrot and bell pepper into small ¼ inch pieces.

3. Heat 3 Tbsp of the olive oil in a large cast-iron skillet or non-stick pan on medium heat. Add the onions and garlic, cover, and sauté for about 5 minutes, until onions begin to soften, stirring once or twice.

4. Add the carrot, bell pepper, cumin, coriander, turmeric, oregano, salt, and pepper. Cover and sauté for about 5 more minutes, until veggies begin to get soft.

5. Raise heat to medium high. Use your hands to crumble the tofu into the pan. The crumbles should be a range of sizes, with the largest about the size of an almond. Mix well.

6. Cover and sauté, stirring occasionally, for about 5 minutes on medium high. If it begins to stick, add the additional 1 Tbsp olive oil. Reduce heat to medium and sauté until the tofu starts to gets crispy in places—this should take about 10 minutes more. While the tofu mixture is cooking, stir it occasionally—allowing it to rest in the pan for several minutes between stirs helps its edges crisp up nicely.

7. Turn off heat, add the nutritional yeast and mustard, and stir.

8. Serve warm, alongside pancakes (page 167) and fruit.

VARIATION:

I usually use fresh tofu for this recipe, but frozen tofu works fine, too. The texture of tofu does change when freezing, becoming a bit spongy and more like scrambled eggs. You can also experiment with different combinations of veggies for this dish—mushrooms and spinach in place of the carrot and bell pepper is quite tasty.

Tempeh "Bacon"

This recipe serves three to four people, but if I'm eating it, it serves no more than two because I want to eat the whole batch! It's sweet, salty, and crispy on the outside, and soft on the inside. It's great for breakfast or brunch, or on a sandwich with avocado and tomato.

Makes: 3-4 servings
Prep time: 5-10 minutes
Marinate time: 20 minutes
Cook time: 15 minutes

For the marinade:
1 Tbsp olive oil
2 Tbsp soy sauce or tamari
2 Tbsp maple syrup
1 tsp smoked paprika
½ tsp garlic powder
¼ tsp salt
¼ tsp pepper

For the tempeh:
1 8-ounce block tempeh
(preferably soy)
2 Tbsp olive oil, for frying

1. Prepare the marinade: In a 9x13 inch baking dish, add all the marinade ingredients. Mix well, then spread evenly over the surface of the dish, which will give you a very thin layer of marinade.

2. Prepare the tempeh: Cut your block of tempeh into about 30 very thin, 4-inch long strips (refer to illustration). To do this, cut the block in half so you have 2 thin slabs. You can cut through the packaging, then easily pop each slab out of the plastic. Slice each half-block lengthwise into about 15 thin strips each. Place each strip into the marinade, and flip each strip over to coat evenly on both sides.

3. Let the tempeh marinate for at least 20 minutes—longer is fine, too.

4. Cook the tempeh: In a large non-stick or cast iron skillet, heat the 2 Tbsp olive oil on medium heat. Prepare a plate with a paper towel on it.

5. Once the oil sizzles when a tiny piece of tempeh is tossed into it, fry the tempeh: take each tempeh strip out of the marinade, dipping it to ensure it's well coated and then allowing excess marinade to drip off. Fill the pan with a single layer of tempeh strips, so that each strip can really cook in the oil. If they don't all fit in a single layer, cook tempeh in several batches.

6. Cook for about 4 minutes, then flip and cook 3-4 minutes on the other side. The tempeh strips should turn brown and get slightly crispy on the outside, and may begin to blacken in just a few spots.

7. As the strips finish cooking, use a fork to spear each strip and place it on the paper towel. If cooking in several batches, repeat until all the tempeh is cooked.

8. Serve hot.

HOW TO CUT THE TEMPEH:

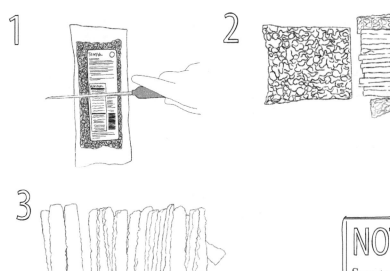

NOTE:
Soy tempeh is preferred here rather than multi-grain tempeh made with rice or millet, because it holds together better when sliced thinly.

Quiche

Quiche makes a great brunch dish, I like to serve it in the summer alongside a cold soup like roasted tomato soup (page 118). The art of quiche is learning the basics and then experimenting with different combinations of seasonal veggies. Kale and mushroom is one of my favorite combos. It's also great with summer squash, tomato, broccoli, artichoke hearts, potatoes, veggie sausage, and a variety of different cheeses. Review the note for help with variations.

Makes: One 9-inch quiche (serves 6)
Prep time: 20 minutes
Bake time: 45-50 minutes

1 9-inch pie crust (page 174)
½ medium onion
1 medium clove garlic
1 cup sliced mushrooms (about 5 medium button mushrooms)
¾ cup chopped kale (about 3 large leaves of kale) or 1 cup raw spinach leaves
¼ cup fresh parsley
10 leaves fresh basil
2 Tbsp olive oil
½ tsp dried oregano
1 tsp salt, divided
½ tsp ground black pepper, divided
3 eggs
1 cup whole milk
¼ cup parmesan cheese
½ cup + ¼ cup grated cheddar cheese, divided

1. Preheat oven to 375°F. Prepare a pie crust in a 9-inch pie pan, and place pan and crust in the freezer to chill.

2. Dice the onion, mince the garlic, and set aside. Wash and slice the mushrooms, and wash and chop kale or spinach. It's nice to cut the veggies into fairly large pieces, so they show up visually in the finished quiche.

3. Coarsely chop the parsley and basil, and set aside.

4. Place olive oil in a medium pan, heat on medium heat, and add the onion and garlic. Cover and cook for about 5 minutes, stirring occasionally, until the onions begin to soften. Add the mushrooms. If using kale, add it here with the mushrooms. Sauté for about 5 minutes, until the mushrooms begin to brown.

5. Add the oregano, ½ tsp of the salt, and ¼ tsp of the pepper. Add the parsley and basil. If using spinach, add it here with the fresh herbs. Continue cooking for about 2 more minutes until the herbs just wilt. Remove from heat and allow to cool slightly. All veggies should be soft, but not mushy.

6. Place the eggs and milk in a bowl or large measuring cup, and whisk together with a fork until evenly mixed. Add remaining ½ tsp salt and ¼ tsp pepper, and mix.

7. Assemble the quiche: Place the veggie mixture in the bottom of the pie crust and spread out evenly over the surface of the crust. Sprinkle with the parmesan and the ½ cup cheddar cheese. Pour the egg mixture over the filling, using your hands or a spoon to lightly mix the filling with the egg, making sure that all the bits of filling are covered in egg and everything is evenly mixed. If you want to, you can arrange the filling so that a few pretty slices of mushroom are visible on the surface of the quiche.

8. Place quiche on a large sheet pan, which will make taking the quiche in and out of the oven much easier and catch any filling that bubbles over while baking.

9. Place pan in the upper half of the oven and bake for 30 minutes. Remove from oven and sprinkle the remaining ¼ cup cheddar cheese evenly over the top of the quiche.

10. Return to oven and bake for 15-20 more minutes. It's done when the center of the quiche is set: if you gently shake the quiche back and forth, the center should hold firm. While baking, the filling may puff up a bit and then settle back down, which is normal.

11. Cool for about 10 minutes before cutting into slices. Serve warm.

VARIATION:

To substitute other veggies in this recipe, the basic formula for one quiche is:
3 eggs
1 cup milk
1 cup total mixed cheeses
1 cup cooked veggies (usually 2 cups raw veggies will cook down to 1 cup).
In most cases, you can cook the veggies with the onion, garlic, and herbs listed above. For veggie sausage, brown it in a separate pan. You can also cut some of the veggies into artful, thin slices to decorate the top of the quiche, such as a cross-section of a bell pepper, tomato, or broccoli floret.

Other favorite veggie and cheese combinations:
Broccoli and veggie sausage with cheddar and jack cheese
Tomato, bell pepper, and artichoke heart with feta and mozzarella cheese

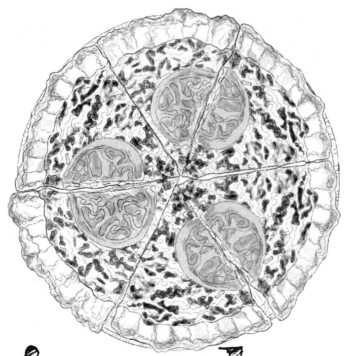

Spinach Ricotta Pie

When I was growing up, spinach ricotta calzone—essentially a pizza pocket filled with a cheesy, spinach filling—was a special treat. This recipe is inspired by my fond memories of that cheesy, spinach-y goodness. Essentially an extra-cheesy quiche, or perhaps a lasagna pie, this dish is an excellent brunch option. It works great for dinner served alongside Tuscan bean stew (page 124) or a simple tomato salad. Ricotta often comes in 15-ounce containers, and either a 15-ounce or 16-ounce container will work just fine here. For a vegan variation, review note.

Makes: One 9-inch pie (serves 6)
Prep time: 20 minutes
Bake time: 40-45 minutes

1 9-inch pie crust (page 174)
½ medium onion
¼ cup fresh parsley
½ pound fresh spinach leaves or half of a 10-ounce package frozen spinach, thawed
2 Tbsp olive oil
1 tsp salt, divided
½ tsp pepper
dash nutmeg
1 pound whole milk ricotta
2 eggs
½ cup grated mozzarella cheese
1 cup grated parmesan cheese
1 medium tomato (optional)

1. Preheat oven to 375°F. Prepare a pie crust in a 9-inch pie pan, and place pan and crust in the freezer to chill.

2. Dice the onion into ½ inch pieces. Wash parsley and roughly chop it. If using fresh spinach, rinse it, keeping the leaves whole. If using frozen spinach, thaw it and squeeze dry, discarding the liquid—you should have about ½ cup of thawed, squeezed spinach.

3. Heat the olive oil in a medium pan, add onion, cover, and sauté for about 5 minutes until it begins to soften and brown. Add spinach, parsley, ½ tsp of the salt, and the pepper and nutmeg. Sauté 3 minutes more, until all spinach has wilted. Remove from heat and let cool for about 5 minutes.

4. Meanwhile, place ricotta in a large bowl and soften it with a wooden spoon. Add the eggs and mix well. Add the mozzarella, parmesan, and remaining ½ tsp salt. Add the cooked spinach mixture, and stir until well mixed.

5. Remove pie crust from the freezer and fill with ricotta-spinach mixture, smoothing the surface of the filling with the back of a spoon. Slice the tomato into thin rounds and arrange rounds artfully on top of the pie.

6. Bake for 40-45 minutes, until the center of the filling has set: it should remain firm when you gently jostle the pie pan.

7. Let stand 10 minutes before cutting and serving.

VARIATION:

To veganize this recipe, replace the ricotta and eggs with 1 recipe cashew cheese (page 21). Double the amount of spinach, using a total of 1 pound total fresh, or one full 10-ounce package frozen. Add 1 cup of your favorite vegan shredded cheese in place of the parmesan, and omit the mozzarella. Top with a sprinkle of your shredded vegan cheese, sliced tomato, and a handful of pine nuts.

Hummus

The word hummus means "chickpea" in Arabic, and versions of the dish originate in Egypt, Palestine, and Lebanon. In the US, hummus has become a bit of a phenomenon as a convenience food, because it's so delicious. Packaged supermarket hummus is made and served differently here than in its countries of origin, but I'm a sucker for the store-bought stuff. Several years ago, I set out to create a recipe for really good homemade hummus that would mirror my favorite varieties. I wanted it to be creamy without too much tahini—just a little tangy, silky smooth, and with a bit of a garlicky bite to it. To develop the recipe, I compared the ingredient labels for several packaged hummus brands, and started experimenting. The resulting recipe is the hummus that I make on a regular basis. It's smooth and creamy, thick enough to hold its own on a sandwich, and also tasty served as a dip.

Makes: About 3 cups (4-6 servings as a main dish, or 12 servings as an appetizer)
Cook time: 1 hour and 15 minutes (if cooking the chickpeas)
Prep time: 15 minutes
Chill time: 2 hours

3 cups cooked chickpeas (1 ½ cups dry, soaked overnight and cooked, or just shy of two 15.5-ounce cans, drained)
3 medium cloves garlic
1 tsp salt
2-4 Tbsp water
½ cups olive oil
3 Tbsp tahini
2 Tbsp lemon juice
1 Tbsp apple cider vinegar
1 tsp ground cumin
1 tsp ground coriander
½ tsp ground black pepper
a few sprigs fresh parsley (optional)

To serve (optional):
olive oil
ground sweet paprika
ground cumin

1. If you are using dried chickpeas, soak them overnight, then drain and rinse. Place in a pot, cover with water, and cook until very soft—1-1 ½ hours. It is important that the chickpeas be very soft, so don't rush them. When they are cooked, drain and rinse the chickpeas.

2. Place the garlic in a food processor and pulse until it is finely chopped, about 15 times. Add the chickpeas, salt, and the 2 Tbsp water. Blend on high for about 15 seconds. Scrape down the sides of the bowl, then, with the food processor running, add the olive oil in a steady stream. Blend for 3-5 minutes, until it is very smooth. This will take a while! If it is too thick for the food processor to function, add the remaining 2 Tbsp water at any point to help it blend.

3. Add the tahini and blend until mixed in, about 30 seconds. Add the lemon juice, vinegar, cumin, coriander, and pepper, and blend for about 1 minute until uniform. If desired, add a few sprigs of parsley and blend for about 20 seconds more, until the parsley is chopped.

4. Scrape hummus out into a serving bowl, and smooth its surface with a rubber spatula. To garnish, use your finger or the tip of a butter knife to make a pattern of indents in the top of the hummus—two concentric circles is nice. Carefully pour olive oil over the surface so that it goes into the grooves that you made. Sprinkle a little cumin and paprika over the top for color. Serve immediately, or cover and refrigerate until serving. If you've used warm chickpeas and want to serve cold hummus, let it chill for 2 hours before serving. Covering the surface with olive oil will help make sure it does not dry out nor discolor as it cools.

NOTE:

Blending the chickpeas while they are still warm helps create a smoother hummus. If you're using canned chickpeas, just make sure to blend until smooth, which may take a few additional minutes. If you're using chickpeas that you've cooked ahead of time and chilled in the fridge, it helps to let them come to room temperature before blending; you can even warm them in a microwave for 60 seconds. Waiting to add the acidic ingredients—lemon juice and vinegar— until after the chickpeas are already fully blended also helps to create a smoother texture.

Chapter Two:

SALADS & VEGGIE SIDES

Work with Dignity CARING FOR OUR BODIES

> "as possible as yeast
> as imminent as bread"
> -LUCILLE CLIFTON[18]

Years ago, I traveled to Chicago as part of Chapel Hill-based chef Vimala Rajendran's team of family members and friends, to cook for the Revolutionary Work in Our Times (RWIOT, pronounced "riot") conference. Vimala's partner, Rush Greenslade, packed pots, pans, and a giant colander into a roof rack carrier on top of their minivan. We piled in at 3 a.m. and drove through gorgeous West Virginia misty valleys and Ohio midday sun toward Chicago. Heading home a week later, we couldn't repack everything as neatly as Rush had, and the colander ended up on my head like a hat. During the drive, we dreamed out loud about opening the family's restaurant, dove deep into hard conversations about healing trauma, and cracked jokes born from the delirium of the long drive—including talking to the colander as if it were a fellow passenger. Vimala has mentored me through various cooking pursuits; later I would work at her restaurant, Vimala's Curryblossom Café,[19] for several years.

It was amazing and wonderful to nourish this collaboration of 250 communist, socialist, and anarchist radicals, scheming and dreaming futures together. And, it was exhausting. I had my first experience of what I call "mermaid feet," where I worked for so many hours in a row that my feet began to hurt like walking on needles with every single step. In the original Hans Christian Anderson version of The Little Mermaid, the mermaid agrees to a horribly patriarchal deal—in order to become human and marry the man of her dreams, she must experience every step on land like daggers in her feet. This detail was omitted from the Disney version of the story.

On the last day, with mermaid feet in full effect, the entire cooking team came out to participate in the morning assembly, so that everyone could thank us. We were invited to stay for a brief centering meditation, led by brilliant healing justice practitioner Yashna Maya Padamsee, who encouraged everyone to fully inhabit our bodies. Members of the cooking team started looking around at each other uncomfortably. As beautiful as Yashna's guidance was, we were all in so much pain that dropping into feeling was not a pleasant experience. We knew that after the 5 minutes were up, we would have to return to the kitchen to prepare lunch for everyone; tuning into our pain would make it hard to do that task with love. Many of us slipped quietly back into the kitchen.

Nested in my memory of that experience are all the times I forgot to care for myself while cooking for others, and also all the times we made do together. Like when, in the very first week of baking for Bread Uprising cooperative, fellow baker Tim Stallmann and I made a spreadsheet of bread orders for the 25 founding-member households, and baked the exact right amount. It wasn't until the bread came out of the oven that we realized we had forgotten to put in a bread order for ourselves! Or when co-worker Ala Jitan and I would close the kitchen at Vimala's Curryblossom Café, full of conversations about navigating the liminal spaces of gender, religion, and liberation. Sometimes, at a certain hour of the night, my brain would shut down from exhaustion, either because I came to work from an already long day of facilitation, or just because I had rolled and baked 100 naan that evening. Scrubbing the griddle, I would say, "I can only talk about Harry Potter now," and Ala would kindly change the subject and ask me something about Hagrid or Hermione.

Cooking for large community events often involves impossibly long, strenuous hours. I strive to move through the kitchen with as much presence as possible, and sometimes it's just hard. Knowing that I am doing important work, I may choose to continue to keep going even when it is physically painful. As a relatively able-bodied caterer with some autonomy, I have the privilege to make those choices based on my own body's capacity.[20] But the food system itself rests directly on a lack of choice: on exploitation of people's bodies in fields, processing plants, and sweltering kitchens. This denial of body autonomy runs through from the enslavement of African people—forced to migrate, grow food, and cook for white profit—to today, where low-wage food service workers, many the descendants of enslaved people, have to fight for basic rights like a liveable wage and the ability to unionize.[21]

Because the food system is shaped by oppression, our food itself carries these stories of exploitation—and the resilience and resistance that goes with them. Most Southern foods come from Black, Indigenous, and poor white food traditions in this region: meals prepared from what is left after the land has been stolen, after a slave owner's family ate their fill, or after a long day's work—yet served up to family with skill and love.[22] Recipes in this Southern tradition, passed down through generations of people who could cook and share them because they survived, carry freedom dreams mixed in with the ingredients. Cooking these foods requires honoring the communities these dishes come from and working to restore sovereignty over land, life, and body.

I am in the kitchen in the summertime, preparing collards.[23] Under the wash water, deep green leaves are dotted with silver air bubbles: beautiful teardrops. Audre Lorde writes that when we allow ourselves the power of feeling our lives fully, our work can become "a conscious decision—a longed for bed which I enter gratefully and from which I rise up empowered."[24] These greens carry both the denial of that human right and the possibility of its fruition. I am dreaming of work with dignity in kitchens everywhere, including care, the resources to thrive, and the safety to choose to be in our bodies.

Quick-Sautéed Collard Greens

This is the way I most often make collards at home, because it's quick, and I like how the edges of the greens get browned and a little bit crispy. You're basically pan-searing them, so the keys are high heat, plenty of oil, and low moisture: the greens are cooked in two rounds to ensure the steam can escape. This method works especially well when the leaves are young and tender, and works great for kale, too. I learned to cook greens this way from Lizzie Jacobs, my co-worker in The Stone House kitchen.

Makes: 4-5 servings
Prep time: 20 minutes
Cook time: 15 minutes

1 medium onion
2 medium cloves garlic
2 pounds collard greens
5 Tbsp olive oil, divided
1 ½ tsp salt
½ tsp ground black pepper
1 tsp apple cider vinegar

1. Cut the onion in half lengthwise, then slice crossways into long, ¼ inch wide ribbons. Cut up the garlic as you wish.

2. Wash the collard greens, shake dry, and de-stem them (refer to note on page 89). Cut into thin strips, and place in a large bowl.

3. Heat about half the olive oil in a wide, heavy-bottomed pan or pot on medium heat. Add the onion, cover, and sauté on medium heat for about 5 minutes, until it begins to soften, stirring occasionally.

4. Raise heat to medium high. Add the garlic, then half the collard greens. Add the salt and pepper, and sauté uncovered for 3 minutes, stirring often. The greens should wilt and reduce in volume—now there is enough room in the pan for the second half of the greens.

5. Push the first batch to one side of the pan and add the second batch next to it. Sprinkle the remaining half of the olive oil on top of the new batch of collards and stir. You can move the greens around in the pan so the first batch is on top of the second batch, allowing the second batch to cook on direct heat in the bottom of the pan. Cook for about 5 more minutes, stirring every minute or so, or until the greens are tender with just a slight crunch to them.

6. Remove from heat, sprinkle the vinegar over the greens, and mix.

7. Serve immediately, or cover until ready to serve.

Slow-Cooked Collard Greens

This is a Southern staple, and I love passing by a garden with a long row of collards growing up out of the red earth. Collards grow throughout most of the year, but because my family is not ancestrally from the South, we didn't grow or cook collards when I was growing up. I have come to love them as a staple comfort food, and learned to cook them years ago from my housemate Denise VanDeCruze. She would put a whole onion in the bottom of the pot, and when the onion was soft and caramelized after hours of cooking, the collards were done. This recipe is adapted from that method, which works because the collards slowly steam themselves, absorbing the flavors of the spices as they cook. It's nice to do this with just a little bit of liquid—that way the greens aren't floating in broth at the end. They turn out soft, creamy, and nutritious, perfect for a cold winter evening.

1 medium onion
4 medium cloves garlic
2 pounds collard greens
3 Tbsp olive oil
1 whole dried ancho chile pepper
1 bay leaf
¼ cup water
2 Tbsp tamari or soy sauce
1 Tbsp apple cider vinegar
½ cube veggie broth, chopped
1 tsp smoked paprika
1 tsp ground black pepper
½ tsp salt

Makes: 5-6 large servings
Prep time: 20 minutes
Cook time: 30 minutes

1. Cut the onion into 8-10 large pieces, and cut up the garlic as you wish.

2. Wash the collard greens, shake dry, and de-stem them (refer to note and illustration). Cut into thin strips, and place in a large bowl.

3. Heat olive oil in a large, heavy-bottomed pot on medium heat. Add the onions, garlic, ancho chile, bay leaf, and then the collards on top. Pour water, soy sauce, and vinegar over collards. Add the chopped veggie broth cube to the pot. Sprinkle collards with smoked paprika, pepper, and salt.

4. Cover and let cook on medium heat for about 10 minutes. Stir and check to make sure there is at least a tiny bit of liquid in the bottom of the pot. Reduce heat to low and cook for about 20 minutes more, stirring 1-2 times to ensure even cooking. The collards are done when the onion is completely soft, the leaves are fading in color, and they taste delicious!

NOTE:

To de-stem collards, hold a single collard leaf by the stem with one hand, and place 2 fingers from your other hand just at the base of the leaf. Quickly run those fingers along the stem towards the far end of leaf, taking the leaf with you. If the leaves are too tough for this, place each leaf underside-up on the cutting board and run a chef's knife on either side of the stem to remove it.

To chop collards into thin strips, lay a de-stemmed leaf flat on the counter and layer more de-stemmed leaves on top of it until you have a small pile of about 10 leaves. Gently roll the pile up into a tight, long roll. Hold one end of the roll with one hand, and with the other use a chef's knife to cut thin slices, about ¼ wide, across the roll. You'll end up with long, thin strips of collards. If you want them shorter, cut them in half.

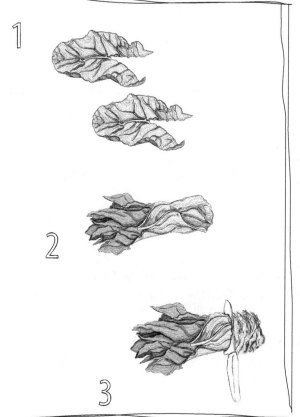

VARIATION:

For a different flavor profile, replace the olive oil with niter kibbeh (page 59). Replace the paprika, bay leaf, and ancho chile with 3 Tbsp grated fresh ginger and half of a chopped jalapeño pepper. This is similar to the way gomen wat, an Ethiopian collard green dish, is prepared. I like to make it this way to serve with mesir wat (page 56) or doro wat (page 58).

Baked Zucchini with Pesto

Pesto is so tasty, and this is a simple way to serve it over veggies. These zucchini "boats" are great as a side dish for lasagna (page 16 and 18) or spaghetti and meatballs (page 20).

Makes: 6 servings
Prep time: 10 minutes
Bake time: 30 minutes

2 Tbsp + ¼ cup pesto,
  divided (page 140)
1 Tbsp fresh oregano leaves
3 medium zucchini (about
  1 ½ pounds)
1 Tbsp olive oil
pinch of salt

1. Preheat oven to 375°F. Prepare pesto (page 140).

2. Wash oregano, shake dry, and pull whole leaves off the stem. Place leaves in a small bowl and set aside.

3. Wash zucchini, cut off stem end, and slice in half lengthwise. Place on a sheet pan or in a 9x13 inch baking dish.

4. Drizzle olive oil over zucchini, then use your hands to toss, ensuring that the oil coats each piece and the pan. Arrange zucchini cut side up, in a single layer. Sprinkle with a tiny bit of salt.

5. Use a butter knife or spatula to spread 2 Tbsp of the pesto evenly over the cut edge of each zucchini piece, reserving the rest until after the zucchini has cooked. Sprinkle with oregano leaves.

6. Bake for 30 minutes. Zucchini should be tender but not mushy.

7. Remove from oven and spread the remaining ¼ cup of pesto evenly over the zucchini pieces. Serve warm.

NOTE: Zucchini can get humongous in the summertime. In order to ensure you have tender zucchini and reasonably portioned pieces for this dish, choose zucchini no bigger than 8 inches long and 2 inches in diameter. You can also make this recipe with yellow crookneck squash.

HOW TO ROAST VEGGIES

Roasting is one of my favorite ways to prepare vegetables. It's almost magical how just olive oil, salt, and pepper can create such crispy, caramelized, fresh, and tasty morsels. I have even been accused of lying when I list the simple ingredients that I put on a roasted veggie side dish, because it tastes too good to be true. You can roast just about any vegetable. Here are a few tips for success.

When preparing roasted veggies, I think about two things: First, what does this meal need? Veggies that work great for roasting include starchy vegetables like potatoes and vitamin-rich ones like broccoli. Whether I'm choosing one vegetable or a combination to roast together, I think about whether I am looking to fill in the carbs for a meal, or the green vegetable. Second, I think about what is in season, and what will be fresh and delicious this time of year.

Tips for crispy, delicious veggies:

1. After washing the veggies, make sure they are dry before cutting them up and roasting. Excess moisture will cause them to steam in the oven rather than roast, making them soft before they can get any crispness on the outside. Dry veggies, on the other hand, will brown nicely.

2. Cut the veggies into medium-large pieces. If the pieces are too large—more than a couple of inches across—they'll brown on the outside before cooking through in the middle. But large, artfully cut chunks of veggies can be really nice for presentation. I split the difference and cut softer veggies like broccoli into 2- to 3-inch long florets, and most root vegetables into 1 ½ inch cubes.

3. Toss the veggies generously in olive oil, which will ensure that the natural sugars on the surface of the veggie pieces will caramelize, giving them a browned, crispy texture on the outside and a sweet, delectable flavor. Toss them in salt and pepper before roasting, then taste and adjust seasonings before serving. You can get creative with different spices and seasonings, but choose dry spices, not water-based seasonings like vinegar or soy sauce.

4. Use a hot oven: 400-425°F is best. This will help the veggies get crispy on the outside.

5. Place veggies in a single layer on a sheet pan and leave the pan uncovered when roasting. This will allow their natural moisture to evaporate and ensure that they can roast on all sides. Stir roasting veggies every 15-20 minutes to ensure even cooking and to prevent them from sticking to the pan.

6. Be mindful of different cooking times when roasting a combination of veggies at once. Veggies like zucchini, broccoli, cauliflower, green beans, okra, and bell pepper will roast quickly—and a hot, 425°F oven is especially important for ensuring that they brown. Garlic, onions, eggplant, carrots, potatoes, sweet potatoes, and winter squash will roast for a medium amount of time—they do best at 400°F, to ensure they cook through. Beets take the longest time to roast. If combining veggies that roast for different amounts of time, roast each on separate pans—or separate areas of the same pan—so you can easily remove each type of vegetable as it finishes roasting. Oven temperature can be flexible here as long as you mind the roasting time and check the veggies for doneness.

7. Be patient. If you just really want the veggies to be done but they're not browning yet, remind yourself that they are going to be so good if you wait.

8. Garlic cloves can be roasted right in their paper husk and removed from it after roasting. Toss them in olive oil and a little salt right in the husk. They will be much easier to peel after roasting, which softens them and helps them pull away from the skin.

9. Use a metal spatula to turn the veggies right after they come out of the oven so they don't stick to the pan. And, of course, you can eat some right off the pan!

Okra and Tomatoes

Okra is a plant of the African diaspora—it made its way to this continent with Black people forcibly brought here as slaves. Jews for Racial and Economic Justice's Jews of Color Caucus puts an okra pod on the Seder plate to honor Black resilience and survival.[25] I love okra, and to cut down on its sliminess, I like to either roast it in long spears (roasted seasonal veggie salad, page 102) or stew it with tomatoes. This stewed option is a Southern classic—the tomatoes seem to help the okra's texture, and the flavors complement each other well. Acquiring fresh, young okra will help ensure success here (refer to note). Okra plants are also gorgeous. If you have the opportunity to grow it, it's fun to harvest the little okras, which point upward from their stem. Mint adds a refreshing flavor to this dish, perfect as part of a summer dinner.

Makes: 4-6 servings
Prep time: 10 minutes
Cook time: 20-25 minutes

1 pound okra (about 2 ½ cups sliced)
1 ½ pounds fresh tomatoes (about 3 ½ cups chopped)
1 medium onion
3 medium cloves garlic
⅓ cup fresh parsley
2 Tbsp olive oil
¾ tsp salt
½ tsp ground black pepper
½ tsp dried oregano, or 1 tsp fresh
½ tsp dried basil

To serve:
10 large leaves spearmint or apple mint

1. Wash the okra and tomatoes. Slice the stem end off of the okra and discard. Cut the okra crossways into rounds ½ to 1 inch thick, and set aside. Core the tomatoes and chop them into large 1-inch pieces.

2. Cut the onion into ½ inch pieces, and finely mince the garlic. Set these aside. Wash the parsley, shake dry, and coarsely chop.

3. Place olive oil in a medium pot and heat on medium heat. Add onion and garlic, cover, and cook for about 5 minutes, stirring occasionally, until onions begin to soften.

4. Add okra, salt, pepper, oregano, and basil and cook, uncovered, stirring frequently, for 5 minutes.

5. Add tomatoes, stir, cover, and cook for 5 minutes. Add parsley, cover, and cook for 5 more minutes. Okra should be tender and tomatoes should still be in distinct chunks that are just beginning to fall apart.

6. Wash the mint, remove from the stem, and chop the mint leaves crossways into fine strips. Sprinkle mint over okra just before serving.

NOTE:

When choosing okra, make sure the pods are small and tender. Many varieties of okra get tough and stringy once they grow to be longer than a middle finger. If I have an okra pod that is questionable, I often do the fingernail test by piercing the outside of the okra fruit with my nail. If my nail won't go in, it's too tough. If I can pierce it, even with difficulty, it's good to use. If you are buying okra from a farmer, do not be rude—if you poke an okra with your fingernail and it passes the test, buy it!

Roasted Potatoes

I love roasted root vegetables of any sort, and these potatoes are particularly tasty because they get nice and crispy like home fries. The rosemary adds a pungent, earthy flavor that makes them extra comforting. They will sing to you when they first come out of the oven as steam escapes from the crispy potato skin.

Makes: 4-5 servings
Prep time: 10 minutes
Cook time: 40-45 minutes

2 pounds Yukon gold potatoes, red potatoes, or a combination of both
2 Tbsp dried rosemary, or 1 large sprig fresh
2 Tbsp + 1 Tbsp olive oil, divided
1 tsp salt
½ tsp ground black pepper
½ tsp garlic powder
2 Tbsp fresh parsley

1. Preheat oven to 425°F.

2. Wash the potatoes well and remove any bruised spots. Leaving the skin on, chop them into large 1 to 1 ½ inch chunks and place in a large bowl.

3. If using fresh rosemary, remove the stem and chop the leaves finely before adding to the bowl. If using dried rosemary, crumble it into the bowl with your fingers.

4. Sprinkle 2 Tbsp of the olive oil over potatoes.

5. Sprinkle the salt, pepper, and garlic powder over potatoes and toss to coat—hands are great for this, or a large metal spoon will do.

6. Grease a large sheet pan with the remaining 1 Tbsp olive oil. Place the herb-coated potatoes on the pan in a single layer. Depending on the size of your pan, you may need two pans.

7. Place in the upper half of the oven and bake for 40-45 minutes, turning with a spatula after 15 minutes and again after 30 minutes. They should be crispy on the outside and soft on the inside.

8. Meanwhile, wash the parsley and pat dry with a towel. Chop finely and set aside.

9. Once the potatoes are cooked, toss with the chopped parsley. Serve hot.

LAZY BAKER METHOD:

Place the cut potatoes directly on the pan(s) and sprinkle evenly with rosemary, all 3 Tbsp of the olive oil, and seasonings. Toss right on the pan, then bake.

Spiced Sweet Potatoes

In late summer and early fall, sweet potatoes are plentiful in North Carolina, and they can be as sweet as candy. Sometimes I leave the peel on my sweet potatoes for a nice chewy texture, but for this recipe, I remove it so the sweet potatoes absorb the flavors from the spices and coconut oil to become such sweet, delicious nuggets. Ajwain, found at most Indian grocery stores or at gourmet markets, gives this dish a pungent kick without heat.

Makes 4-6 servings
Prep time: 15 minutes
Cook time: 40-50 minutes

2 Tbsp virgin coconut oil
3 large sweet potatoes (about 2.5 pounds)
1 tsp salt
1 tsp ajwain seeds
2 tsp ancho chili flakes (review note, or substitute chili powder blend)

1. Preheat oven to 425°F.

2. If the coconut oil is solid, bring it to a liquid state by measuring the oil into a small glass jar, then microwaving for 40 seconds; or by placing the jar in hot water for 15 minutes and stirring occasionally until the oil melts.

3. Wash and peel the sweet potatoes. Chop into large 1 to 1 ½ inch cubes.

4. Place sweet potatoes on a large sheet pan and drizzle with the coconut oil. Sprinkle with salt, ajwain, and chili flakes. Toss to coat evenly.

5. Bake for 40-50 minutes, turning with a spatula after 15 minutes and again after 30 minutes. The sweet potatoes should be soft on the inside, with crispy edges.

NOTE

This dish is flavorful yet mild. If you want it spicy-hot, add 1 tsp of red pepper flakes or ½ tsp ground cayenne pepper along with the ancho chili flakes.

ANCHO CHILI FLAKES

Gone are the days when I would use flavorless, generic chili powder blends whose ingredient labels boast that it contains "spices." I love to purchase whole, dried chilies from the local Latin American supermarket, which sells about 8 different varieties in bulk. When choosing chilies, they should be slightly flexible—not brittle—and smell sweet and fragrant. Ancho chilies, which are dried poblano peppers, are my favorite. Guajillo chilies are also a tasty, relatively mild option to add to your mix. Here's how to toast and blend your own chili powder.

1. Purchase 5 large, mild dried chilies from a market.

2. Toast the chilies to bring out the flavor: Preheat oven to 350°F. Place the chilies on a pan and roast in the oven for 7-10 minutes, just until the skin blisters. Some of them may puff up. Remove from the oven and let cool. They will become brittle.

3. Discard the stems and the seeds. Place the remaining peppers in a spice grinder or mortar and pestle and coarsely grind.

4. Store the flakes in an airtight glass jar for up to 2 months, and add to almost any dish. Five ancho chilies make about ⅓ cup of chili flakes.

Coconut Mashed Sweet Potatoes

I first made this recipe for a retreat at The Stone House, as part of a make-your-own taco bar. It's simple and tasty, and works great as a taco or burrito ingredient or as a side dish of its own. As the name suggests, it's quite coconut-y.

Makes: 5-6 servings
Cook time: 1 hour
Cool time: 15 minutes
Prep time: 15 minutes

2 ½ pounds sweet potatoes (choose medium-sized ones, about 4)
¼ cup unsweetened coconut flakes (optional)
1 cup full-fat canned coconut milk
1 Tbsp coconut or olive oil
1 tsp garlic powder
1 tsp salt
1 tsp ancho chili flakes (optional, page 97)

1. Preheat oven to 400°F.

2. Wash the sweet potatoes and place them whole on a sheet pan. Poke each one a few times with a fork. Bake for 30 minutes. Remove from oven, turn each potato over, and return to oven. Bake until very soft, at least 30 more minutes, or longer for large sweet potatoes. You can speed up baking time for large potatoes by cutting them in half beforehand. They are done when the skin has pulled away from the sweet potato flesh, and the flesh is very soft when poked with a fork.

3. Let cool for 10-15 minutes, until you can comfortably handle them.

4. Meanwhile, if using the coconut flakes, spread them out on a pan, and place in the oven to toast until golden brown, about 4 minutes. Set aside to cool.

5. Peel the skin off the sweet potatoes and discard. Place potatoes in a large bowl. Mash with a potato masher or a wooden spoon until they are relatively smooth.

6. Add the coconut milk, olive or coconut oil, garlic powder, salt, and ancho chili flakes (if using). Beat with a spoon until well mixed and fluffy. Place in a serving bowl and top with toasted coconut flakes. Serve warm.

NOTE:

I usually include the toasted coconut topping if serving as a side dish, but omit it if the sweet potatoes are going into tacos or burritos.

Herbed Potato Salad

This is a vinegar-based potato salad, chock full of fresh herbs. I like to leave the skin on the potatoes for extra color and flavor, but you can remove it if you prefer. When potatoes are in season, it's extra nice to use a combination of several varieties, including purple potatoes. You can also make this recipe with other fresh herbs if you have them on hand: thyme and oregano are tasty in different combinations with dill, parsley, basil, and sage. Any way you make it, it's perfect for an outdoor meal.

Makes: 6 servings
Prep time: 15 minutes
Cook time: 15 minutes
Chill time: 1 ½ hours

For the potatoes:
1 quart water
1 tsp salt
2 pounds red, gold, or purple potatoes

For the salad:
½ small red onion (about ¼ cup chopped)
2 medium cloves garlic
2 Tbsp fresh dill
¼ cup fresh parsley
10 large leaves fresh basil
1 tsp chopped fresh sage (optional)
6 Tbsp olive oil
2 Tbsp apple cider vinegar
2 Tbsp red wine vinegar
¾ tsp salt
½ tsp ground black pepper

1. Cook the potatoes: In a medium pot on high heat, heat the water to boiling with the 1 tsp salt. While the water heats, wash potatoes and remove any bruised spots. Chop into large cubes, about 1 inch wide.

2. Once the water boils, add the potatoes and cook for about 15 minutes until soft, not mushy. A fork should go into a piece of potato easily.

3. Meanwhile, prepare the dressing and herbs. Dice the onion into small ¼ inch pieces. Finely mince the garlic. Finely chop the dill, parsley, basil, and sage (if using). Set these aside.

4. Place the olive oil, apple cider vinegar, red wine vinegar, ¾ tsp salt, and pepper in a tightly-lidded mason jar and shake to mix.

5. Once the potatoes have cooked, drain them in a colander and place in a medium bowl. While the potatoes are still hot, pour the dressing over them. Sprinkle the onion, garlic, and herbs over potatoes, and mix gently.

6. Chill in the refrigerator until cold, about 1 ½ hours. Speed up this process by stirring the salad every 30 minutes or so. Be careful not to overmix, as the potatoes can become mushy. Serve cold.

LAZY BAKER METHOD: Instead of mixing up the dressing in a separate jar, measure out each dressing ingredient directly onto the cooked potatoes. Add onions, garlic, and herbs, and mix.

Green Bean and Fennel
Salad with Balsamic Vinegar

This recipe is a tasty way to serve green beans in the heat of summer, when they are in season. I love the sweetness that the balsamic vinegar adds to this salad when it caramelizes on the roasted veggies. The combination of fennel, basil, and red onion is delightful, but I've made the latter two optional if you prefer a simpler salad. This dish is delicious served warm or cold.

Makes: 6 servings
Prep time: 15 minutes
Bake time: 35 minutes
Chill time: 30 minutes (optional)

2 pounds fresh green beans
1 bulb fennel
¼ cup olive oil
¼ cup balsamic vinegar
1 tsp salt
½ tsp ground black pepper
½ tsp garlic powder
2 Tbsp fresh parsley
2 Tbsp fresh basil (optional)
2 Tbsp red onion (optional)

1. Preheat oven to 400°F.

2. Wash and de-stem the green beans, leaving them whole. Remove the fronds from the fennel bulb, reserving 2 pieces of frond and discarding the rest. Slice the fennel bulb crossways into thin ¼ inch pieces—they should break apart into wishbone-shaped slivers of fennel.

3. In a large bowl, toss the green beans and fennel slivers with the olive oil, balsamic vinegar, salt, pepper, and garlic powder. Spread evenly on a large sheet pan and roast for 30-35 minutes, turning with a spatula after 20 minutes. The veggies are done when green beans are soft and their color has muted, and fennel has just a slight crunch to it.

4. Meanwhile, finely chop the reserved fennel frond, parsley, basil, and red onion (if using). Set these aside in a small bowl.

5. Once green beans and fennel are cooked, transfer to a large bowl. Add the fresh herbs and red onion, and toss to mix.

6. To serve cold, chill in the refrigerator for at least 30 minutes. Or, serve immediately.

LAZY BAKER METHOD:

Toss the green beans and fennel in the seasonings right on the pan, rather than in a bowl. After chopping the fresh herbs, set them aside in the large bowl in which you plan to serve the finished salad. You can clean up the cutting board while the veggies roast. Then, once roasted, sprinkle the herbs over the pan of beans to ensure they mix in evenly. Transfer back to the bowl—all you'll need to wash up is the roasting pan.

Lemony Green Beans with Fresh Herbs

This is a simpler, quicker green bean recipe that's still full of flavor. The green beans are steamed in boiling salted water, and then dressed. This dish is especially good with fresh-squeezed lemon juice, and is great served warm or cold.

Makes: 6 servings
Prep time: 15 minutes
Cook time: 10 minutes
Chill time: 30 minutes (optional)

For the green beans:
2 pounds fresh green beans
2 cups water
$\frac{1}{2}$ tsp salt

For the dressing:
$\frac{1}{2}$ cup lemon juice
2 Tbsp olive oil
$\frac{1}{4}$ cup fresh parsley
2 Tbsp fresh basil
$\frac{1}{4}$ cup fresh dill
$\frac{1}{4}$ tsp salt
$\frac{1}{4}$ tsp ground black pepper

1. Wash and de-stem the green beans, leaving them whole.

2. Cook the green beans: Heat 2 cups of water with the $\frac{1}{2}$ tsp salt in a medium pot on high heat until boiling. Reduce heat to medium high, add the green beans, and cook for 8-10 minutes, until bright green in color and slightly soft.

3. Meanwhile, make the dressing: Juice the lemon and place juice in a small, tightly-lidded jar with the olive oil. Wash and chop the parsley, basil, and dill, and add to the dressing. Add the $\frac{1}{4}$ tsp salt and the pepper. Shake well to mix.

4. Drain the green beans in a colander, and place in a large bowl. Pour the dressing over them and toss to coat.

5. Serve immediately. Or to serve cold, chill in the refrigerator for at least 30 minutes before serving.

CHOOSING GREEN BEANS:
Green beans are best when they are fresh and tender: they get tough if left on the plant too long. When buying, check to make sure there are no brown spots and that they snap easily. You can actually snap one in half to make sure—if it breaks easily, without stringiness, it's perfect. If buying from a farmer, make sure to buy the bean you snapped—don't abandon a broken bean!

Roasted Seasonal Veggie Salad

This is a summer favorite, and it's great at any time of year. I like to use different local veggies depending on what is in season. The veggies are roasted, then tossed with fresh herbs and chilled to make a refreshing salad. It's especially nice served over a bed of mixed greens—the juices from the salad become the salad dressing.

Makes: 5 servings
Prep time: 20 minutes
Cook time: 30 minutes
Chill time: 1 hour and 15 minutes

For roasting the veggies:
2 pounds fresh veggies
(variations on facing page):
   1 large eggplant
   ½ pound okra
   ½ pound broccoli crowns
1 large red onion
4 medium cloves garlic
1 tsp salt
1 tsp ground black pepper
1 tsp garlic powder
3 Tbsp olive oil, divided

For the salad:
¼ cup fresh parsley
2 sprigs fresh mint (about 2 Tbsp, chopped)
2 sprigs fresh basil (about 2 Tbsp, torn)
1 tsp fresh or dried oregano
2 Tbsp fresh lemon juice

1. Preheat oven to 425°F.

2. Wash and chop the veggies: Slice the eggplant into rounds about ¼ inch thick. Place in a bowl and set aside. Remove the stem end of the okras and slice each okra lengthwise into 2 long spears. Cut the broccoli crowns into large tree-shaped pieces. Dice the red onion into large 1-inch pieces. Peel the garlic and leave the cloves whole. Place okra, broccoli, onion, and garlic in a second large bowl.

3. Season the veggies: Place salt, pepper, and garlic powder in a small bowl and mix. Divide the spice mixture evenly between the eggplant bowl and the okra bowl, and toss each bowl of veggies with the spices. Add 1 Tbsp of the olive oil to the okra bowl and toss. Drizzle 1 Tbsp olive oil over the eggplant bowl, and toss until evenly coated.

4. Use the remaining 1 Tbsp olive oil to coat 2 large sheet pans. It seems like a lot, but you won't be adding any additional oil to the dressing, so the oil in which the veggies are roasted soaks into the veggies and essentially serves as part of the salad dressing!

5. On one of the pans, arrange the eggplant in a single layer. On the other, spread out the okra mixture into as close to a single layer as possible. If either veggie mixture doesn't fit on your pan, roast in 2 separate batches rather than packing it in.

6. Roast the veggies for 15 minutes, then remove from oven and use a spatula to stir the okra mixture and flip over each eggplant piece. The eggplant should be brown and crispy on the bottom when you flip it, and the okra mixture should be browning where the veggies touch the pan.

7. Return pans to oven. Bake the okra mixture for about 10 more minutes, and the eggplant for about 15 minutes. The veggies should still be slightly crunchy and golden brown. The eggplant should be crispy on the outside and soft on the inside.

8. Use the spatula to make sure the veggies aren't stuck to the pan; let them rest on the pan at room temperature for about 15 minutes until no longer steaming.

9. Meanwhile, wash, dry, and chop the parsley and mint. Use scissors to snip the basil leaves into a few pieces without agitating them too much. De-stem the oregano.

10. Once veggies have stopped steaming, place them in a large bowl. Sprinkle with parsley, mint, basil, oregano, and lemon juice. Stir gently until just mixed.

11. To serve cold, chill for 1 hour before serving.

VARIATIONS: Okra, eggplant, and broccoli is my favorite veggie combination for this salad. I like to use combinations of three different seasonal veggies, and you can use any veggies that roast well. It's great with cauliflower (cut into trees like the broccoli), green beans (de-stem and leave whole), and bell pepper (chop into large pieces)—roast these as described for broccoli and okra above. Zucchini or summer squash can be cut it into rounds like the eggplant and roasted in a single layer on a pan, but will only need to roast for 20-25 minutes in all. The zucchini rounds should still be a little crunchy so that they hold their shape in the salad. You could also include seasonal fruit like fresh figs (cut in half and roast for 15-20 minutes) or pears. Cherry tomatoes also make a nice addition (cut in half and add raw when adding the fresh herbs). Here are a few ideas for seasonal combinations based on an NC harvest calendar:

    Spring: Asparagus, cauliflower, and new potatoes
    Summer: Zucchini, mini peppers, and green beans with cherry tomatoes
    Fall: Broccoli, carrots, and fresh figs
    Winter: Brussels sprouts, carrots, and turnips

LAZY BAKER METHOD: Rather than tossing the veggies in the olive oil and spices in separate bowls, place cut veggies directly on the pan. Sprinkle or brush with olive oil and spices, and toss directly on the pan.

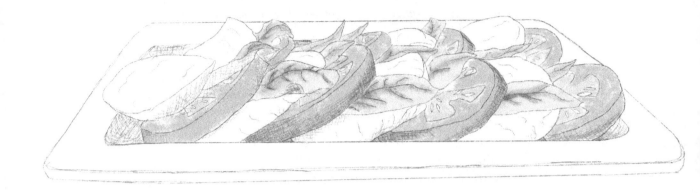

Caprese Salad

Makes: 4 servings as a side dish,
 or more as an appetizer
Prep time: 15 minutes

Tomatoes, fresh mozzarella, and basil are such a tasty combination. In the heat of summer, I like to make this dish with heirloom tomatoes in a variety of shades, creating a rainbow of yellow, red, and purple. Balsamic reduction (page 141) adds extra sweetness to this dish without making it overly juicy.

1 pound slicing tomatoes (about 2
  large or 3 medium tomatoes)
½ tsp salt
½ tsp freshly ground black pepper
2 Tbsp olive oil
1 tsp balsamic vinegar
8 ounces fresh mozzarella cheese
2 large sprigs fresh basil (about 20
  leaves)
2 Tbsp balsamic reduction (page
  141)

1. Slice tomatoes into about 12 large, thick rounds and place in a bowl. Sprinkle with salt, pepper, olive oil, and balsamic vinegar. Gently mix.

2. If the mozzarella is packaged in water, drain it, discarding the liquid. Slice the mozzarella into thin rounds, aiming to have about the same number of pieces as you have tomato slices. Add these to the bowl and gently toss. The goal here is to quick-marinate the mozzarella in the tomato juices, without breaking apart any of the pieces.

3. Wash the basil and dry with a towel. Remove whole leaves from the stem and discard stems.

4. Take individual tomato and mozzarella slices out of the marinade and arrange them on a platter. There are a couple of ways to arrange this dish: As a salad, it's nice to create rows of slightly overlapping tomato and mozzarella—alternating 1 slice of tomato, 1 piece of mozzarella, and 1 basil leaf (refer to illustration). As an appetizer, it can be nice to lay all of the tomato slices flat on the platter, placing a slice of mozzarella and then a basil leaf on top of each so you have 12 neat stacks. Discard excess liquid.

5. Use a teaspoon to drizzle balsamic reduction over the dish. Sprinkle with a little additional salt and pepper, and arrange remaining basil leaves on top. Serve immediately.

VARIATION:

To make vegan, I recommend Miyoko's Creamery brand vegan fresh mozzarella, which is quite tasty, even when raw. You can also omit the mozzarella and make a pretty, simple salad with tomatoes, basil, and dressing.

Spicy Tomato Salad

Makes: 6 servings
Prep time: 20 minutes

This recipe is based on timatim, an Ethiopian tomato and jalapeño salad. It is a delicious summer salad to make with heirloom tomatoes. When fresh tomatoes are not plentiful, I make it with roma tomatoes, as they tend to have more flavor in the wintertime and also hold together well.

2 pounds fresh tomatoes (about 6 cups chopped)
2-inch piece fresh ginger root (about 2 Tbsp grated)
1 jalapeño pepper
½ small white or red onion (about ¼ cup diced)
1 Tbsp olive oil
1 Tbsp unseasoned rice vinegar
½ tsp agave nectar
1 tsp salt
1 tsp ground black pepper
1 tsp berbere (optional, page 57)

1. Wash tomatoes, ginger, and jalapeño. Chop the tomato into ½ inch cubes, and place in a strainer or colander for about 10 minutes to drain off some of the juices.

2. Meanwhile, prepare the rest of the salad: Grate ginger. Remove the seeds from the jalapeño and discard—unless you like it really spicy, in which case, include them—and finely mince the pepper. Dice the onion into ¼ inch pieces.

3. Place the drained tomatoes in a large bowl. Add ginger, jalapeño, and onion. Sprinkle with olive oil, rice vinegar, agave nectar, salt, pepper, and berbere (if using). Mix well.

4. Serve immediately, or chill until ready to serve.

NOTE: Even with the pepper's seeds removed, this salad is a little spicy. If you prefer a milder heat level, use just ¼ or ½ of the jalapeño.

Summer Cucumber Salad with Dill

Makes: 6 servings
Prep time: 15-20 minutes

Cucumbers are plentiful in the early summer in NC, and make for a refreshing treat on a hot day. I have long loved eating them fresh off the vine—one of my favorite childhood photos shows me as a toddler, joyfully running around the back yard with a fresh-picked cucumber from my mother's garden in my hands. I first created a cucumber salad recipe when cooking for the Rooted In Community (RIC) youth food justice conference in 2010. Fellow chef Melanie Wilkerson suggested that we make a cucumber salad to go with lunch, and I was in charge of coming up with recipes for that meal. The recipe has evolved since then, and this version has a hint of sweetness and a nice, radish-y kick. The nigella seeds add a bit of a nuttiness, crunch, and a nice color contrast—find them at an Indian grocery store. There's lots of room for experimentation here with different fresh herbs: try it with basil, sage, or mint in place of the dill and parsley if you like.

1 ½ pounds cucumbers (3 medium or 2 large)
2-4 radishes (to taste)
½ medium white onion
2 Tbsp fresh parsley
2 Tbsp fresh or frozen dill
⅓ cup white vinegar
1 Tbsp agave nectar or granulated sugar
1 Tbsp olive oil
1 tsp kalonji/nigella seeds (optional)
¾ tsp salt

1. Wash and half-peel the cucumbers, so that you have alternating white and green stripes going down the cucumber lengthwise; then slice them into thin rounds. Wash the radishes and slice into thin rounds. Slice the onion into long, thin slivers—as thin as you can get them. Place the cucumber, radish, and onion in a large bowl.

2. Wash the fresh parsley and dill, pat dry with a towel, and coarsely chop. (If using frozen dill, simply crush it while still frozen rather than chopping it.) Add the herbs to the salad bowl.

3. In a small jar or measuring cup, make a dressing by mixing the vinegar, agave or sugar, olive oil, nigella seeds (if using), and salt. Stir until the sugar is dissolved, then pour it over the veggies.

4. Serve immediately, or eat within a day for the freshest flavor.

LAZY BAKER METHOD:

If using agave rather than granulated sugar, measure the dressing ingredients directly onto the veggies in the salad bowl, and mix it all up. This won't work with sugar, as the sugar crystals need to dissolve in the dressing first.

NOTE:

My favorite type of cucumber to use for cucumber salads are the long, thin-skinned English/hothouse cucumbers, but you can make this recipe with any type of cucumber. Check to make sure the peel of your cucumbers is soft enough to eat by poking the cucumbers' end once with your fingernail—if the tip of your nail goes into the skin easily, you don't need to peel them except for aesthetic reasons. If your fingernail doesn't go through easily, the skin is a bit tough and you'll want to peel the cucumber all the way rather than making decorative stripes.

Cucumber Salad with Sesame and Fresh Ginger

This recipe is gingery and pungent, and I like to serve it alongside Thai Red Curry (page 34). In the wintertime, when it's hard to find good cucumbers, you can use the same dressing to make a tasty cabbage salad (review note).

Makes: 6 servings
Prep time: 30 minutes

2 Tbsp sesame oil
2 tsp raw sesame seeds
½ tsp brown mustard seeds
1 ½ pounds cucumber (3 medium or 2 large)
4 small scallions
2 Tbsp fresh basil
2 Tbsp fresh cilantro
2-inch piece fresh ginger root (about 2 Tbsp grated)
⅓ cup unseasoned rice vinegar
1 tsp agave nectar or granulated sugar
¾ tsp salt
¼ tsp ground black pepper

1. In a small pan, heat the sesame oil on medium heat until hot. Add sesame seeds and mustard seeds, and toast for about 3 minutes, until the mustard seeds pop. Remove from heat and let cool.

2. Meanwhile, wash and half-peel the cucumbers, so that you have alternating white and green stripes going down the cucumber lengthwise; then slice them into thin rounds. Slice the scallions in half lengthwise, then into pieces about 1 inch long. Place cucumber and scallions in a large bowl.

3. Wash, pat dry with a towel, and coarsely chop the basil and cilantro. Add the herbs to the salad bowl.

4. Wash the ginger, grate it finely, and place grated ginger in a small jar or measuring cup. If you have any stringy parts left over that won't grate, squeeze the juice from them over the cucumbers, then discard the pulp.

5. Make a dressing by adding the sesame oil mixture, vinegar, agave or sugar, salt, and pepper to the grated ginger. Stir until the agave or sugar is dissolved, then pour the dressing over the veggies.

6. Serve immediately, or eat within a day for the freshest flavor.

VARIATION: This recipe also works great as a cabbage salad. Simply replace the cucumbers with 1 medium head of green or savoy cabbage. Finely chop the cabbage into long, thin pieces. Add the scallions, herbs, and dressing, and toss.

NOTE: Toasting the mustard seeds until they pop removes their bitterness, so you're left with a slightly spicy, nutty flavor. It should take about the same amount of time for the sesame seeds to brown as it takes for the mustard seeds to pop. If you can't find brown mustard seeds, yellow ones will do.

Red Cabbage & Carrot Slaw

I started making this recipe as a slaw to serve with potato enchiladas, beans, and rice. I love that it is tangy and fresh, with a subtle nutty flavor from the toasted mustard and sesame seeds. It's great with all kinds of meals as a lemony cole slaw, an alternative to the standard creamy NC slaw.

Makes: 5 large servings
Prep time: 15-20 minutes

2 Tbsp olive oil
1 tsp mustard seeds
1 Tbsp raw sesame seeds
½ medium head red cabbage (about 1 pound)
2 large carrots
½ bunch fresh cilantro (about 1 cup)
¼ cup lemon juice
2 Tbsp apple cider vinegar
1 tsp garlic powder
1 tsp ground cumin
¾ tsp salt

1. In a small pan, pour in the olive oil, mustard seeds, and sesame seeds. Toast on medium heat for about 3 minutes, until the mustard seeds pop. Remove from heat and let cool.

2. Meanwhile, slice the cabbage into long, thin pieces, almost like linguine: Slice the head of cabbage in half lengthwise, reserving one half for a different use. Place the other half facedown on a cutting board and carefully slice it into thin strips. You can leave the strips as they are, or cut them in half to make them a little shorter. Peel and grate the carrots. Coarsely chop the cilantro.

3. Place cabbage, carrots, and cilantro in a large bowl and mix. Add the lemon juice, vinegar, garlic powder, cumin, and salt. Pour the olive oil and toasted seeds over the salad. Mix well.

4. Serve immediately, or keep in the refrigerator until serving. This salad is best served the same day so that the cabbage is still crispy, but it will keep for 2 days in the fridge.

> NOTE: I love this salad either with just red cabbage or with a mix of red and green. I find that the red cabbage is a bit sweeter and has a fuller flavor than the green, but when I'm making it in quantity, I use one head each of red and green cabbage, as the color combination is especially nice this way. Try it with both red and green cabbage and decide what you prefer!

Kale Salad

This recipe came into my kitchen through co-worker and friend Lizzie Jacobs. I had never heard of kale salad until I met her, and it was always a staple on her menus. Besides being tasty, kale salad is a pretty interesting science project: when massaging the otherwise crunchy leaves with olive oil, the oil breaks down the cell walls of the kale, softening it as if it's been lightly cooked. Lemon and soy sauce add a pleasant, tangy flavor to this dish, and the avocado compliments the kale nicely. You can add different veggies in place of or in addition to the sprouts, like grated carrots or halved cherry tomatoes.

¼ cup raw pumpkin seeds
¼ cup raw sunflower seeds
2 Tbsp raw sesame seeds
1 pound fresh kale (review note)
3 Tbsp olive oil
2 Tbsp lemon juice
2 Tbsp tamari or soy sauce
1 large avocado
4 ounces alfalfa, clover, or pea sprouts

Makes: 4-6 servings
Prep time: 15 minutes
Cook time: 8 minutes

1. Heat a small saucepan on medium heat. Add pumpkin seeds and sunflower seeds. Toast for 2-3 minutes, stirring very frequently, until pumpkin seeds begin to pop and seeds have browned.

2. Place toasted seeds in a small bowl. Add sesame seeds to the hot pan, then immediately turn off heat. Allow sesame seeds to toast in the hot pan for about 5 minutes, stirring occasionally, until they turn golden brown. Add to bowl with the other seeds.

3. Wash, shake dry, and de-stem the kale by holding the stem end in one hand, and with the other hand pinch the stem just at the base of the leaf. Quickly run this second hand along the stem, pulling the leaf off with it and leaving the stem in the first hand. Discard stems.

4. Tear the leaves into small pieces and place in a large bowl.

5. In a small bowl, mix olive oil, lemon juice, and tamari or soy sauce. Pour over the kale and massage the kale with your hands for several minutes. The salad will decrease in volume, which lets you know that the kale is breaking down, absorbing the flavors from the dressing, and developing a nice, soft texture.

6. Sprinkle seeds over kale and mix well.

7. Just before serving, cut the avocado into chunks and add to kale. Wash and drain the sprouts, and add half of them to the kale. Mix gently until kale, avocado, and sprouts are combined. Artfully arrange remaining half of sprouts on top of the salad—I like to tuck little bunches of sprouts all around the edge of the serving bowl.

LAZY BAKER METHOD:

Measure the olive oil, lemon juice, and tamari or soy sauce directly onto the kale rather than mixing it up in a separate bowl.

NOTE:

You can make this salad with any kale, but I prefer to use a curly-leafed kale rather than the smooth lacinato kale, because I find that the latter breaks down a bit too much. My favorite for this recipe is red Russian kale—the purple one! It's so pretty, has a nice texture, and has a less plant-y taste than green curly kale.

Chapter Three:

SOUPS

Queer Possibility
CHOSEN FAMILY RECIPES

"May the taste of honey linger
Under the bitterest tongue."
-ADRIENNE RICH[26]

For me, carrot soup is one of those dishes that carries home. It was a staple in my house growing up, and the smooth, creamy, carroty goodness filled the house with a sweet smell. Even though the ingredients are simple enough that we really did not need to reference the recipe after making it a few times, we always pulled out the recipe card. The card was handwritten by my grandmother on my mom's side, Frida Rubin, who passed when I was nine years old. Seeing her handwriting was a treat that reminded me of her loving notes in the cards and letters she would send me as a young child.

Over the years, my mom has done the work of creating family trees—piecing together memories, photographs, and letters to get a picture of where we come from. It is such a treasure to have the album she put together for me, along with a tree mapping out our ancestors and distant cousins. A few people reappear in the photographs who are not part of our family by blood or marriage, like my great-great-uncle's ex-girlfriend, who remained close with his family in the United States after they broke up and he returned to Russia; and several of my grandmother's best friends.

My grandmother built relationships with her friends across time and space. There was Gertrude Pinkney, who she met in library school. They were close their entire lives, even when Gertrude stayed in Detroit and my grandmother moved first to Chicago, then to Maryland, and her children grew up like cousins to my mom. And there was Dottie Bial. My mom remembers when Dottie got married—to a rabbi—and felt it was no longer appropriate to ride a bicycle as a rabbi's wife. She gave her bike to my mom, then a young child, who rode it for years.

I often think about whether and how queer bonds show up in our family histories. What I mean is all sorts of bonds of love, friendship, and mutual support that go beyond a nuclear family structure. Where is the space on a branching family tree for the relationships in our lives that don't stem from a married partnership or don't result in children? Often these histories can be hidden or denied, and need to be pieced back together. Often there are no clear words for these people, and a simple family tree doesn't suffice. How do we demonstrate that we are real to each other? How do we show up beyond fragments of memory, with material evidence of our existence?

Food can be a bridge beyond words. The comfort of soup in winter, bowl steaming and soft, nourishes us like holding each other tight so we know we are not alone. The carrot soup recipe that my grandmother wrote down on that card, which I have adapted to be vegan, comes from Dottie. While they were straight, married women, Dottie and my grandmother were lifelong family to each other. Witnessing the ways that my ancestors formed these bonds of love and mutual care helps me not only to honor them, but also to dream up possibilities of more expansive, queer lineages.

It is out of both necessity and choice that LGBTQ+ people name and honor the people who have impacted our lives beyond our families of origin. So often, we might not get to access so-called family recipes because we were cut out of the family tree, disinvited from gatherings, or told that we are only welcome if we leave the queer parts of ourselves at the door. Whether or not we have access to our family trees, we find our people, build upon these relationships, make lineage out of these threads, and pass their stories down generations.

Sweet, salty, and creamy flavors mix on my tongue in resonance with the beauty, pain, and possibility of queer lives. We carry forward a long tradition of survival by sharing foods that sustain us through hard times, foods that connect us across generations, and foods that remind us of joy, desire, and resistance.

Carrot Soup

This is my vegan version of a family recipe from one of my grandmother's close friends, Dottie Bial. After I became a vegetarian at age ten, it was a staple that my family would make for our Rosh Hashanah meal, along with round challah and a bean salad. It's simple to make, full of carroty goodness, and creamy because of the potatoes. You will need a blender or immersion blender for this recipe.

Makes: 8 cups of soup (4-6 servings)
Prep time: 15 minutes
Cook time: 35 minutes

1 large onion
2 large red or Yukon gold
  potatoes (about ½ pound)
1 large stalk celery
6 large carrots (about 1¼
  pounds)
3 Tbsp olive oil
2 tsp garlic powder
1 tsp + ½ tsp salt, divided
½ tsp ground black pepper
5 cups water
1 cube veggie broth, chopped
1 cup full-fat canned coconut
  milk
2 Tbsp finely chopped fresh
  parsley (optional, for garnish)

1. Chop the onion into large 1-inch chunks. Wash the potatoes and celery, and cut into 1-inch chunks. Wash and peel the carrots, then chop them into rounds about ½ inch thick.

2. Place olive oil in the bottom of a large pot and add all the veggies—first the onions, then potatoes, then celery and carrots on top. Place on medium heat, cover, and cook for about 15 minutes, stirring 2 or 3 times. Onions should be tender, but the potatoes and carrots should still be crunchy.

3. Add the garlic powder, 1 tsp of the salt, and the pepper to the pot and mix. Add 5 cups of water just to cover, and the chopped veggie broth cube. Heat to boiling, then reduce heat and simmer for about 10 minutes, or until veggies are soft.

4. Remove pot from heat. If you have an immersion blender, use it to blend the entire contents of the pot until very smooth. Or let it cool slightly, then purée in batches in a regular blender.

5. Just before serving, add the coconut milk and remaining ½ tsp salt, and stir. If using the parsley, finely chop and add it to the pot, or use it to garnish each bowl. Serve hot.

THE IMMERSION BLENDER IS YOUR FRIEND

The immersion blender is a finicky friend that can be very helpful to you in the kitchen, but can also lash out at you with its sharp teeth. As long as you treat it right, all will be well.

I never knew about immersion blenders until I started cooking professionally. In my house growing up, if we needed to blend something—carrot soup, for example—we would just wait for it to cool a bit, then purée it in batches in a regular blender. When I started cooking in quantity, I found this to be incredibly inefficient—not only do you have to wait for the soup to cool and then reheat it, but you need at least one extra pot or bowl to put the blended soup into, while the portion of soup that's still waiting to be blended sits in the original pot. It's not too bad if you're just making enough soup for 6 people and can blend it in 2 batches, but making soup for 30 people becomes a very frustrating process. I was thrilled to find that I could use an immersion blender to purée right in the cooking pot!

The immersion blender works best for soups, dressings, and other liquid foods. If it's too thick for a regular blender to blend, an immersion blender probably won't work, either. Different models of immersion blenders have different types of motors, and the higher-powered your immersion blender is, the better it will work for blending a large batch or a thick substance.

In many ways, the immersion blender is the ultimate lazy baker tool, but it can also be quite hazardous. Multiple people I know have sustained immersion blender-related injuries that landed them in urgent care when trying to clear the blades of food and accidentally touching the "on" button. Now, whenever I use one, I make a point to remind myself to unplug the power cord before putting my hand anywhere near the blender blades.

Vegan Cream of Broccoli Soup

Puréed pumpkin seeds and a variety of herbs add a lovely creamy flavor and lots of depth to this savory soup. It's perfect for a winter afternoon, served with rolls (page 162 or 164). This soup has a thick, smooth base, with little chunks of broccoli flowers in it for a bit of texture. It uses the entire broccoli stalk—a trick I learned from Tim Stallmann. If you have extra broccoli stems left over from a different recipe, you can add them in as well. Feel free to substitute fresh herbs instead of dry if you have them on hand. You will need a blender or immersion blender for this recipe.

Makes: 8 cups of soup (4-6 servings)
Prep time: 15 minutes
Cook time: 45 minutes

For the pumpkin seed cream:
½ cup raw pumpkin seeds
1 cup warm water

For the soup:
1 large onion
3 medium cloves garlic
2 large stalks celery
1 large russet potato (about ½ pound)
1 large bunch broccoli (about 1 ½ pounds)
¼ cup fresh parsley
¼ cup olive oil
1 bay leaf
1 tsp dried thyme
½ tsp dried oregano
1 tsp dried rosemary
½ tsp dried sage
1 cube veggie broth, chopped
1 ½ tsp salt
½ tsp ground black pepper
4 cups water
3 Tbsp nutritional yeast

1. Start the pumpkin seed cream: Place pumpkin seeds in a small bowl or large measuring cup, cover with 1 cup of warm water, and soak for about 30 minutes.

2. Meanwhile, make the soup: Chop the onion into large 1-inch pieces and set aside. Clean and chop the garlic, celery, and potato, and set these aside in a medium bowl. Wash the broccoli. Cut the crown off of the stem and set the crown aside. Peel off the tough outer part of the stem and discard it. Chop up the stem and set aside in a small bowl. Finely chop the crown until you have 2 cups of little pieces of broccoli flower—set aside in a separate bowl. Chop the rest of the crown into large pieces and add these to the bowl with the broccoli stem. Wash, dry, and finely chop the parsley, and set aside.

3. Heat the olive oil in a large, heavy-bottomed pot on medium heat. Add the onions, cover, and sauté for about 5 minutes, until they begin to soften. Add the garlic, celery, potato, and bay leaf. Cover and cook for about 10 minutes, stirring a few times.

4. Add the chopped broccoli stem and large pieces of crown, reserving the 2 cups of finely chopped crown for later. Add the thyme, oregano, rosemary, sage, veggie broth cube, salt, and pepper. Stir, cover, and cook on medium heat until you can easily insert a fork into the broccoli stem, about 10 minutes more.

5. Add the water, turn heat to medium high, and bring to a boil. Reduce heat to low and simmer for about 5 minutes. Turn off heat, remove bay leaf, and use an immersion or regular blender to blend the soup until it is silky smooth. If using an immersion blender, blend the hot soup directly in the pot. If using a regular blender, let the soup cool slightly until it feels safe to blend.

6. Return the pot of soup to the stove, turn the heat to low, and add the bay leaf back into the pot. Add the chopped broccoli crowns, parsley, and nutritional yeast. Cover and cook for about 10 minutes, until the broccoli crowns are soft.

7. Meanwhile, purée the pumpkin seed cream: Place pumpkin seeds and all of their soaking water in a blender and blend on high for 3 minutes. You should have a smooth, thick cream. If it is not smooth, scrape down the sides of the blender and purée for another minute.

8. Take the pot of soup off the stove. Stir in the pumpkin seed cream just before serving. Serve hot.

Roasted Tomato Soup

Makes: 7 cups of soup (4-5 servings)
Prep time: 20 minutes
Bake time: 55 minutes
Chill time: 3 hours

For the roasted veggies:
2 pounds fresh tomatoes (about 6 medium tomatoes)
1 medium onion
5 medium cloves garlic
½ large green bell pepper
½ large orange or red bell pepper
2 Tbsp olive oil
2 tsp granulated sugar
½ tsp salt

For the soup:
½ cup raw pine nuts
1 tsp dried oregano
½ tsp smoked paprika
¼ tsp dried thyme
½ tsp salt
¾ tsp ground black pepper
3 cups water

This chilled soup gives the essence of summer tomatoes in a smooth, cool, nutty soup. Like most of my soup recipes, I developed it to serve alongside pizza at the Center for Documentary Studies at Duke—this one doubles as a dipping sauce for the crust. It's also tasty alongside vegan grilled cheese made with pesto. If you don't want to use pine nuts, be sure to review the note for substitution options. You will need a blender or for this recipe.

1. Preheat oven to 450°F.

2. Wash and core the tomatoes, and cut each one in half. Place in a large bowl. Chop the onion and bell pepper into large 1 ½ inch pieces, and add to the bowl. Peel the garlic cloves and add to the bowl, leaving them whole. Add olive oil, sugar, and salt, and toss.

3. Line a large sheet pan with parchment paper. The sugars from roasting tend to burn onto the pan, so this will make for easier cleanup—if you don't have parchment, lightly oil the pan. Dump veggies onto pan, then arrange tomatoes so they are cut-side up.

4. Roast for 45 minutes, turning all but the tomatoes with a spatula after 30 minutes. Remove pan from oven.

5. Toast the pine nuts: Turn the oven down to 350°F and place nuts on a small baking pan. Toast in oven for 5-7 minutes, until golden brown.

6. Cool all ingredients for about 30 minutes.

7. Place tomato mixture, including any juices, in a blender. Add toasted pine nuts and all the spices. Blend for about 3 minutes, until silky smooth. If the 3 of cups water will fit in your blender, add at any time. Otherwise, mix water and soup base together in a large bowl after soup is blended.

8. Chill for 2 ½ hours, and serve cold.

VARIATIONS: The sugar helps the roasting veggies caramelize. You can also substitute 1 Tbsp agave nectar.

Pine nuts too expensive? Almonds, walnuts, and pumpkin seeds all work great instead.

LAZY BAKER METHOD:

Forty-one minutes into roasting the veggies, create a little space on one side of the sheet pan and place the pine nuts next to the veggies. Roast the veggies and nuts for the remaining 4 minutes and remove promptly to ensure they don't burn.

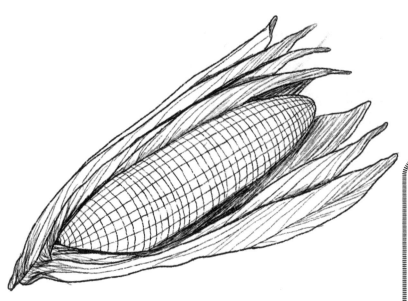

Smoky Corn Chowder

This flavorful corn chowder recipe was born on a cold winter evening when I was cooking dinner for a friend and wanted to use up the delicious frozen corn that I'd preserved the summer before. It's great any time of year, but if you want to make this recipe in winter, review the note on preserving your own fresh corn ahead of time. You will need a blender or immersion blender for this recipe.

Makes: 10 cups of soup (5-6 servings)
Prep time: 20 minutes
Cook time: 50 minutes

For the corn:
5 large ears fresh corn or 1 pound frozen corn (about 4 cups of corn kernels)
1 cup water
½ tsp salt

For the soup:
1 poblano pepper
1 green bell pepper
1 cup full-fat canned coconut milk

For the base:
1 medium onion
4 medium cloves garlic
2 large stalks celery
2 medium potatoes (red or gold potatoes work well)
3 Tbsp olive oil
2 tsp dried oregano
1 tsp dried sage
1 tsp smoked paprika
1 cube veggie broth, chopped
1 ½ tsp salt
1 tsp ground black pepper
5 cups water
2 Tbsp all-purpose flour (gluten-free option: corn or potato starch)

The voices of farmers in Warren County, North Carolina, echo in my head each time I buy an ear of fresh corn: "Don't break the cold chain." What, you ask? The sugars in the kernels are what makes sweet corn, well… sweet. Once harvested, it only has a short amount of time at room temperature before the sugars turn to starch, making your once candy-sweet corn now taste more like a dull grain. Whether you're buying corn from a farmer or grocery store, or harvesting it yourself, make sure to get those ears into the fridge as soon as possible, so the cold chain won't break. Once the chain is broken, you can't get it back! The promise of a sweet ear of corn motivates me to hurry home, or pack a cooler if I'll be out and about for a while.

1. Heat oven to 400°F.

2. Steam the corn: Clean the ears of corn, discarding husks and silk. Place the 1 cup water and ½ tsp salt in a small pot. Heat on high until it boils, then add the corn and cover. Steam for about 4 minutes, just until the corn becomes brighter in color. Remove corn from pot and allow to cool until you can comfortably handle it, then cut kernels off the cob. You can save the salted water to use in place of some of the water in the soup.

3. Roast your poblano and bell pepper: Place whole peppers on a pan in the oven and roast for 30 minutes, turning peppers over halfway through. Once they come out of the oven, place in a paper or plastic bag to steam for 10 minutes. Remove from bag, cut the peppers open and remove the seeds and stem. The skin should peel off easily; discard it. Dice the soft pepper pieces into small ¼ inch pieces, about the size of a corn kernel, and set aside.

4. Meanwhile, prepare the soup base: Chop the onion, garlic, celery, and potatoes into large 1 ½ inch pieces. Place the olive oil in a large pot and heat on medium heat. Add the veggies, cover, and sauté for 15 minutes, stirring occasionally. Add the oregano, sage, smoked paprika, chopped veggie broth cube, salt, and pepper. Stir.

5. Add the water, turn heat to high, and bring to a boil. Reduce to a simmer for 10 minutes, or until all veggies are soft—a fork should go through the potatoes easily.

6. Remove pot from heat. Using an immersion blender, purée the entire contents of the soup pot until smooth. If using a blender, let soup cool slightly, then blend until smooth.

7. Add the flour: To ensure there are no floury lumps, remove about 1 cup of the soup base into a small bowl, add the flour to the bowl, and stir vigorously with a fork or whisk until smooth. Once well combined, add this flour mixture back into the pot and stir with a wooden spoon. Heat the soup on medium low, stirring for about 5 minutes until it thickens.

8. Add the corn kernels and chopped peppers to the soup. Simmer on low for 5-10 minutes.

9. Just before serving, stir in the coconut milk. Serve hot.

TIPS FOR FREEZING CORN:

Plan ahead to set yourself up for a delightful corn chowder in the wintertime. Buy fresh corn from a farmer in the summer: in NC, at the big state farmers markets in Raleigh and Greensboro, you can buy a massive bag of corn for $20—plenty to share with friends. Blanch or steam it as described in step 2, cut it off the cob, and freeze it in quart or gallon bags. You'll have super-sweet fresh corn in the winter to make hot, tasty chowder. And, since you already blanched it before freezing, just add the corn kernels directly to the soup in step 8.

LAZY BAKER METHOD:

This is a recipe where I usually work as I go, preparing one set of ingredients while the others are cooking. This cuts down on prep time, but requires managing a lot of steps at once. If you feel comfortable working this way, wait to blanch the corn until after the peppers are in the oven. Then, blanch the corn and prepare the soup base as the peppers continue to roast.

VARIATIONS:

Poblano peppers vary in heat level, and using one may make this chowder a little spicy. If you want it spicier, replace the bell pepper with a second poblano. If you want it milder and a little sweet, replace the poblano with a red or yellow bell pepper.

Versatile Fall Veggie Soup

As soon as the weather starts to turn cold, I want to eat this soup every day. I created this recipe in 2012, inspired by a recipe for sancocho de gallina that I clipped from the Spanish-language newspaper Horizonte.[27] Sancocho has variations across Latin America, and often contains sweet chunks of corn on the cob that you pull out of the soup and eat right off the cob. This is fun for vegetarians, because it's sort of like eating a chicken leg but without the ick factor. The recipe here has several options for combinations of ingredients that you can choose based on what you have in the kitchen, or the flavors that you prefer to eat. My two favorite combinations are lima beans, carrots, white potatoes, and butternut squash with parsley and dill; and pinto beans, carrots, sweet potatoes, and yuca with cilantro and a dash of cumin.

Makes: 12 cups of soup (6 servings)
Prep time: 15 minutes
Cook time: 45-50 minutes

1 medium onion
2 medium cloves garlic
2 large stalks celery
3 cups diced root vegetables
  (choose 3: carrots, sweet
  potatoes, white potatoes, yuca,
  butternut squash)
2 Tbsp olive oil
1 tsp dried oregano
1 ½ tsp salt
½ tsp ground black pepper
½ tsp ground cumin (optional)
½ cup fresh herbs (choose:
  parsley and dill and omit the
  cumin, or cilantro and include
  the cumin)
2 ears fresh corn
7 cups water
1 cube veggie broth, chopped
2 cups cooked beans (choose
  1-2 varieties: pinto, lima, white
  beans, kidneys, chickpeas)

1. Dice the onion and celery into ½ inch pieces. Mince the garlic. Set aside.

2. Prepare your root vegetables: Wash and peel the ones you have chosen, and chop them into ½ inch pieces roughly the same size as the onions and celery. If using a butternut squash in combination with other veggies, you'll just need half of the squash (refer to note). If using yuca, which I highly recommend, review note.

3. Choose a pot large enough to comfortably hold 3 quarts of soup. Heat the olive oil in the pot over medium heat.

4. Add the onions, garlic, and celery and sauté until onions begin to soften, about 5 minutes, stirring occasionally.

5. Add the root vegetables, oregano, salt, and pepper to the soup pot and stir. If using cumin, add it here. Cover the pot and cook for 10-15 minutes, stirring once or twice, until the vegetables begin to soften.

6. Meanwhile, coarsely chop the fresh herbs and set aside. Shuck the corn, remove any corn silks, and break each cob into large 2-inch chunks Most corn breaks surprisingly easily with two hands, but a large sharp chef's knife will also work.

7. Add half of the fresh herbs to the pot and stir.

8. Add the water, veggie broth cube, and beans. Cover, turn heat to medium high, and bring to a simmer. Turn heat to low and simmer for 20-25 minutes, or until veggies are soft.

9. Add the rest of the fresh herbs and the corn cobs. Simmer for 5-10 minutes, until corn is bright and tender.

10. Serve hot.

COOKING WITH YUCA:

Yuca is a delicious, starchy root vegetable from South America, and has many other names around the world: cassava, manioc, and tapioca. It cooks up soft, with a distinct creamy texture and nutty flavor. At supermarkets in the US, it will usually have a waxy coating, and is very brittle and difficult to cut into small pieces. To use yuca in this soup, you can peel the tuber and cut it into about 3 large chunks. Throw the large pieces directly into the soup with the diced root vegetables. After the soup has simmered for 20 minutes, remove the yuca chunks and slice them down the center, so you can pull out the tough string in the middle. Then dice the cooked yuca and add it back into the pot to continue cooking.

You can also purchase frozen, peeled yuca, which comes in large chunks, at most Latin American supermarkets. Add these pieces, whole and frozen, when you add the veggies to the soup pot. After the soup has simmered and they are cooked, pull them out to remove the string, and dice as above.

COOKING WITH WINTER SQUASH:

To easily peel a butternut squash, slice it in half lengthwise, then cut off the ends and remove the seeds. Cut each half in 2, resulting in 4 large pieces of squash. It should now be relatively easy to use a vegetable peeler for each piece. I don't recommend trying to peel acorn squash, as the ridges make that a challenge—save it for a dish that calls for roasting it in large chunks, then peel it after it's cooked.

Tuscan Bean Stew

I started making this soup as a hearty dish to serve with spinach ricotta pie (page 80). It's now one of my favorite winter dishes to make at home. I like to make a big batch, portion it into serving-size containers, and freeze for a grab-and-go lunch. Traditionally, it is served with crusty bread and parmesan cheese, but I even enjoy it plain.

Makes: 14 cups of soup (6-8 servings)
Prep time: 20 minutes
Cook time: 45 minutes

1 medium onion
¼ cup + 1 Tbsp olive oil, divided
1 large carrot, peeled
2 large stalks celery
3 medium cloves garlic
1 bay leaf
2 tsp dried oregano
1 tsp dried rosemary
1 tsp dried thyme
1 tsp dried basil
1 tsp smoked paprika
1 tsp ground black pepper
2 tsp salt, divided
6 cups water
1 cube veggie broth, chopped
½ large red bell pepper
1 14.5-ounce can diced tomatoes
2 ½ cups cooked cannellini beans (refer to note)
2 ½ cups cooked kidney beans
1 small bunch lacinato kale (about ½ pound)
½ cup fresh parsley
2 large vegan Italian sausages (recommended, but omit for a gluten-free option)

To serve:
vegan parmesan cheese (optional)

NOTE:

I usually cook 1 cup each dry cannellini and kidney beans to use in this soup. Keep the cannellini and kidney beans in 2 separate pots during this process so they retain their distinct color and flavor. Soak beans overnight, then drain and rinse. Place beans in a pot, re-cover with water, add a little salt, and simmer beans for 1-1 ½ hours, until soft. Alternatively, you can use a total of 3 16-ounce cans of beans, 2 of one variety and 1 of the other.

1. Dice the onion into small ¼ inch pieces. Place in a large pot with ¼ cup of the olive oil and heat on medium heat. Stir, cover, and cook for about 5 minutes, until onions begin to soften.

2. Dice the carrot and celery into ¼ inch pieces, and finely mince the garlic. Add these and the bay leaf to the onions, cover, and cook for about 5 minutes more.

3. Add the oregano, rosemary, thyme, basil, smoked paprika, black pepper, and 1 tsp of the salt. Stir and allow to cook for a few minutes so the spices can infuse.

4. Add the water and veggie broth cube, raise heat to high, and bring to a boil. Immediately reduce heat to a simmer.

5. Chop the bell pepper and add to the pot, along with the canned tomatoes and both types of beans. Simmer for about 15 minutes, until carrots are completely soft.

6. Meanwhile, wash and de-stem the kale; chop into large 1- to 2- inch pieces. Rinse the parsley, shake dry, and chop. Set kale and parsley aside.

7. If using the vegan sausages, cut them into thin rounds and place in a small pan with the remaining 1 Tbsp olive oil on medium heat, cooking for about 3 minutes on one side until lightly brown; flip over and repeat.

8. Add the kale, sausage, and parsley to the soup pot. Cook for about 10 minutes, until kale is tender. Stir in the remaining 1 tsp salt.

9. Serve warm, garnished with vegan parmesan cheese if desired.

COOKING IS MAGIC

Cooking is spell-making for nourishment; and what goes into the food matters, because it goes directly into our bodies. This can be about the physical ingredients, like how I became a vegetarian at age ten because I loved animals and didn't want to take dead ones into my body. It is also about how we care for each other with the magic, emotions, and energy that ingredients can carry. I once received a gift of fresh herbs from a supervisor who was firing me from a job at a Jewish institution because of my principled stance in support of Palestinian liberation. The gift was a kind gesture of generosity and regret, but after I dried the herbs and put them into jars, I realized that this experience of repression was not something I wanted other people to take into their bodies. So, when I added the oregano to a Tuscan bean stew, I sprinkled in some salt I had harvested from the ocean during the new moon of Rosh Hashanah, and put an intention of release and healing into the pot with it.

I've also learned to be mindful of unintentional magic. One autumn many years ago, I made a long-anticipated confession of love to an old friend. It felt good to finally speak that truth even though he did not reciprocate, and the intensity of the moment had me noticing every detail of the bright camellia blossoms outside my kitchen door. I felt love swirling in the air, joy and sadness mixing within me and spilling out. That weekend, cooking for a social justice training, I witnessed multiple participants professing their love for each other over the course of three intense days. I was not trying to put the romantic giddiness of unrequited love into that chili or those cookies, but all the crushes that happened felt like too much of a coincidence. I was grateful when we all made it out of that weekend alive, just with so many tears.

Lentil Soup with Ginger and Fennel

I created this soup years ago for a winter solstice gathering. It was a hit—the sweet earth-tones of the ginger and fennel, combined with lentils and a few vegetables, make for a simple and soothing meal on a cold day.

Makes: 14 cups of soup (6-8 servings)
Prep time: 15 minutes
Cook time: 1 hour

2 cups French or brown lentils
   (make sure to get whole, not split, lentils)
1 medium to large onion
3 medium cloves garlic
2 large stalks celery
2 large carrots
3-inch piece fresh ginger root
   (about 3 Tbsp grated)
2 Tbsp olive oil
1 ½ tsp whole fennel seeds
1 bay leaf
2 tsp + ½ tsp salt, divided
½ tsp ground black pepper
1 cube veggie broth, chopped
10 cups water
4 packed cups fresh spinach, or 1
   10-ounce package frozen spinach

1. Rinse the lentils and place them in a bowl, covered in cold water, to soak until they need to be added to the soup.

2. Dice the onions into medium ½ inch pieces, and finely mince the garlic. Set aside. Dice the celery and carrots into ½ inch pieces. Finely grate the ginger.

3. In a large pot, heat the olive oil on medium heat. Add the onions and garlic, and sauté for about 5 minutes, stirring occasionally, until the onions begin to soften.

4. Add the celery, carrots, ginger, fennel seed, and bay leaf to the pot. Cover and cook for about 10 minutes, stirring occasionally.

5. Drain the lentils in a large strainer or colander, and rinse until water runs clear. Add lentils to the pot along with 2 tsp of the salt, and the pepper, veggie broth cube, and water. Turn heat to high and bring to a simmer. Immediately reduce heat to low and simmer for 30 minutes.

6. If using fresh spinach, remove any large stems and add the leaves whole to give the soup a nice texture. If using frozen spinach, just add it to the pot as is—no need to thaw it first. Add the remaining ½ tsp salt to the pot. Simmer for 15 minutes more, or until the lentils are tender.

7. Serve hot, with bread and a salad.

COOKING FOR RETREATS: DIFFERENT TYPES OF HUNGER

I used to manage the kitchen at The Stone House, a retreat center whose programs focused on spirituality and social justice. Sometimes, we cooked for organizers coming for strategic planning retreats. We also cooked for activists coming to take a much-needed break from their work. And, we often cooked for meditation retreats and other groups engaged in contemplative spiritual practices. Human bodies can have different kinds of hunger when engaged in different activities, and I learned how to plan menus for groups focusing their time in different ways. This is some of what we would think about when planning menus for different groups.

When people are sitting all day in deep relaxation and concentration, engaged in spiritual practice, they often need simple, light, but deeply nourishing food—lots of salads and soups. Too much salt or flavor can be overwhelming. For meditation retreats, breakfast would be simple and hearty, with a hot cereal, hard-boiled eggs, and fruit and yogurt. Lunch would be the biggest meal of the day, with a full menu featuring a hearty main dish and several sides. Dinner would be the lightest meal, to help the body wind down for sleep—usually soup, salad, and bread. We would usually serve dessert once a day, with lunch.

Conversely, for groups doing strategic planning, we would ensure that lunch was lighter—not too carb-heavy, or else people would be tempted to fall asleep in the afternoon. Dinner was a hearty meal with a dessert included, a tasty reward after a hard day's work. And, of course, plenty of coffee was always available.

If cooking for a workday where people were out on the land, lifting, hauling, and digging, we would make sure everyone got plenty of liquids. Breakfast would be full of protein and carbs to carry people through the day, and lunch was hearty too. Food would have plenty of sugars and salts to help replace those lost through sweating and physical exertion.

For groups taking a much-needed break from organizing work, we wanted them to feel pampered. Dishes full of flavor, plenty of sweets, and special requests for participants' specific comfort foods were on the table. And no matter the group, in addition to thinking about the type of activity people were engaged in, it was always important to think about what sorts of foods would make each group feel at home, and what sorts of specific health considerations the participants might be bringing.

Vegan Chicken Soup

...to feed the soul. Add noodles or matzo balls, if you like. Leave the vegan chicken out and just enjoy veggies in a tasty broth. However you like it, eat it up and enjoy. This soup is pure comfort for me, and it is even better made ahead and eaten the next day.

Makes: 10 cups of soup (4-5 servings)
Prep time: 20 minutes
Cook time: 40 minutes

½ large onion
1 large carrot
1 large stalk celery
2 medium cloves garlic
¼ cup fresh parsley
¼ cup fresh or frozen dill
2 Tbsp + 1 Tbsp olive oil, divided
1 bay leaf
¼ tsp dried basil
¼ tsp dried oregano
1 cube veggie broth, chopped
1 ½ tsp salt
½ tsp ground black pepper
6 cups water
7 ounces Delight Foods soy patties or other mock chicken (review note)
¼ pound thin spaghetti (optional)

NOTE:

Delight Foods soy patties can be found in the freezer section of some natural foods stores in NC. They are delicious. If you want to make a gluten-free soup, simply omit the soy patties and the noodles. For an inexpensive, gluten-free protein in place of the patties, add ½ cup dry TVP (textured vegetable protein) with the water in step 6. For additional substitution options, visit "In My Kitchen" on page 9.

1. Slice the onion in half lenthwise, cut into thin ribbons, then cut each ribbon in half. Peel the carrots and cut into thin matchsticks, about 2 inches long. Thinly slice the celery. Chop the garlic as you like.

2. Wash, shake dry, and coarsely chop parsley and dill. Set aside. If desired, you can include the stems—chop them finely and set aside separate from the leafy herbs, and add stems to the soup pot with the dry herbs in step 5.

3. Heat 2 Tbsp of the olive oil in a large pot on medium-low heat. Add the onion, cover, and sauté for 5 minutes, stirring occasionally, until it begins to soften.

4. Add the carrot, celery, garlic, and bay leaf. Cover and sauté for 10 minutes more, stirring occasionally. The onion should begin to brown and the celery and carrot should be crunchy, but beginning to soften.

5. Add the basil, oregano, chopped veggie broth cube, salt, and pepper. Stir.

6. Add the water, turn heat up to high, and bring to a boil. Immediately reduce to low, cover, and simmer for about 15 minutes, or until veggies are no longer crunchy.

7. Meanwhile, brown the soy patties: Place the remaining 1 Tbsp olive oil in a medium pan, and heat on medium heat. Place frozen, whole patties in pan. Cook until lightly browned, 3-5 minutes on one side; then flip and cook 3-5 minutes on the other. Remove from heat and let cool until safe to touch. Slice the cooled patties into short strips, similar in size to the carrots.

8. Meanwhile, if adding noodles, prepare them: Heat a small pot of water on the stove. Break the spaghetti in half and cook it al dente according to package directions. Drain and rinse with cold water. Place the cooked spaghetti on a cutting board and chop into 1-inch pieces.

9. Add parsley, dill, spaghetti (if using), and soy patty pieces to the soup pot. Simmer for 5 minutes more, and serve hot. You can also make the soup ahead of time and keep it on low heat for an hour or so before serving, or make it the day before and reheat the next day. If making ahead, add the soy patties and half the parsley and dill here, adding the spaghetti and remaining herbs just before serving.

LAZY BAKER METHOD:

Rather than prepping your veggies before you start, chop the onion and start cooking it while you chop the carrot, celery, garlic, and herbs. This will save you a few minutes on prep time. If one of the veggies cooks for a few minutes longer than recommended, it's not a big deal. You can also save time by boiling the water in a kettle so it's already hot when you add it to the soup in step 6.

VARIATION:

If you want to change the quantity of the veggies here, you can add more carrots, less celery, more soy patties, or any other variation. If you want a thinner broth, just add more water, and add an additional ¼ tsp salt for every additional cup of water.

Matzo Balls

Matzo balls are tasty little dumplings that are great in vegan chicken soup (preceding recipe) during Passover—or any time of year, really. These matzo balls are chock full of herbs and flavor; not too dense, but also not billowy little clouds. The aunties say to make sure you never uncover the pot when preparing matzo balls, otherwise they will turn out rock-hard. Is this true? I can't say, because I never uncover the pot! There are three versions here for your various dietary needs: a traditional version made with eggs and matzo meal, a gluten-free version made with almond meal, and a vegan version. Keep the matzo balls separate from the soup broth until serving for an allergy-friendly meal: just one broth for everyone, with different matzo ball options for people to add to each individual bowl.

Traditional Matzo Balls

Makes: 8 matzo balls (serves 4)
Prep time: 10 minutes
Chill time: 20 minutes
Cook time: 20 minutes

2 Tbsp onion
1 Tbsp fresh or frozen dill
1 Tbsp fresh parsley
½ cup matzo meal
½ tsp garlic powder
½ tsp salt
1 Tbsp olive oil
2 eggs
6 cups water, with 1 tsp salt
  added

1. Prepare vegan chicken soup (page 128) so that you have a broth in which to serve your matzo balls.

2. Finely mince the onion. Wash the dill and parsley, dry with a towel, and finely chop.

3. Mix up the matzo balls: Place matzo meal, garlic powder, and the ½ tsp salt in a bowl and mix well with a spoon. Add onion, dill, and parsley, and mix well. Make a well in the center, and place olive oil and eggs in it. In the well, beat the eggs and oil until well mixed. Then, mix with the matzo meal until a sticky dough forms.

4. Cover bowl and place in the fridge to chill for 20 minutes. After chilling, the dough will be sticky but somewhat firm.

5. Steam the matzo balls: In a wide pot with a tight-fitting lid, heat the 6 cups salted water to boiling on the stove. Scoop walnut-sized portions of dough with a spoon, then use wet hands to form into balls. Keep in mind that they will expand as they cook!

6. Once the water is boiling, quickly drop the matzo balls directly into the water in the pot, one at a time, to form a single layer. Cover immediately. Turn heat down to medium low, and simmer for 20 minutes. If a little steam is escaping from the lid, you can just trust that they are cooking nicely.

7. After 20 minutes, open the pot and use a slotted spoon to remove matzo balls from the pot. Place them on a large plate, in a 9x13 inch baking dish, or—to keep them as perfect spheres—into an empty egg carton coated with plastic wrap.[28] I like to keep them dry until serving so that they stay light and airy.

8. To serve, add the matzo balls to the soup broth. You can add them either to the pot or to each bowl. If your soup broth is hot, the matzo balls will reheat in minutes when you plop them into the steaming broth.

Gluten-Free Matzo Balls

This non-traditional matzo ball was inspired by an almond-based paleo muffin. Once, I was trying out muffin recipes, and one version came out so much like matzo balls that I decided to use the concept as the basis for this gluten-free version. These matzo balls are nice and fluffy, but a bit dry, so make sure they get soaked in broth before serving.

Makes: 8 matzo balls (serves 4)
Prep time: 10 minutes
Cook time: 15 minutes

1. Prepare vegan chicken soup (page 128) so that you have a broth in which to serve your matzo balls.

2. Finely mince the onion. Wash the dill and parsley, dry with a towel, and finely chop.

3. Mix up the matzo balls: Place almond meal, garlic powder, and salt in a bowl and mix well with a spoon. Add onion, dill, and parsley, and mix well. Make a well in the center, and pour in olive oil and eggs. In the well, beat the eggs and oil until well mixed. Then mix with the matzo meal until a sticky dough forms.

4. Steam the matzo balls: Do not place them directly in water or they will fall apart! You must use a steamer to keep the balls out of the water while cooking them in a moist environment. Place about 1 ½ inches of water in the bottom of a wide pot. Spray the surface of a steamer basket with cooking oil spray to make removing the matzo balls easier, and place the basket in the pot. If you don't have a steamer basket, review note for a makeshift option.

2 Tbsp onion
1 Tbsp fresh or frozen dill
1 Tbsp fresh parsley
¾ packed cup almond meal
½ tsp garlic powder
½ tsp salt
1 Tbsp olive oil
2 eggs
water for steaming

5. Cover the pot and heat the water to boiling on the stove. Scoop walnut-sized portions of dough with a spoon, then use wet hands to form into balls. The balls will be wet and will probably settle into a dome shape rather than a sphere.

6. Once the water is boiling, quickly transfer the matzo balls in the steamer, leaving 1 ½ inches of space between each. Cover immediately. Turn heat down to medium low and steam for 15 minutes.

7. After 15 minutes, remove from heat. Open the pot. The matzo balls should have expanded significantly, and be dome-shaped and light. Use a spatula to scrape each matzo ball off the steamer, and place them on a large plate until serving.

8. To serve, add the matzo balls to the soup broth. You can add them either to the pot, or to each bowl. If your soup broth is hot, the matzo balls will reheat in minutes when you plop them into the steaming broth.

IF YOU DON'T HAVE A STEAMER BASKET that fits inside a pot, you can create a makeshift steamer: Place a small ceramic or metal bowl with a flat bottom in the center of a wide pot. Pour about 1 ½ inches of water into the bottom of the pot. Balance a large plate that just fits inside the pot on top of the bowl, so that it sits inside the pot above the water level. Spray the surface of the plate with cooking oil spray to make removing the matzo balls easier. Follow the directions above, placing the matzo balls on top of the plate. Beware that as the water boils, the plate and bowl may shake and rattle a bit.

Vegan Matzo Balls

These matzo balls are tasty and have a nice texture—the trick is steaming them, rather than boiling, so they hold their shape. If you are making vegan matzo balls during Passover, be sure to check with whomever you're sharing the soup whether baking soda and flaxseed are ingredients they are willing to eat.[29] The flax can be easily replaced with ground chia seed, but without the baking soda, unfortunately, the matzo balls become unpleasantly dense rocks.

2 Tbsp onion
1 Tbsp fresh dill
1 Tbsp fresh parsley
¾ cup matzo meal
½ tsp baking soda
½ tsp garlic powder
¼ tsp salt
3 Tbsp olive oil
¾ cup hot water
2 tsp golden flaxseed meal
½ tsp vinegar or lemon juice
water for steaming

Makes: 8 matzo balls (serves 4)
Prep time: 10 minutes
Cook time: 15 minutes

1. Prepare vegan chicken soup (page 128) so that you have a broth in which to serve your matzo balls.

2. Finely mince the onion. Wash the dill and parsley, dry with a towel, and finely chop.

3. Mix up the matzo balls: Place matzo meal, baking soda, garlic powder, and salt in a bowl and mix well with a spoon. Add onion, dill, and parsley. Drizzle in the olive oil, and mix well. In a small bowl or measuring cup, mix the hot water and flaxseed meal. Add to the matzo meal mixture and mix until a sticky dough forms. Let the dough rest for about 2 minutes: it should become less sticky.

4. Steam the matzo balls: Do not place them directly in water or they will fall apart! You must use a steamer to keep the balls out of the water while cooking them in a moist environment. Place about 1 ½ inches of water in the bottom of a wide pot. Spray the surface of a steamer basket with cooking oil spray to make removing the matzo balls easier, and place the basket in the pot. If you don't have a steamer basket, review note on facing page for a makeshift option.

5. Cover the pot and heat the water to boiling on the stove. Scoop walnut-sized portions of dough with a spoon, then use wet hands to form into balls. Keep in mind that they will expand as they cook!

6. Once the water is boiling, quickly transfer the matzo balls to the steamer, leaving 1 ½ inches of space between each matzo ball. Cover immediately. Turn heat down to medium low and steam for 15 minutes. (Unlike the gluten-free version, these must be cooked in a steamer, rather than baked. Since they have no eggs to help leaven them, it's the added moisture from the steam that helps them rise).

7. After 15 minutes, remove from heat. Open the pot. The matzo balls will be a little bigger than when you put them in, and they should be dome-shaped and look glossy. Use a spoon or spatula to remove matzo balls from the steamer and place them on a large plate. For vegan matzo balls, it's important to store them on the plate, not in the broth—they will fall apart if left soaking in the water for too long.

8. To serve, add the matzo balls to each soup bowl. If your soup broth is hot, the matzo balls will reheat in minutes when you plop them into each steaming bowl.

Chapter Four:
SALAD DRESSINGS, SAUCES, & SALSAS

Comfort Food
REFLECTIONS ON COOKING FOR STUDENT ACTION WITH FARMWORKERS

"Got food?
Thank a farmworker."
-STUDENT ACTION WITH FARMWORKERS bumper sticker[30]

In the world of appreciation for delicious, healthy food, farmworkers often get lost in the conversation. Consumers might think about supporting local farmers, or consider the impact of their food choices on their own bodies and on the planet. Grocery stores market to these trends, emphasizing local or organic sourcing while erasing farmworkers. Unless we have a direct connection to work in the fields, many of us don't talk about the migrant workers who grow most of the food we eat in the United States. There is much racial and economic justice work to be done to transform our food system. This includes supporting small family farms, particularly Black farmers, and supporting cooperatives; and it must include fighting for justice alongside migrant farmworkers.

I deeply appreciate the work Student Action with Farmworkers (SAF) does to lift up farmworker experiences, organize in the fields, and empower students from farmworker families. Their work is a combination of leadership development, documentary work, organizing, advocacy, and direct service. When I moved back to Durham in 2005, I lived in a collective house with many SAF staff, who encouraged me in my culinary enterprises; one of my first catering gigs was cooking for SAF's Into the Fields summer internship program.

I developed my potato enchilada recipe when, after cooking for several Into the Fields retreats, SAF asked me to cook for their high school youth program for the first time. The meal was for a community gathering with students, parents, and families, and Rosie Rangel, the youth director at the time, asked me to make a comforting meal that would put everyone at ease. At the time, I was only cooking vegetarian food, so for this group of Latinx families, she suggested either enchiladas or chiles rellenos as the main dish. I was honored to participate, and I set to work on recipes.

When I brought my first recipe test of potato enchiladas to a friend's house, she told me, "this tastes like lasagna enchiladas." I laughed, feeling my Italian grandmother's presence within me—this was a repeat of how her beloved chili recipe tasted like minestrone. Food is love, which means that I bring myself and my ancestors to the food I cook, along with deep respect for the individuals and communities I cook for and within. I kept working at the recipe, until I was confident that it was delicious enough to nourish these hardworking families who deserved a feast in their honor. The enchiladas no longer taste like lasagna, but the love is still there.

Cooking for SAF's programs has been one of the most joyous parts of my career in the kitchen. Cooking for retreats, I got to accompany these brilliant young people and spend a weekend preparing their meals. Oftentimes, I would get to know youth because they came to hang out at the kitchen table while I cooked breakfast, telling me about their own kitchen experiments and asking for advice about dishes they were learning to make at home.

Whoever we are cooking for, we are nourishing them for that practice and for the work ahead, both physically and spiritually. When I used to cook for silent meditation retreats, the cooking team stayed in silence in the kitchen, holding space for the participants within the silence of the retreat. In holding space for the SAF youth, I make food to honor and nurture their growth and possibility as young leaders alongside the learning they are doing at the retreat itself. It is their leadership that will bring justice for the farmworker communities from which they come; and farmworker justice is a foundational piece of building a just and sustainable food system for everyone.

Enchilada Sauce

When I first started making enchiladas, I always bought canned enchilada sauce. I wanted to make my own, so I developed this recipe through a process of trying out different ingredients over the years. It's quick to make, and tasty—a tangy red sauce that is great over potato enchiladas (page 44), or as a condiment with beans and rice.

Makes: 4 cups, enough for 16 enchiladas.
Prep time: 10 minutes

½ medium onion
½ fresh poblano or green bell pepper
1 medium clove garlic
1 14.5-ounce can crushed tomatoes
¼ cup canola oil
2 Tbsp tomato paste
2 tsp sweet paprika
1 tsp ancho chili flakes (page 97, or substitute chili powder blend)
½ tsp ground dried chipotle pepper (or smoked paprika)
½ tsp ground cumin
½ tsp garlic powder
½ tsp salt
1 cup water

1. Cut the onion and pepper into large chunks.

2. Place onions, peppers, and all other ingredients in a blender.

3. Blend on high for about 1 ½ minutes, until smooth.

4. Use immediately, or store in the refrigerator for up to a week.

NOTE: Made with the chipotle pepper powder, this sauce has a little kick to it. If you prefer it mild, replace with smoked paprika for a smoky flavor without the heat.

Peanut Sauce

This peanut sauce is tangy and just a little bit sweet. I love it over noodles (page 36), either warm or cold. It also makes a nice dip for raw veggies or almond-crusted tofu (page 24) if served as an appetizer. Use fresh ginger for the most flavor, but ground ginger will do in a pinch.

Makes: 2 cups
Prep time: 10 minutes

¾ cup peanut butter (preferably creamy)
2 Tbsp olive oil
2 Tbsp lemon juice
2 Tbsp apple cider vinegar
2 Tbsp soy sauce
1 Tbsp agave nectar or honey
1 Tbsp grated fresh ginger root, or 1 tsp ground ginger
½ tsp garlic powder
½ tsp ground coriander
½ tsp salt
½ tsp ground black pepper
¾ cup water

1. Place all ingredients in a quart-sized mason jar with a tight-fitting lid.

2. Shake vigorously, until everything is well-combined.

3. Taste and add more salt or sweetener, if desired.

NOTE: Fresh ginger keeps well in the freezer, and it is actually easier to grate when frozen than when fresh. Store it in a freezer-safe container, and take it out about 5 minutes before grating to let it soften slightly. If you don't use the whole piece of ginger, place the rest back in the freezer immediately, to use later.

VARIATION: To make a thicker sauce to serve as a dip, use ½ cup of water instead of the full ¾ cup.

Tomato Sauce

Some people might call this cheating, but I like to make my sauce from canned tomatoes. It's delicious, cooks much more quickly than with fresh tomatoes, and is convenient to make at any time of year. You can buy canned crushed tomatoes; or can your own whole tomatoes in season, then use them to make a tasty sauce in mid-winter.

1 medium onion
3 medium cloves garlic
3 Tbsp olive oil
¼ cup + ½ cup fresh parsley, divided
½ large green or red bell pepper
1 bay leaf
1 tsp dried oregano leaves (or 1 Tbsp fresh, chopped)
1 tsp dried basil leaves (or 1 Tbsp fresh, chopped)
½ tsp salt
½ tsp ground black pepper
⅓ cup tomato paste (about half of a small 6-ounce can)
1 28-ounce can crushed tomatoes
2 tsp agave nectar or honey

Makes: 4 cups, about 6-8 servings
Prep time: 10 minutes
Cook time: 45 minutes

1. Dice the onion and bell pepper into ¼ inch pieces and finely mince the garlic.

2. In a heavy saucepan, heat the olive oil on medium heat. Add the onion and garlic, and sauté for about 5 minutes, stirring occasionally, until the onions begin to soften.

3. Chop all of the parsley, setting ½ cup aside in a small bowl. Add the remaining ¼ cup to the pot—you can include chopped parsley stem here. Dice the bell pepper into ¼ inch pieces. Add the diced bell pepper and the bay leaf, oregano, basil, salt, and black pepper. Stir, cover, and cook for about 7-8 minutes until the peppers begin to soften and the onions are slightly transparent.

4. Add the tomato paste, and stir to break it up. Add the crushed tomatoes.

5. Cover and bring to a simmer, then immediately reduce heat to low. Simmer for 20-25 minutes, stirring occasionally to prevent sticking: simmering allows the flavors to infuse and combine.

6. Add the agave or honey and the remaining ½ cup parsley, mix well, and let cook for another 5 minutes.

7. Your sauce is ready to serve, or to use to make lasagna (pages 16 and 18) or pizza (page 178).

NOTE: Extra sauce will keep in the fridge for up to a week. It also freezes well: First, cool sauce in the fridge, then transfer to an empty yogurt container or heavy, resealable freezer bag to keep for several months.

VARIATION: If you like a veggie-full sauce, this sauce works well with different combinations of veggies. Try adding ½ cup of chopped mushrooms, zucchini, or eggplant when you add the bell pepper. For a chunkier sauce, cut the onion, pepper, and any veggies into half-inch pieces instead of little ¼ inch ones.

Vegan Pesto

Pesto is the essence of summer for me, with its pungent aromas of fresh basil and garlic. You can make pesto with any fresh green herb, including wild-harvested plants like chickweed, but I am partial to the combination of basil and parsley here. The optional lemon juice here adds a nice little kick, too. I like to make a big batch in the height of summer, portion it into ice cube trays or half-pint containers, and freeze. They thaw quickly for year-round use in recipes like pasta salad (page 72), or as a tasty snack on toast or crackers.

Makes: About 1 ½ cups
Prep time: 10 minutes

1 packed cup fresh basil
1 packed cup fresh parsley
¼ cup raw sunflower or
  pumpkin seeds
2 medium cloves garlic
¾ cup olive oil
2-3 Tbsp nutritional yeast
¾ tsp salt
1 tsp lemon juice (optional)

1. Wash the basil and parsley, and dry with a towel. Remove the tough end of the stems (some stem is fine—review note). Rough chop the herbs into large pieces about 2 inches long, then measure to make sure you have a full cup of each. Set aside.

2. Place the sunflower or pumpkin seeds and garlic in a food processor, and pulse until finely chopped.

3. Add parsley, basil, olive oil, nutritional yeast, salt, and lemon juice (if using). Blend on high for about 1 minute, until ingredients are thoroughly chopped and combined.

4. Serve over pasta, as an ingredient in salad dressing, as a spread on toast, over vegetables, or pretty much for anything.

NOTE: Since you are blending the basil and parsley, you can include part of the stem. I usually cut off an inch of the parsley stem end and discard it, then rough chop the whole bunch of parsley into about 4 large pieces. To de-stem the basil, I use my fingernails to cut through the stem; if there's a part that I can't easily cut through with my nails, I know it's too tough and discard the stem from that point downwards. Usually this means I keep 2-3 inches of stem for each sprig of basil leaves, and discard the rest.

NOTE: If you don't have a food processor, you can finely chop everything with a chef's knife. Or you can try mixing up the pesto in a blender. In a blender, add the olive oil first, then the seeds and garlic. Once these are blended, add the herbs a little bit at a time, making sure each addition is well-blended before adding the next. This will help make sure the large quantity of fresh herbs doesn't clog up the blender.

Balsamic Reduction

I like to call this balsamic molasses because of its thick consistency and candy-like sweetness. It's made by slowly cooking down the vinegar to ⅓ of its original volume, while its natural sugars caramelize. I usually make it for caprese salad (page 104), but often end up drizzling the leftovers over salads and roasted veggies, or using it as a spread on toast. You can also mix it with mayo for a tasty sandwich spread.

1 cup balsamic vinegar

Makes: ⅓ cup
Cook time: 25-30 minutes

1. Place balsamic vinegar in a small saucepan. Heat on medium heat until it simmers. Immediately turn down to the lowest possible heat and simmer slowly, uncovered, for 25 minutes. Stir every 5-10 minutes with a rubber spatula. It will bubble gently, and after about 20 minutes, there should be clusters of small bubbles covering most of the surface of the vinegar, interspersed with patches of flat surface.

2. After 25 minutes, check doneness by placing a few drops onto a teaspoon. Let cool for about 30 seconds, then tilt the spoon to the side. If you can still pour it but it moves slowly, and looks just a tiny bit thinner than honey or molasses, it is done—remove from heat. If it is still quite runny, continue cooking for up to 5 minutes more.

3. Let cool for at least 30 minutes before using. At that point, it will still be slightly warm, but fine to use. Keep in mind that it will thicken up as it cools.

4. Store in the refrigerator in a tightly sealed container for up to 1 month. Bring to room temperature before using.

> NOTE: You want to make sure to remove the reduction from the heat before it begins to rise and puff up in the saucepan. If this begins to happen, it means that the sugars, cooking as the vinegar reduces, are heading into the next stage and may become too hard to pour. Immediately remove the reduction from heat and let cool. If it's not easily pourable, try adding 1 Tbsp of water, and you may still be able to use it.

Lemon Tahini Dressing

Makes 2 ½ cups
Prep time: 10 minutes

When I was in college, there was a café on campus where you could get a great big salad for $2.50. Someone told me about Annie's Goddess Dressing, which they offered in the café, and I would always go in and order salads with that tangy tahini goodness over mixed greens, cherry tomatoes, and olives. In the springtime, I would get my salad from the basement café, walk around to the front porch of the student union, and sit out there, basking in afternoon sunlight. When I was growing up, my mom used to make a tahini dressing we affectionately called "Rubin's Own." I decided that I needed to create a dressing that would remind me of family and of those college spring afternoons. This dressing also makes a great dip for veggies (refer to note on facing page). This recipe makes a lot, so halve it if needed.

1 Tbsp chopped yellow or red onion
1 medium clove garlic
¾ cup olive oil
¾ cup tahini
½ cup lemon juice
2 Tbsp apple cider vinegar
1 Tbsp soy sauce or tamari
1 Tbsp honey or agave nectar
1 tsp dried oregano (or 1 Tbsp fresh)
½ tsp salt
½ tsp ground black pepper
½ cup water
2 Tbsp fresh parsley
1 Tbsp fresh basil (or 1 tsp dried)

Method #1

To make in a blender: Place the onion and garlic in the blender. Cover with olive oil, then add all ingredients except for the water, parsley, and basil. Blend for about 30 seconds until puréed. Add the water and blend until emulsified—the dressing should become smooth and lighter in color. Add the parsley and basil and blend for about 15 seconds, until the herbs are chopped and evenly distributed.

Method #2

To make in a quart mason jar: Finely chop the onion, garlic, parsley, and basil. Place these along with all remaining ingredients in a mason jar, close tightly, and shake until smooth and emulsified.

This dressing will keep for 1 to 2 weeks in the fridge. When chilled, it thickens up, but will thin out again as it comes to room temperature.

VARIATION: To make as a dip for veggies, use half the amount of water (¼ cup). If you want it even thicker, use just a couple tablespoons of water to give it a smooth, emulsified consistency without thinning it out.

HOW TO STEAM BROCCOLI

I love to eat salad as a main dish with lemon tahini dressing, mixed greens, cherry tomatoes, shaved carrots, Kalamata olives, cooked chickpeas, and steamed broccoli. Sesame and chickpeas together make a complete protein! Here's how to steam the broccoli and then chill it for a salad.

Prep time: 2 minutes
Cook time: 5 minutes

In a small pot with a lid, heat to boiling:
> 1 cup water
> ½ tsp salt

Trim most of the stem off of:
> 1 large head of broccoli

Once the water boils, reduce heat to medium and place the broccoli crown in the pot with its stem side down. Cover and steam for 5 minutes. Immediately remove from pot, and let cool on a plate. You can save the water to use for veggie stock—keep in mind that it is pretty salty.

Once safe to handle, cut the broccoli into little broccoli trees. Cover and chill in the refrigerator until ready to use.

Strawberry Balsamic Vinaigrette

I love the sweet, fruity flavor of this dressing, served over a springtime salad with baby lettuce, sugar snap peas, cucumber, and sliced fresh strawberries. In the heat of summer, using blackberries in place of the strawberries is delicious as well. This recipe makes a lot, so halve it if needed.

Makes: 2 cups
Prep time: 10 minutes

5 medium-large fresh strawberries
1 handful fresh parsley (about ¼ cup)
1 medium clove garlic
¾ cup olive oil
1 Tbsp agave nectar or honey
1 tsp dry basil
½ tsp salt
¼ tsp ground black pepper
½ cup balsamic vinegar
¼ cup water

1. Wash, de-stem, and halve the strawberries. Wash and roughly chop the parsley.

2. In a blender, place all ingredients except the balsamic vinegar and water. Blend on high until the strawberries are puréed and everything is well combined.

3. With the blender running, slowly pour in the balsamic vinegar and then the water. The dressing should be nicely emulsified and light brown in color. Store in the refrigerator in an airtight container for 1-2 weeks, and remove from fridge 15 minutes before serving so the dressing will pour easily.

WINTER VARIATION:

Use 3 Tbsp strawberry jam in place of the fresh strawberries, and omit the agave nectar. Made with jam rather than fresh berries, the dressing will keep for a month in the fridge.

SUMMER VARIATION:

Substitute ½ cup fresh blackberries in place of the fresh strawberries.

Cilantro Lime Dressing

This fresh, slightly spicy dressing is great over salad or as a condiment with tacos. One summer at lunchtime, a 5-year-old came back for seconds of the bright-green dressing. I was hovering by the buffet line and he said to me, "This is good, is it made of grass?" I love that he thought it must be made from grass, and wanted to eat it anyway. It's tasty! The recipe is adapted from one that my former co-worker Miriam Biber used to make. It makes a lot, so halve it if needed.

Makes: 2 ¼ cups
Prep time: 10 minutes

1 packed cup cilantro
  (leaves and stem)
½ jalapeño pepper
1 medium clove garlic
1 cup canola or olive oil
2 tsp agave nectar or honey
½ tsp ground black pepper
½ cup lime juice
3 Tbsp tamari or soy sauce
3 Tbsp water

1. Wash and rough chop the cilantro. You can include the stems in this recipe—just trim off any brown parts first. Cut the jalapeño in half and discard the seeds.

2. Place cilantro, the half jalapeño, garlic, oil, agave or honey, and black pepper in a blender and purée for 45 seconds until smooth.

3. Mix the lime juice, tamari, and water in a measuring cup. With the blender running, slowly pour this mixture into the blender, and blend for about 30 seconds until emulsified.

4. Store in the refrigerator in an airtight container. This dressing will keep for several weeks, but it is best when used within a week.

NOTE: For a milder version, use ¼ of a fresh poblano pepper in place of the jalapeño.

Avocado Sauce

Creamy and tangy, this dressing works as a condiment with mock chicken "carnitas" (page 42), potato enchiladas (page 44), or beans and rice—I like to use it as a vegan option in place of sour cream. It's also delicious as a salad dressing and as a dip for raw veggies. You'll want to make it a different thickness depending on how you're using it, so I give several options here.

1 large ripe avocado
½ cup olive oil
1 medium clove garlic
2 tsp agave nectar or honey
½ tsp ancho chili flakes (page 97, or substitute chili powder blend)
½ tsp salt
½ tsp ground black pepper
¼ cup lime juice
2 Tbsp red wine vinegar or unseasoned rice vinegar
½ to ¾ cup water (review note)
¼ cup fresh parsley or cilantro

Makes: About 2 cups, 8-10 servings as a condiment
Prep time: 10 minutes

1. Open the avocado, remove the pit, and scoop the avocado flesh into a blender. Add the olive oil and garlic, then the agave, chili flakes, salt, and pepper. Blend on high for about 30 seconds, until smooth and well mixed.

2. Add the lime juice and vinegar. Blend until combined. With the blender running, slowly pour in the water, so the sauce emulsifies. Blend for about 1 minute until sauce is thick, smooth, and light in color.

3. Wash the parsley or cilantro, shake dry, and remove any brown parts. Chop into several large pieces and place in blender. Blend for about 30 seconds, until the herbs are well minced and combined with the rest of the sauce.

4. Serve immediately, or store in the refrigerator in an airtight jar for up to 5 days.

NOTE: To make a thick sauce or dip, use the lesser amount of water. To make a salad dressing that pours more easily, use the greater amount of water. I like to use the cilantro when making this as a dip and the parsley when making it as a salad dressing.

Avocado Green Tomato Salsa

Avocados are one of my favorite foods—I love them on pretty much anything. This salsa is chunky like pico de gallo, and tangy and tasty as a dip. Sometimes I like to eat it right out of the bowl with a spoon. I started making this salsa in search of a dish similar to guacamole, but a bit more substantial and not quite as expensive to make. This recipe is fairly mild—if you want it spicier, add some chopped jalapeño pepper, or even a little bit of cayenne.

1 pound ripe, firm avocados (2 large or 3 small)
1 pound tomatillos or ripe yellow and green tomatoes
½ cup fresh cilantro
½ small to medium red onion
1 poblano pepper
3-4 Tbsp lime juice
1 ½ tsp ground cumin
½ tsp garlic powder
1 tsp salt
½ tsp ground black pepper

Makes: 4-5 cups, about 10 servings
Prep time: 15 minutes
Chill time: 30 minutes

1. Choose avocados that are just ripe—if you press gently with your finger on the outer skin, you should feel some give without it being mushy.

2. Dice the avocados. You want to dice the avocados without breaking them into mush, so a sharp knife is key. I like to cut the avocados in half, remove the pits, peel the skin off of each avocado half, and then cut the peeled avocado into neat cubes. Place diced avocado in a large bowl.

3. Wash the tomatillos or tomatoes, dice them into ½ inch pieces, and place in a large bowl.

4. Wash the cilantro and dry it lightly with a towel, and coarsely chop it. Dice the onion and poblano into small ¼ inch pieces. Add all of these to the bowl.

5. Add the lime juice, cumin, garlic powder, salt, and pepper. Mix gently until just combined.

6. Serve immediately, or cover tightly with plastic wrap and chill before serving.

> NOTE: All of these ingredients are readily available at Latin American supermarkets. If it's summertime and you can find ripe yellow or green heirloom tomatoes at a farmer's market, they make a really tasty salsa. If not, tomatillos work great: be sure to remove their papery outer coating before washing. I don't recommend making this salsa with red or orange tomatoes, as the red juices will mix with the green of the avocado and create a salsa with a brownish tinge.

Peach Tomato Salsa

I love to make this fresh salsa in the summer when peaches and tomatoes are plentiful, sweet, and juicy. It's great as a snack served with chips, or as a taco topping. If good fresh peaches are hard to find, I often replace them with mangoes. I don't usually peel my peaches, but if using mangoes, you'll definitely want to peel them.

1 pound fresh tomatoes
1 pound peaches (review note)
½ cup fresh cilantro
½ small to medium red onion
1 medium clove garlic
½ fresh poblano or green bell pepper
½ fresh jalapeño pepper (optional)
¼ cup lime juice
1 tsp apple cider vinegar
1 ½ tsp ground cumin
1 tsp salt
½ tsp ground black pepper

Makes: 4-5 cups, about 10 generous servings
Prep time: 15 minutes
Chill time: 30 minutes

1. Wash the tomatoes, core, and dice into ½ inch pieces. Place in a large strainer or colander for about 5 minutes to drain off some of the juices.

2. Meanwhile, dice the peaches into cubes the same size as the diced tomato. If you have freestone peaches, slice each peach in half, twist to open, and remove the pit. To get nice, even cubes, place half of a peach cut side down on the cutting board, and cut a slice parallel to the cutting board, so you have 2 round slices of peach from one half. From there, it's easy to dice each slice into cubes. Place diced peaches in a large bowl.

3. Wash the cilantro, dry it lightly with a towel, and rough chop it. Mince the onion and garlic. Dice the poblano or green bell pepper into small ¼ inch pieces. Add all of these to the bowl.

4. If you like a spicier salsa, mince the jalapeño (including the seeds) and add to the bowl. If you like it milder, discard the seeds before mincing, or omit the jalapeño altogether.

5. Add the drained tomatoes to the bowl. Pour the lime juice over the salsa. Add the vinegar, cumin, salt, and pepper. Mix well.

6. Serve immediately, or chill before serving. This salsa is best made fresh, but will keep for about 3 days in the refrigerator.

> NOTE: This recipe works best with slightly under-ripe peaches. It's also tasty with soft, overripe peaches—it's just a pain to cut the peaches when they're soft. Try not to store your peaches in the refrigerator: they can become grainy, especially when taken in and out of the fridge repeatedly. If you've stored your peaches on the counter, you may want to chill the salsa before serving so that it gets nice and cool.

Herb Butter

This garlicky butter works great for garlic bread, or as a great spread on rolls. The recipe makes enough for 2 baguettes worth of garlic bread. If using unsalted butter rather than salted, add about ½ tsp salt.

Makes: ½ cup
Prep time: 10 minutes
Cook time: 4 minutes
Chill time: 1 hour and 30 minutes

2 medium cloves garlic
½ cup (1 stick) salted dairy or
  vegan butter (Earth Balance
  works well)
2 Tbsp fresh parsley
2 Tbsp fresh herbs: sage, basil,
oregano, or thyme
¼ tsp garlic powder
⅛ tsp ground black pepper
pinch salt

1. Finely mince the garlic.

2. Place half of the butter in a small saucepan and cook on medium heat until melted. Add the garlic and sauté for about 2 minutes, until the garlic turns a golden brown. Remove from heat and let cool for about 5 minutes.

3. While the butter mixture cools, wash, dry, and finely chop your fresh herbs. Any combination of the herbs listed here will be great: I like to use 2 Tbsp parsley plus 1 Tbsp each of two additional herbs from the list. You should have ¼ cup total of herbs, including the parsley.

4. Add the garlic powder, pepper, pinch of salt, and fresh herbs to the butter mixture. Mix well.

5. Place the remaining half of the butter in a small bowl, and pour the melted butter mixture over it. Use a spoon to soften it, mixing the cold butter completely with the melted butter until you have a partially melted mixture with an even consistency.

6. If using to make garlic bread, spread butter on the bread immediately, without refrigerating.

7. If using as a spread for rolls, transfer to a small bowl, cover, and refrigerate for 1 ½ hours so it can thicken. Store in the refrigerator for up to two weeks—remove from fridge 10-15 minutes before serving to make it soft and spreadable again.

Chapter Five:
SAVORY BAKING ADVENTURES

Sharing the Sacred
BREAD FROM THE EARTH

"what shows us our face in a stranger,
who teaches us what we clutch shrivels
but what we give goes off in the world
carrying bread to people not yet born."
-MARGE PIERCY[31]

Sunlight streams in the through the kitchen window. The earthy smell of yeast and honey greets my nostrils as I uncover the ripe, round dough, dividing and twisting it in a steady rhythm. On Friday afternoons, I feel my ancestors behind me, moving my hands across smooth dough, braiding together our dreams. Generations of women carried out this weekly task of preparing rich, precious loaves for the holiest time of the week—Shabbat, a time of rest much needed after hard work. I connect with those who prepared bread for families, for community, for union meetings and radical gatherings—a different kind of holy work. I breathe gently, allowing them to move through the kitchen with me, infusing the challah with our survival, with a depth of knowing our lineage that is more rejuvenating even than sleep.

I learned to bake challah from my mother.[32] As a child, I braided my hair every day, and I don't remember whether I learned to braid bread or hair first. The gentle thump of the thick ropes of dough on the table as I cross them over each other again and again. For Rosh Hashanah, it was always a round loaf—round like the cycle of the year, and full of raisins for a sweet year. I worked hard to tuck in the ends so the circle braid had no discernible beginning or end. We threw old bread crumbs into the creek and let go of the old year's regrets, and ate sweet, fresh challah and apples dipped in honey with our hopes for the new year coming.

This bread is made holy through our efforts and those of the Holy One. The Jewish blessing before eating bread, "Blessed are you, Yah our G!d, spirit of the universe, who brings forth bread from the earth," teaches us that bread is miraculous—a gift from the Divine like manna. The bread sits on our table like a sacrifice on the Temple altar, creating sacred space in the home. We bake two loaves for Shabbat, recalling the story that, as our people wandered in the wilderness after escaping slavery, we received and gathered two portions of manna on Friday so that we could have a day of full rest on Shabbat. In my chavurah, we toss portions of the bread to each other after blessing it on Friday nights. It comes down to us like manna from the heavens, soft-edged and steaming, touched by love.

Ritual around bread, so essential for creating the sacred space of the Shabbat table, can also extend that sacred space into the streets. For several years, Jewish Voice for Peace attended the annual Historic Thousands on Jones Street march in Raleigh, North Carolina with baskets of fresh-baked challah.[33] Offering it to fellow marchers, we literally broke bread with people across faith and culture. When we break bread in community like this, we co-create the streets as a sacred space. The act of sharing makes possible our dreams, prayers, and hard work toward a world free from hunger and full of collective liberation.

Sharing can also be complicated. For years, I would bristle when non-Jews asked me to bake challah for them or to share my recipe, filled with the heart-wrenching sensation of something precious being ripped away. I owe my understanding of why I carry recipes in my body like this to Indigenous and Black activists' teachings about the dangers of cultural appropriation. Within a system of white European Christian supremacy, some of us are taught to consume everything—from the earth's precious gifts to each other—while others are left to be plundered.[34] In the face of these systems, it can be hard to protect the sacred without clutching it so tightly that it loses its living breath. I am committed to resisting consumption and theft, and to sharing with respect, mutuality, and vulnerability. My own relationship to what is sacred to me also reminds me to support Indigenous peoples' defense of sacred land, water, and cultural traditions—so often targeted for theft and destruction.

Whatever our sacred foods are, they come to us with rituals and a lineage that we carry into the future because we want to pass on their life-giving connection. We might make an offering of these foods, say a particular blessing, or prepare them only at a certain time of year. We might have learned to make them from elders in our family or community. They might remind us of home, or of specific places and people. They might be something we eat every day that makes the simple day itself holy. When we prepare sacred foods from our lineages, our ancestors move through the kitchen with us, giving us recipes and wisdom for how to move beyond recipes. These foods move holiness through us. They can remind us to refuse to consume and be consumed, humbling us before the Holy in awe of our aliveness and interdependence. Our food lineages come to us, we transform them with our lives, and we choose pieces of the whole to pass on. As Marge Piercy writes, in this way we carry a bread of possibility "to people not yet born."

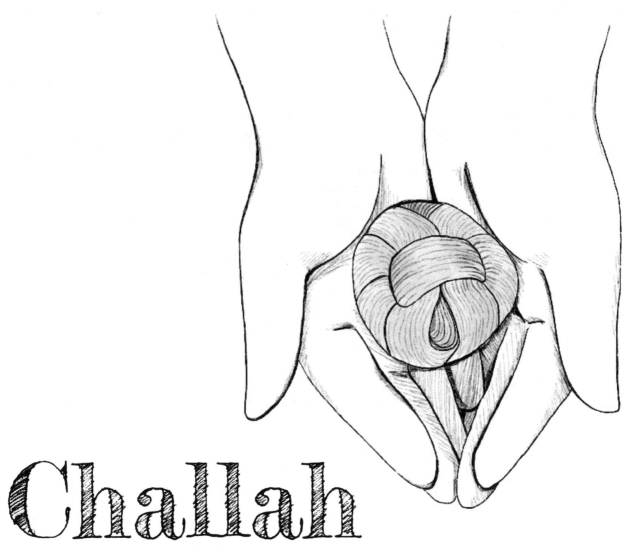

Challah

This is an exercise in trust. Many of us who come from cultures that have been subjected to marginalization and genocide have recipes that carry our survival in them. For me, an Ashkenazi Jew, challah is such a food of sacred space and cultural memory. It is a rich, delicious treat, and it is also meant for a specific purpose—I make it only for Shabbat, holidays, and special occasions. I always bless it, and if I am making a large quantity, I will take an offering out of the dough. You are being entrusted here with potent cultural magic, and I ask that you treat it with care. I am sharing these recipes so that my people can have access to them, to make and share bread for times of celebration, coming together, and ancestral connection.

"CHALLAH IS TAKEN"

Challah refers both to this bread of celebration, and to an offering of dough removed from any type of bread before baking. If you come across a store-bought box of matzo, most likely "challah is taken" will be written on the side. This means the dough offering has been made and you don't have to worry about making it yourself. Making a challah offering is an instruction given in the Torah (Leviticus 15:18-21). In the practices of the ancient Temple, challah (חַלָּה) was the name for an offering of cakes (often translated as loaves) made from flour and oil, brought to the Temple by the people. The word comes from the root ח-ל-ל, meaning to bore or pierce—probably describing the way these cakes were made, or their appearance. People would bring two challot, one to be burnt as an offering, and the other to be eaten by the Temple priests.

Today, the challah offering is only required for large batches of dough, so it is not a practice that I engaged in as a home baker. When I was working at La Gemma bakery in Wilmington and made challah for sale for the first time, I felt that making the dough offering would allow me to maintain the sacred practices of baking at my job. Because we are in diaspora and there is no Temple to which we can bring our challah offering in contemporary times, we burn it. Every Friday morning, as I made the challah at the bakery, I would draw myself up to my full height, tear off a portion of the dough, say the blessing, and braid it into a tiny loaf. Baking it until it was inedible to humans, I would take a moment of holy time and offer it to the birds and the mice in the woods behind the bakery. This followed the minhag hamakom (custom of the place): when I talked with the bakery owner about how I was thinking of sanctifying my challah baking, he shared that he sometimes made flour offerings there.

To make a challah offering, allow the dough to rise. Pull off a walnut-sized piece of dough before you divide the dough to shape it. As you pull it off, say the blessing, written here in the feminine:

בְּרוּכָה אַתְּ יָהּ אֱלֹהֵינוּ מַלְכַּת הָעוֹלָם אֲשֶׁר קִדְּשָׁתְנוּ בְּמִצְוֹתֶיהָ וְצִוַּתְנוּ לְהַפְרִישׁ חַלָּה מִן הָעִסָּה

B'rukhah at Yah, Eloteinu malkat ha'olam, asher kidshatnu b'mitzvoteiha v'tzivatnu l'hafrish challah min ha'isah.

Blessed are you, Holy Breath and Source, divine Queen of the universe, who makes us holy through Her guideposts and guides us to separate the challah offering from the dough.

Hold up the dough and say, "This is challah!" Then you can braid it into its own tiny, beautiful loaf. Baking the offering in an empty oven or over a flame used specifically to char it—not alongside the bread itself—is a traditional practice. But, in a world of climate catastrophe, you might choose to use less fuel and bake it alongside the bread. Bake it to a burnt crisp to ensure it doesn't get accidentally eaten, and offer it however you make offerings, along with any additional blessings you make.

Vegan Challah

Makes: 2 loaves; 1 loaf serves 5 people
Prep time: 40 minutes
Rise time: about 2-3 hours, depending on temperature (at least 30 minutes for the sponge, 45 minutes for the dough, and 30 minutes for the loaves)
Bake time: 30 minutes

1 ¾ cups water, at wrist temperature
2 tsp active dry yeast
4 cups all-purpose flour, divided, plus up to ½ cup extra for kneading
1 ½ cups whole wheat bread flour
¼ cup golden flaxseed meal
¼ cup mild-flavored oil such as canola oil
¼ - ⅓ cup agave nectar or maple syrup
1 ½ tsp salt
1 Tbsp soy milk or aquafaba (page 189), to brush over loaves

Make an intention:

For a restful Shabbat, to be in your body and connect with your ancestors while you bake, for liberation for all.

Make the sponge:

In a large bowl, pour in water and yeast. Add 2 cups of the all-purpose flour and mix to form a thick batter. Cover with a damp towel, some plastic wrap, or a plate. Place in a warm spot, like on top of a refrigerator. Let sit for 30 minutes to 1 hour, until airy and bubbly.

Make the dough:

Stir the sponge to deflate it. Place flax meal, oil, agave or maple syrup, and salt on top, and mix well. Add the 1 ½ cups whole wheat bread flour and the remaining 2 cups all-purpose flour. Mix until a dough forms. Turn out onto a lightly floured countertop, and knead for 5 minutes, adding the remaining ½ cup flour as needed. The dough should be firm, but may be a little sticky. Oil a large bowl, form the dough into a ball, and place in the bowl. Flip the dough over so the top of it is oiled as well. Cover with a damp towel, some plastic wrap, or a plate, and place in a warm spot, like on top of the refrigerator. Let rise 45 minutes to 1 hour, until doubled in size.

Shape and Bake: (Visit pages 158-159)

> NOTE: Jewish communities from different parts of the world have varied bread traditions, including many different varieties of challah. The recipes here are a quantification of a challah-making process I have intuited over the past fifteen years. When I am mixing up the dough, I only measure certain ingredients—the water, to ensure that I know how much bread I will have; the yeast, so that it will rise right; and the eggs/flax and salt, so that it will delight the tongue. I add the flour, oil, and sweetener by feel. I encourage you to listen to the bread, your ancestors, and intuition as you become comfortable with these recipes.

A Traditional Challah

Makes: 2 loaves; 1 loaf serves 5 people
Prep time: 40 minutes
Rise time: about 2-3 hours, depending on temperature (at least 30 minutes for the sponge, 45 minutes for the dough, and 30 minutes for the loaves)
Bake time: 30 minutes

1 ½ cups wrist temperature water
2 tsp active dry yeast
5 cups all-purpose flour, divided, plus up to ½ cup extra for kneading
1 ½ cups whole wheat bread flour
4 eggs
¼ cup mild-flavored oil such as canola oil
¼ - ⅓ cup honey
1 ½ tsp salt
1 Tbsp water, mixed with reserved
1 Tbsp egg, for egg wash

NOTE: The non-vegan recipe calls for a little less water than the vegan recipe, because eggs contain moisture whereas flax meal soaks it up.

Make an intention:

For a restful Shabbat, to be in your body and connect with your ancestors while you bake, for liberation for all.

Make the sponge:

In a large bowl, pour in water and yeast. Add 2 cups of the all-purpose flour and mix to form a thick batter. Cover with a damp towel, some plastic wrap, or a plate. Place in a warm spot, like on top of a refrigerator. Let sit for 30 minutes to 1 hour, until airy and bubbly.

Make the dough:

Stir the sponge to deflate it. Crack eggs into a small bowl and whisk lightly with a fork. Add all but 1 Tbsp of the eggs to the sponge. Reserve that 1 Tbsp in the small bowl, and add 1 Tbsp of water to it. Mix again with the fork and set aside—this will be the wash that you brush over the loaves just before baking. Add the oil, honey, and salt to the sponge and mix well. Add the 1 ½ cups whole wheat bread flour and the remaining 3 cups all-purpose flour. Mix until a dough forms. Turn out onto a lightly floured countertop, and knead for 5 minutes, adding the remaining ½ cup flour as needed. The dough should be firm, but may be a little sticky. Oil a large bowl, form the dough into a ball, and place in the bowl. Flip the dough over so the top of it is oiled as well. Cover with a damp towel, some plastic wrap, or a plate, and place in a warm spot, like on top of the refrigerator. Let rise 45 minutes to 1 hour, until doubled in size.

Shape and Bake: (Visit pages 158-159)

LAZY BAKER METHOD: Instead of putting the dough to rise in a clean bowl, scrape out the bowl you used to mix it up. Even if a few bits of dry dough remain stuck to the bowl, it's fine to lightly oil the bowl and return the dough to it.

How to Shape and Bake the Challah

SHAPE THE LOAVES

1. Turn the dough out onto a clean countertop. It should be fluffy and come out of the bowl in a round shape. Use a large chef's knife or a dough scraper, plus your geometry skills, to cut the circle in half. Cut each half into 3, 4, or 6 pieces, depending on what type of braid you want to do. I like to cut the dough into pie wedges in order to keep the strands the same size.

2. Roll each piece of dough into a long rope about 1 inch in diameter. You want the ropes to be fairly thick to ensure that you have nice big pieces of challah to tear off and eat. Braid as a 3-strand, 4-strand, or 6-strand depending on your preference (review instructions on facing page for how to make a four-strand braid).

3. Place the loaves on a parchment-lined sheet pan, leaving generous space on either side of each loaf. Brush loaves with soy milk, aquafaba (page 189), or egg wash. Place in a warm spot one last time, and let rise until a small indent remains when you poke the loaf with a finger, about 30 minutes to 1 hour. If you are a bread-baking novice, visit Tips for Bread Baking on page 161 for advice about rising times.

4. After you put the loaves to rise, preheat the oven to 375°F.

BAKE THE LOAVES

Place loaves into the hot oven, close, and immediately turn oven down to 350°F. Bake for 30 minutes, rotating the pans after the first 15 minutes—most ovens don't bake evenly, so switch which pan is on the top and bottom racks, and turn the pans around for optimal baking. After 30 minutes, check that the bottom of the loaf sounds hollow when you tap it—if so, it's ready. If not, bake for 5 more minutes. Remove from oven and move the loaves from the pan to a wire rack to cool. Cover with a towel while cooling so the crust stays soft.

Bless and serve.

HOW TO BRAID

A 3-strand braid has nice, large pieces and is easy to make, but gives a loaf that is a little flat. A 6-strand braid is nice and tall, but the pieces are a little small if you're tearing the bread. A 4-strand is my current favorite, because it has the large pieces of a 3-strand braid with the height of a 6-strand braid. Growing up, we always did a 3-strand braid, and I still braid this way when making a round loaf for Rosh Hashanah, representing the cycle of the year: it's easier to make it look seamlessly round. You can practice your braiding with yarn while your bread rises![35]

Here are instructions for making a 4-strand braid:

1. Place all four strands side by side and pinch the far end together tightly. Place strand 4 over strand 2.

2. Place strand 1 over strand 3.

3. Place strand 2 over strand 3.

4. Repeat this pattern (4 over 2, 1 over 3, 2 over 3) until the loaf is fully braided.

5. Tuck any stray ends underneath and pinch together to hold.

6. Admire your work!

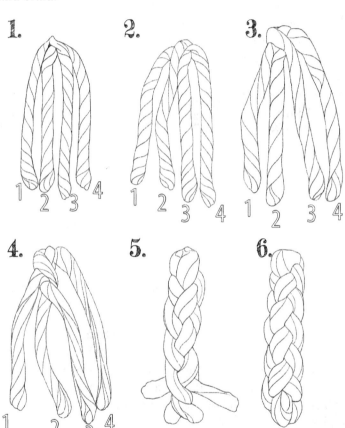

VARIATION: GAY CHALLAH

To make gay challah, mix up the dough and then divide it into 6 equal parts right before kneading. I use a kitchen scale to make sure the parts are equal. Add about ⅛ tsp gel food coloring to each ball of dough (use a different color for each) and knead until food coloring is evenly distributed—this usually takes more than 5 minutes for each color. Let each ball of dough rise, then divide each colored ball in 2 and braid two 6-strand loaves that each contain one strand of each color.

Gluten-Free Shabbat Bread

I am a firm believer that vegan and gluten-free recipes don't have to taste exactly like their dairy or glutenous counterparts—they just need to be delicious in their own way. This bread does not look or taste exactly like challah, but is a tasty, gluten-free bread to bless and eat on Friday nights. Like challah, this is a sacred bread for me—I treat it with respect and only make it for sacred occasions. This can be expansive: in addition to making it for Shabbat, I baked up a version of this bread for communion at the very queer ordination of my friend Rev. Alba Onofrio.

1 ½ cups almond meal
1 cup tapioca starch
½ cup white rice flour
1 Tbsp baking powder
1 tsp guar gum
1 tsp salt
1 tsp carob powder (optional)
¼ cup canned coconut milk
1 tsp apple cider vinegar
¼ cup olive oil
¼ cup honey, agave nectar, or maple syrup
2 Tbsp golden flaxseed meal
¼ cup hot water
½ cup raisins (optional)

Makes: 1 loaf; serves 5
Prep time: 15 minutes
Bake time: 35 minutes

1. Preheat oven to 375°F.

2. In a large bowl, mix together the almond meal, tapioca starch, white rice flour, baking powder, guar gum, salt, and carob (if using).

3. In a small bowl or measuring cup, mix coconut milk and vinegar. Add olive oil and sweetener.

4. In a separate small bowl, whisk together the flaxseed meal and hot water until gooey. Add the flax mixture and the coconut milk mixture to the almond meal mixture, and mix well. Work quickly at this point, because the bread will begin to rise from the reaction of the vinegar and baking powder, so you'll want to shape the loaf as soon as possible. If using the raisins, add them and mix. Scoop the dough into a parchment-lined pie pan or round 9-inch cake pan. Use wet hands to form the dough into a nice dome shape, leaving 1-2 inches of space all around it.

5. Bake at 375°F for 15 minutes, then turn oven down to 350°F and bake for an additional 20 minutes, or until it is golden-brown and a toothpick inserted in the center comes out clean.

6. Cool on a rack for 10 minutes before serving.

> **NOTE:** Without the carob, this bread takes on a golden color similar to challah. With the carob, it is a light brown, earthy color. Choose whichever you prefer for a holy bread.

TIPS FOR BREAD BAKING

Yeasted bread is a wonderful living creature that appreciates lots of care, rest, and different amounts of warmth depending on how it is feeling. This can be intimidating for first-time bakers, and challenging for people on a tight schedule. You'll have the most success if you let yourself get to know your bread dough and allow its cycles to guide you for an afternoon.

Tip #1: Make sure to let the bread rise for as long as it needs, even if that means longer than the amount of time noted in the recipe. Rising time (also called proofing time) can vary greatly based on temperature and humidity: on a frigid winter day, the dough can take five hours to rise, and in the heat of summer, just 30 minutes. You can check if the bread has risen enough by poking the dough gently with a finger. If it springs back, it needs more time. If the indent remains, it's likely ready.

It is especially important to be patient with your bread dough when baking with 100% whole wheat flour. Because whole wheat dough is a bit denser than white dough and doesn't have as much gluten to hold its structure, nor as many natural sugars for the yeasts to eat, it takes longer to rise. Whole wheat breads often have a reputation for being dense—this is because they aren't given ample rising time! Adequate time is especially important in the final rise, which will give the bread or rolls their height. For a sandwich loaf, allow the dough to rise until it's at least an inch above the height of the bread pan before putting it in the oven.

I am very enthusiastic about patience when it comes to bread, but it is also important not to over-proof your bread. Over-proofing can yield a loaf that looks fluffy but deflates when baking, has a giant hole in the center, or tastes sour because the yeasts have eaten up all the sugars and produced a lot of excess alcohol. Be patient, but don't forget about the rising dough! Find that sweet spot and your bread will be fluffy, sweet, and delicious.

Tip #2: When baking at Bread Uprising, I learned about a phenomenon called oven spring.[36] When bread goes into a hot oven, it gets a rising boost, growing taller and fluffier during the first 10-15 minutes of baking. This springing up happens because the carbon dioxide produced by the yeast, and the steam produced by the hot bread dough, expand inside of the air pockets in the dough while the surface of the dough is still soft and able to stretch. This works best in a hot oven, which is why many recipes in this book ask you to preheat the oven to a high temperature, then immediately turn it down once the bread is inside.

Dough also requires a sturdy structure in order to spring up in the oven. Stretching the surface of the dough to form a tight skin when shaping the rolls or loaf will help to trap those air bubbles and get a good spring. At the same time, if the skin on a loaf is too tight, the pressure will expand out at the weakest point, creating unpleasant cracks or bubbles. You can avoid this by letting your loaves relax for a bit between shaping and baking, and you can also slash the top of the loaf a few times with a sharp knife to release some of the tension so that the dough will expand up along the slash—a bread knife or serrated paring knife works best for this.

Tip #3: Both crusty bread and soft rolls have their place in the world. If you want a thick, hard crust, use a clean spray bottle to spray the loaves with water just before placing them in the oven. Bake at a hot temperature, at least 425°F. The hot temperature will cause the water to turn to steam, giving the bread a nice crust. Turn the oven down after 20 minutes to allow the center of the loaf to continue baking.

If you prefer a soft crust, bake at a lower temperature, but not less than 350°F. Cover the bread with a towel when it comes out of the oven to allow the steam rising off the bread to soften the crust as it cools.

Whole Wheat Sandwich Bread and Dinner Rolls

This is Bread Uprising's famous 100% whole wheat sandwich bread recipe. When I was a teen, my mom wrote up a versatile whole-grain bread recipe that we kept on the fridge for years. I used to bake it regularly for my family, making several loaves at once. Bread Uprising's recipe was inspired by that family recipe, fellow baker Tim Stallmann's family recipe, and the Tassajara Bread Book's *method of making a "sponge" that sits overnight to allow the dough to develop more flavor.[37] At Bread Uprising, we used local sorghum molasses, giving the bread a rich, dark color and a nice flavor. If you haven't baked with 100% whole wheat flour before, review Tips for Bread-Baking (page 161) before you begin!*

Makes: 1 dozen dinner rolls
  (to make 1 loaf, review note)
Prep time: 25 minutes
Rise time: about 10 ½ hours
  (8 hour overnight rise, 1 ½
  hour dough rise, and 1 hour
  roll rise)
Bake time: 20-25 minutes

For the sponge:
1 ½ cups (350 grams) cold tap water
½ tsp active dry yeast
1 ½ cups (215 grams) whole wheat bread
  flour

For the dough:
¼ cup (50 grams) canola oil
2 Tbsp (40 grams) honey (can substitute
  agave nectar or maple syrup)
1 Tbsp (20 grams) molasses
1 ¼ tsp salt
2 cups (285 grams) whole wheat bread
  flour
up to ½ cup additional whole wheat bread
  flour for kneading

SHAPING ROLLS

You can make a large number of rolls quickly by placing one roll on a clean, unfloured countertop, and gently placing your hand over it. Cupping the roll very lightly under your fingers, move your hand quickly around in a circle, allowing the roll—pressed against the countertop—to move within your hand. As you pass it back and forth between your thumb and fingers, a smooth surface will form all around the roll. This works because the roll sticks just slightly to the countertop as you move, creating enough tension to stretch the surface of the roll—it's important not to flour the countertop at all. But, you can put a little flour on your hands, so the dough doesn't stick to you. Once you get some practice at this technique, you can try forming 2 rolls at once—one in each hand.

1. Make the sponge: Place the water in a bowl large enough to hold at least triple the amount of water. Add the yeast and stir until it dissolves. Add the 1 ½ cups flour and stir until you have a smooth, thick batter. Cover loosely with plastic wrap or the lid of a pot. Place on a sheet pan just in case it overflows, and let rest at room temperature for 8 hours or overnight.

2. Make the dough: Uncover the sponge and stir it. Add canola oil, honey, molasses, and salt, and stir until well mixed. Add the flour and mix. When the dough comes together into a ball, scrape all the dough out onto a clean, lightly floured countertop, and knead for about 4 minutes. As you knead, add up to ½ cup additional flour into the dough if needed (the amount of flour needed may vary depending on the humidity, but do not add too much flour, as the rolls could become dry). The dough should be evenly mixed, firm, and just a little sticky. Form into a smooth ball.

3. Lightly oil a bowl, drop the ball of dough into the bowl, then flip the dough over so the entire ball is coated in oil. Cover with a warm, damp cloth or with plastic wrap. Set in a warm spot and let rise until about doubled, about 1 ½ hours.

4. Flip the dough out of the bowl onto a countertop, so you have a circular ball of dough in front of you. Use a large chef's knife or pan scraper to cut the dough into 12 equal portions. If you have a kitchen scale and want the rolls to be exactly equal, you can weigh out 75 gram portions of dough for each roll. Otherwise, cutting the dough like a pie into 12 relatively equal wedges works just fine.

5. Line a large sheet pan with parchment paper.

6. Shape the rolls: Form each roll, one at a time, into a neat sphere by stretching the surface of the dough around to one side, so you have one smooth side (the top of the roll) and one messier side (the bottom). Stretching the gluten strands taut on the surface of the dough helps the roll hold its shape while it rises and bakes.

7. Place rolls on the sheet pan, leaving 2 inches of space between each roll. Cover with a damp towel and allow to rise for about 1 hour until soft and fluffy.

8. While the rolls rise, preheat oven to 375°F. Place rolls in upper half of the oven and immediately turn oven down to 350°F. Bake for 20-25 minutes at 350°F, or until the tops have a light brown color. Rolls should be browned on the bottom, and the bottom should sound hollow when you tap it with your finger.

9. Remove from oven, place on a rack to cool, and cover rolls with a clean towel while cooling to ensure that the crust remains soft.

10. Once completely cool, serve, or store in airtight container until ready to use.

VARIATION: SANDWICH BREAD

This recipe makes one sandwich loaf. Follow steps 1-3. After the initial 1 ½ hour rise, oil a 9x5 inch loaf pan. Form the dough into a ball, then into a smooth log with rounded ends, using both hands to stretch the surface of the dough tight. Place in pan, smooth side up. Let rise until fluffy, about 1 hour. Preheat oven to 400°F, place bread in oven, and immediately turn oven down to 375°F. Bake at 375°F for 45-50 minutes, until golden brown on the top, sides, and bottom. The bottom of the loaf should sound hollow when tapped with your finger. Let cool before slicing.

White Sandwich Bread and Dinner Rolls

Fluffy. Bready. Delicious eaten warm with vegan butter or to accompany soup on a cold day. I developed this recipe in my catering business, and we also made it at Bread Uprising. One of my favorite ways to bake and serve these rolls is in a flower-shaped cluster of eight rolls.

Makes: 1 dozen dinner rolls
  (to make 1 loaf, review note)
Prep time: 25 minutes
Rise time: about 9 hours and 40 minutes
  (8 hour overnight rise, 1 hour dough rise,
  and 40 minute roll rise)
Bake time: 20 minutes

For the sponge:
1 ½ cups (350 grams) cold tap water
½ tsp active dry yeast
1 ½ cups (215 grams) white bread flour, also called unbleached bread flour

For the dough:
2 Tbsp (25 grams) canola oil
1 Tbsp (20 grams) honey (can substitute agave nectar or maple syrup)
1 tsp salt
1 ¾ cups (240 grams) white bread flour
up to ½ cup additional white bread flour for kneading

1. Make the sponge: Place the water in a bowl large enough to hold at least triple the amount of water. Add the yeast and stir until it dissolves. Add the 1 ½ cups flour and stir until you have a smooth, thick batter. Cover loosely with plastic wrap or the lid of a pot. Place on a sheet pan just in case it overflows, and let rest at room temperature for 8 hours or overnight.

2. Make the dough: Uncover the sponge and stir it. Add canola oil, honey, and salt, and stir until well mixed. Add the flour and mix. When the dough comes together into a ball, scrape all the dough out onto a clean, lightly floured countertop, and knead for about 4 minutes. As you knead, add up to ½ cup additional flour into the dough if needed (the amount of flour needed may vary depending on the humidity, but do not add excessive flour, as the rolls could become dry). The dough should be evenly mixed, and soft yet stretchy. Form into a smooth ball.

3. Lightly oil a bowl, drop the ball of dough into the bowl, then flip the dough over so the entire ball is coated in oil. Cover with a warm, damp cloth or plastic wrap. Set in a warm spot and let rise until about doubled, about 1 hour.

4. Flip the dough out of the bowl onto a countertop, so you have a circular ball of dough in front of you. Use a large chef's knife or pan scraper to cut the dough into 12 equal portions. If you have a kitchen scale and want the rolls to be exactly equal, you can weigh out 70 gram portions of dough for each roll. Otherwise, cutting the dough like a pie into 12 relatively equal wedges works just fine.

5. Line a large sheet pan with parchment paper.

6. Shape the rolls: Form each roll, one at a time, into a neat sphere by stretching the surface of the dough around to one side, so you have one smooth side (the top of the roll) and one messier side (the bottom). Stretching the gluten strands taut on the surface of the dough helps the roll hold its shape while it rises and bakes.

7. Place rolls on the sheet pan, leaving about 2 inches of space between each roll. Cover with a damp towel and allow to rise about 40 minutes until soft and fluffy.

8. While the rolls rise, preheat oven to 375°F. Place rolls in upper half of the oven and immediately turn oven down to 350°F. Bake for 20 minutes, or until golden brown on top and cooked through.

9. Remove from oven, place on a rack to cool, and cover rolls with a clean towel while cooling to ensure that the crust remains soft.

10. Once completely cool, serve, or store in an airtight container until ready to use.

WHAT IS A SPONGE?

A sponge is a wet, yeasted batter that rests overnight. Also called a pre-ferment, this is a special bread-baking method that yields extra flavorful breads. It's a little like a sourdough starter, but with added yeast and a short enough rising time that it does not develop a sour flavor. The batter is made with water, a little bit of yeast, and flour. The amount of yeast added in a sponge is much less than you would need if making a dough without a sponge, because the yeast grows as it sits overnight. There's no point in adding sweetener, as the yeast will just eat it all up, grow really fast, run out of food, and then start to die before the night is through. When making a sponge, the amount of water and flour is fairly flexible—you'll want it to be about the consistency of pancake batter. Its resting time is fairly flexible as well—anywhere from 8-14 hours at room temperature. You'll want to cover the sponge container so it stays moist, but not with an airtight lid—it is alive and will explode if the yeast's gasses are not able to escape. I like to place my covered sponge bowl on a large sheet pan as well, just in case the sponge gets excited and overflows.

VARIATION: SANDWICH BREAD

This recipe makes one sandwich loaf. Follow steps 1-3. After the initial 1 hour rise, oil a 9x5 inch loaf pan. Form the dough into a ball, then a smooth log with rounded ends, using both hands to stretch the surface of the dough taut. Place in pan, smooth side up. Let rise until fluffy, about 40 minutes. Preheat oven to 400°F, place bread in oven, and immediately turn down to 375°F. Bake at 375°F for about 40 minutes, until golden brown on the top, sides, and bottom. The bottom of the loaf should sound hollow when tapped with your finger. Let cool before slicing.

DINNER ROLL FLOWERS

Made as a special holiday treat at Bread Uprising, these flowers make a nice centerpiece for a dinner party. Two dozen rolls will make three dinner roll flowers. I like to use a combination of one recipe each whole wheat and white rolls. You can also make one roll flower as a centerpiece, and bake the rest of the batch of rolls on a pan to serve from a basket.

Here's how to do it:

Make one recipe each of white (page 164) and whole wheat (page 162) rolls. Mix up the whole wheat dough an hour ahead of the white dough: whole wheat dough takes longer to rise, so it needs this head start at every stage of the process except the sponge stage.

Choose either white or whole wheat dough to be the center of a flower, and the other to be the petals. For a whole wheat center, take the dough from 2 rolls and combine them into 1 large roll. Place this large whole wheat roll on a greased or parchment-lined sheet pan and allow to rise for 20 minutes before shaping the white rolls. Then shape 6 white rolls and arrange them around the whole wheat center, leaving about 1 ½ inches of space between each roll and the center. Continue to proof for 30-40 more minutes, or until rolls are fluffy and the gap between the rolls has closed up.

To make a flower with the reverse color pattern—a white center and whole wheat petals—arrange the 6 whole wheat petals in a circle on the pan, leaving about 6-7 inches of open space in the center. Allow to proof for 20 minutes. Then place a double-sized white roll in the center, and continue to proof for 30-40 more minutes.

If you want to try a colorful, kid-friendly experiment, make a double batch of white rolls. Before rising, separate out ¾ of the dough and knead food coloring into it (review note about gay challah, page 159). Use the plain white dough to form the flower centers, and the brightly-colored dough to make the petals. You can shape all of these rolls at the same time, since they will rise at the same rate.

Bake roll flowers at 350°F for 25-30 minutes.

Pancakes

I developed this recipe when I was running monthly vegan brunches at Ninth Street Bakery in Durham, and it's now my favorite pancake recipe, vegan or not. I love how soft and fluffy these pancakes are, and the cornmeal gives them a nice nutty flavor.

Makes: About 18 small pancakes, 4-6 servings
Prep time: 10 minutes
Cook time: 15-20 minutes

2 cups plain unsweetened soy or almond milk
1 cup water
1 Tbsp + 1 tsp apple cider vinegar
2 ½ cups all-purpose flour
½ cup cornmeal
2 Tbsp baking powder
2 Tbsp sugar
2 tsp salt
¼ cup canola oil, plus a little more for cooking
½ tsp vanilla (optional)

1. In a small bowl or large measuring cup, mix the non-dairy milk, water, and apple cider vinegar. Set aside to curdle.

2. In a large bowl, combine the all-purpose flour, cornmeal, baking powder, sugar, and salt. Mix with a whisk to combine and aerate.

3. Form a well in the center of the flour mixture and pour the vinegar mixture into it. Add the canola oil and vanilla, if using. Mix gently with a spoon or whisk until just combined, with a few small lumps remaining—do not overmix, or the pancakes may take on a gummy texture.

4. Brush a large skillet lightly with oil and heat on medium heat until a drop of water dropped from your finger sizzles. Using a small measuring cup, drop ¼ cup dollops of batter onto the skillet, allowing them to spread out naturally. Once a pancake gets a few bubbles all over its surface, flip it over. Cook for a total of about 4 minutes on each side.

5. You can keep the first round of pancakes in a baking pan in a 250°F oven while you're making the rest, if desired. Serve warm, with maple syrup and vegan butter.

> VARIATION: Add ½ cup chopped walnuts or pecans, 1 cup blueberries, or ½ cup chocolate chips to the batter before cooking. You can also make different sizes of pancakes, to your liking.

Cinnamon Rolls

This was one of our most beloved recipes at Bread Uprising, and we would make a batch of at least 9 dozen when their time came around on the baking rotation. The dough is not too sweet, and the brown sugar filling is super cinnamon-y, making the rolls perfect as a breakfast treat. If you like them sweeter, pile on the glaze to your heart's content. This recipe also includes options for freezing unbaked rolls, to be baked fresh for a tasty breakfast.

Makes: 1 dozen cinnamon rolls
Prep time: 40 minutes
Bake time: 25-30 minutes
Rise time: 9 hours and 45 minutes
  (8 hour overnight rise, 1 hour
  dough rise, and 45 minute roll rise)

For the sponge:
1 ½ cups (350 grams) cold tap water
1 ¼ tsp active dry yeast
2 cups (280 grams) all-purpose flour

For the dough:
¼ cup canola oil (50 grams)
3 Tbsp (60 grams) honey (can substitute agave nectar or maple syrup)
1 tsp (6 grams) salt
2 tsp (4 grams) ground cinnamon
3 cups (410 grams) white bread flour
up to ½ cup additional white bread flour for kneading

For the filling:
1 cup (200 grams) light brown sugar, loosely packed
½ cup (100 grams) canola oil
¼ cup (25 grams) cinnamon
½ tsp ground cloves

1. Make the sponge: Place the water in a bowl large enough to hold at least triple the amount of water. Add the yeast and stir until it dissolves. Add the 1 ½ cups flour and stir until you have a smooth, thick batter. Cover loosely with plastic wrap or the lid of a pot. Place on a sheet pan just in case it overflows, and let rest at room temperature for 8 hours or overnight.

2. Make the dough: Uncover the sponge and stir it. Add canola oil, honey, salt, and cinnamon, and stir until well mixed. Add the flour and mix. When the dough comes together and becomes difficult to mix, scrape all the dough out onto a clean, lightly floured countertop, and knead for about 4 minutes. It should be evenly mixed, and firm yet stretchy. Form in into a smooth ball.

3. Lightly oil a bowl, drop the ball of dough into the bowl, and flip the dough over so the entire ball is coated in oil. Cover with a warm, damp cloth or with plastic wrap. Set in a warm spot and let rise until about doubled, about 1 hour, give or take, depending on the weather.

4. Meanwhile, make the filling: Place brown sugar, canola oil, cinnamon, and cloves in a small bowl or large measuring cup and mix well.

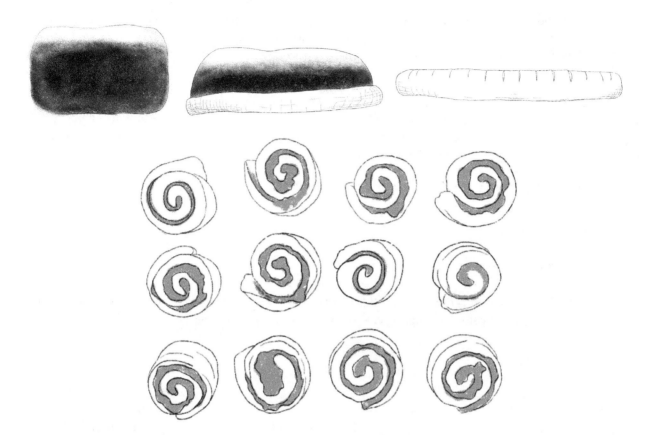

5. Form the rolls: Turn the dough out onto a smooth surface. The dough should be firm enough that you don't need to flour the surface, but if you do, flour it very lightly. Use your hands to flatten and stretch the dough into an approximate rectangle shape. Then use a rolling pin to roll it into a rectangle about 18 inches wide, 12 inches deep, and half an inch thick.

6. Use your hands or a spatula to spread the filling in a thick layer on top of the rectangle of dough. Cover the entire surface of the dough, going all the way to the edges on 3 sides. Leave about 1 inch clear on the long edge farthest away from you (review illustration). Use a finger to brush this edge with a small amount of water, which will help the rolls hold together.

7. Starting from the long edge closest to you, roll the dough into a tight, spiraled roll. When you reach the edge that you moistened with water, stretch the filling-free dough over the outside of the roll and press gently to seal. Flip the whole roll over so the seam is on the bottom.

8. Slice the long roll into cinnamon rolls: First, use a large serrated knife to mark off 12 rolls. You can estimate, or use a ruler to measure and make a small cut to mark every 1 ½ inches along the roll. Marking them off before you begin cutting will ensure that you end up with the expected number of rolls. Then, slice through at each place you marked. Lay each roll on a parchment-lined sheet pan, cut side up, leaving 2-3 inches between each. If the tail unfastens from a roll, just re-wrap it and tuck it under the roll.

9. Let rise for about 45 minutes until fluffy. Meanwhile, preheat the oven to 375°F and place an oven rack in the upper third of the oven. Once the rolls are fluffy, place the pan in the oven and immediately turn the oven down to 350°F. Bake for 25 minutes—if your oven bakes unevenly, rotate the pan after the first 15 minutes.

10. Let cool, then glaze with simple glaze (below). Use a knife to spread the glaze like a frosting, or for less of a sugar rush, use a teaspoon to lightly drizzle a small amount of glaze over the rolls. The surface of the glaze will harden after about 30 minutes: if you want to store extra cinnamon rolls in a plastic bag, make sure to let the glaze harden before covering them so that it will stick to the rolls, not the plastic.

••

Simple Glaze:

⅔ cup powdered sugar
1 Tbsp water
⅛ tsp vanilla extract

Place all ingredients in a large measuring cup or a small bowl and mix vigorously with a spoon or fork. Use immediately, or store in a tightly closed container for up to a week.

VARIATION: I like to arrange cinnamon rolls on the pan as described here, so they spread out wide while baking and pull apart easily. If you prefer to make cinnamon rolls that are a bit taller, pack them into an oiled 9x13 inch baking dish instead of spreading them out on a sheet pan. They'll rise up nice and tall, and the edges will stay soft because they're packed in close. Bake for 30 minutes so that they cook through.[38]

NOTE: To keep honey (or other sweeteners) from sticking to your measuring cup, measure the oil first and then brush a little of the oil into the tablespoon measure that you're using for the honey.

MAKE-AHEAD OPTIONS: You can mix up the rolls the night before to bake them in the morning, or make a double batch and place half of them in the freezer to bake later.

Overnight refrigerator method: Mix up the sponge in the morning. At night, make the dough and shape the rolls. Immediately after shaping the rolls and placing them on the pan, cover the whole pan with plastic wrap and place in the refrigerator. Let rise 8-10 hours. In the morning, let sit at room temperature for 30 minutes, then bake.

Freezer storage method: After the rolls are shaped and have risen on the pan, cover the whole pan with plastic wrap and place it in the freezer to store for up to 3 weeks. To bake, first let the frozen rolls thaw on the pan at room temperature for 1-2 hours, until they are soft to the touch and just slightly cool. Then bake.

Bread Uprising Granola

I started making granola while cooking at The Stone House retreat center. When I came on staff as a cook, I noticed a recipe in the kitchen notebook called Stone House Granola, from Mariana Ruíz. I adapted it significantly, and it became our Bread Uprising granola recipe, including local NC ingredient staples like pecans, honey, and sorghum molasses. It's nice and crunchy, and just lightly sweet.

Makes: 10 cups
Prep time: 15 minutes
Cook time: 35 minutes

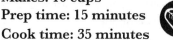

6 cups (690 grams) rolled oats
½ cup (70 grams) raw pumpkin seeds
½ cup (60 grams) raw pecan halves, broken into pieces
½ cup (70 grams) raw sunflower seeds
2 tsp ground cinnamon
2 tsp ground cardamom
½ tsp salt
½ cup (100 grams) canola oil
¾ cup (225 grams) honey or maple syrup
¼ cup (80 grams) molasses (preferably light sorghum molasses)
1 cup (120 grams) raisins

1. Preheat oven to 325°F and place oven rack in the top half of the oven.

2. Measure all dry ingredients into a large bowl: Oats, pumpkin seeds, pecans, sunflower seeds, cinnamon, cardamom, and salt. Mix well.

3. Add the canola oil, honey, and molasses to the dry ingredients. Mix until all the oats and seeds are well coated. A wooden spoon works well for this, but your hands work better.

4. Place parchment paper on a large sheet pan. Spread granola evenly on the pan in a layer no more than 1 ½ inches deep to ensure even baking—if the pan is too small, you'll need to use two pans.

5. Place pan in oven and bake for about 35 minutes in all. After 15 minutes, use a spatula to turn the granola, bringing the granola from the outside edges of the pan into the middle, and the part in the middle toward the outside. Place back in the oven, and after another 10 minutes, repeat this process. After 10 minutes more, test for doneness.

6. To test for doneness, take a few oats from the center of the pan, and leave them on the counter for a couple of minutes to cool. If they are crunchy when cool, it's done. If not, bake for 5 more minutes and test again. The granola will not seem crunchy when hot, but will harden up as it cools.

7. After it is cool, add raisins and mix until evenly distributed. Store in an airtight container, like a glass mason jar, for up to a month.

NOTE: Want clusters in your granola? After it comes out of the oven, let it cool without stirring it. Behold! You will have big clusters that you can break up. If you want to avoid clusters, turn the granola with a spatula right when it comes out of the oven, and once more while it is cooling.

Vegan Biscuits

I like my biscuits fluffy, flaky, and buttery. I developed this recipe to bring more of that deliciousness into the world. I've found that it takes a hot oven, lots of vegan butter, and gentle handling to make good, fluffy biscuits. The magical folding method here makes sure the biscuits are extra flaky and fluffy. Make sure to roll them out thick! Follow these steps, and you will be rewarded with yummy, biscuit-y goodness, perfect for springtime brunch.

Makes: 12 three-inch wide biscuits
Chill time: 2 hours (optional)
Prep time: 20 minutes
Cook time: 12-14 minutes

4 cups all-purpose flour, plus about ½ cup extra for rolling out the biscuits
1 ½ cups plain unsweetened soy or almond milk
2 tsp apple cider vinegar
2 Tbsp baking powder
¾ tsp salt
½ cup plus 2 Tbsp cold vegan butter, such as Earth Balance (1 ¼ sticks, or 5 ounces)

1. If possible, measure out the flour and chill it for at least 2 hours before beginning. This will help the vegan butter hold its shape when you cut it in, which yields a fluffier biscuit. If you don't have time for this, that's okay too.

2. Preheat oven to 450°F and place an oven rack in the upper half of the oven.

3. Pour the soy or almond milk in a small bowl. Add the vinegar, stir to mix, and set aside to curdle.

4. Place the flour, baking powder, and salt in a large bowl. Mix with a whisk to combine and aerate.

5. Cut the vegan butter into thin pieces and scatter it throughout the flour mixture. Use a pastry blender to cut it into the flour mixture until the pieces of butter are about the size of large peas, or just a little larger.

6. Make a well in the center of the flour, and add the vinegar mixture. Stir with a spoon just until evenly blended.

7. Fold the biscuit dough: Turn out dough onto a heavily floured countertop or board. Use your hands to pat the dough gently into a rectangle about 2 inches thick, then fold it in half. Press the the dough out again and fold it over. Repeat this process about 5 times, sprinkling a little flour if needed to prevent sticking. Folding the dough will trap tiny air pockets inside the layers of dough. The air pockets expand during baking, helping the biscuits to rise. The folding is key; it's also important not to over-handle the dough.

8. Now you're ready to roll out the biscuits and cut them. Make sure there's plenty of flour on your countertop so they won't stick to it. Flour a rolling pin and gently roll the dough out until it's 1 to 1 ½ inches thick. Rolling the dough thick is one of the secrets to a nice tall biscuit.

9. Cut the biscuits out with a 2 ½ inch round biscuit cutter or drinking glass. Dip the cutter's edge in flour so the dough doesn't stick to it. Maximize use of the dough by cutting circles as close together as possible. Place biscuits on a parchment-lined sheet pan, leaving about 1 ½ inches of space between them.

At this point, you'll want to handle the remaining dough as little as possible, but do use all of it so you can have lots of tasty biscuits! Take the remaining dough scraps and gently form them into a ball. Roll it out again and cut more biscuits. Repeat until you've used all the dough.

10. Place the pan in the hot oven. Bake for 12 to 14 minutes, rotating the pan after 8 minutes. Biscuits are done when they are golden brown on top and the sides look flaky, not doughy.

11. Serve warm. Yum!

LAZY BAKER METHOD:

Measure the soy or almond milk in a large measuring cup and add the vinegar directly to it there, rather than mixing them in an additional bowl. Use your pastry blender to whisk the dry ingredients, rather than dirtying a whisk.

NOTE: If you have a kitchen scale, weighing vegan butter is the best way to measure it—it can be cumbersome, messy, and inaccurate to try to shove it into a measuring cup. If you're stuck with measuring it by volume, make sure that the vegan butter you're using is regular, not whipped—whipped butter will give you less butter per cup.

NOTE: This recipe scales up well, and I find it especially satisfying to pull 4 dozen of these biscuits out of the oven and watch them fly out of the serving basket. If doubling or quadrupling the recipe, reduce the amount of baking powder by one-fourth. A doubled recipe will have 3 Tbsp baking powder, and a quadrupled recipe will have 6 Tbsp.

Vegan Pie Crust

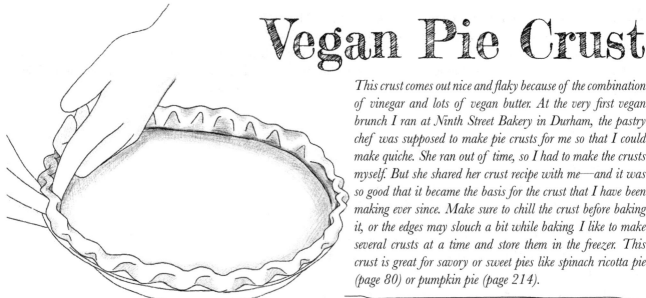

This crust comes out nice and flaky because of the combination of vinegar and lots of vegan butter. At the very first vegan brunch I ran at Ninth Street Bakery in Durham, the pastry chef was supposed to make pie crusts for me so that I could make quiche. She ran out of time, so I had to make the crusts myself. But she shared her crust recipe with me—and it was so good that it became the basis for the crust that I have been making ever since. Make sure to chill the crust before baking it, or the edges may slouch a bit while baking. I like to make several crusts at a time and store them in the freezer. This crust is great for savory or sweet pies like spinach ricotta pie (page 80) or pumpkin pie (page 214).

Makes: 1 single 9-inch pie crust
Prep time: 15 minutes
Chill time: 1 hour

1. In a small bowl, mix 6 Tbsp water with the vinegar, and place in the refrigerator to chill.

> 6 Tbsp cold water
> $\frac{1}{2}$ tsp white or apple cider vinegar
> 1 $\frac{1}{2}$ cups all-purpose flour, plus
>   extra for rolling the crust
> 1 $\frac{1}{2}$ tsp sugar
> $\frac{1}{4}$ tsp salt
> $\frac{1}{2}$ cup cold vegan butter such as
>   Earth Balance (1 stick, or 4 ounces)

2. In a medium bowl, whisk together the flour, sugar, and salt. Slice the vegan butter into thin $\frac{1}{4}$ inch pieces, and scatter it throughout the flour mixture. Using a pastry blender, cut the vegan butter into the flour mixture until the butter is approximately the size of large peas. Large chunks of butter will help give the crust its flakiness, so don't cut them too small!

3. Sprinkle 4 Tbsp of the water-vinegar mixture over flour mixture and use a fork to mix. Try forming the dough into a ball: if won't hold together, add 1-2 Tbsp more of the liquid and gently mix. The dough should be slightly crumbly, but you should be able to form it into a ball that just holds together.

4. Roll out your crust. The easiest way I have found to do this is to roll it out between two pieces of plastic wrap. Place one piece of plastic wrap on the counter. Form the dough into a ball and place in the center of the plastic wrap, then pat down gently. Cover with a second large piece of plastic wrap and roll the dough out with a rolling pin until it is between $\frac{1}{8}$ and $\frac{1}{4}$ inch thick. Remove the top sheet of plastic wrap and place your pie pan upside down on top of the crust. Place one hand under the bottom sheet of plastic wrap and a second hand on the pie pan. Quickly and gently flip the whole thing over, so that the crust is now sitting in the pie pan. Press the crust into the pan, then carefully remove the second sheet of plastic wrap from the top of the crust.

5. Use scissors to trim the edges of the crust so they hang down about 1 inch over the edge of the pie pan. Use the scraps to patch up any parts of the crust that might need it. Then tuck the edges under so that the crust has a nice thick rim. Use 3 fingers to crimp the edge, giving it a wavy texture (refer to illustration).

6. Poke the crust all over with a fork to create tiny holes—this will help prevent it from puffing up while baking.

7. Place in the refrigerator for at least 1 hour, or in the freezer for at least 30 minutes. Once the crust has chilled and is hard to the touch, you can use it immediately or place it in a plastic bag and return it to the freezer to store for several months. Depending on the pie recipe, you might bake the crust empty, or fill it before baking.

NOTE: When rolling the crust between layers of plastic wrap, you won't need additional flour for rolling. If you are rolling on a countertop or board, sprinkle the surface and the rolling pin with a few tablespoons of flour before rolling to prevent sticking.

LAZY BAKER METHOD: Use the pastry blender to whisk the dry ingredients, rather than dirtying a whisk. I like to make several crusts at once and freeze them to use as needed—if doing this in foil pie pans, you can stack them inside of each other and store the whole stack in one large plastic bag.

Pizza Crust

In the summer, every Friday is pizza day for students at the Center for Documentary Studies at Duke—this is the pizza crust that I used to make for those lunches. It's part whole grain while still being nice and airy, full of herbs, and just lightly sweet. The crust recipe is inspired by the calzone dough in the Moosewood Cookbook,[39] *a favorite cookbook from my childhood.*

Makes: One 14-inch pizza (serves 4)
Prep time: 25 minutes
Rise time: 1 hour for the first rise
  (plus 10 minutes for the second rise)
Bake time: 8 minutes for crust
  (plus 10-15 minutes with the toppings on)

1 cup wrist temperature water
1 tsp active dry yeast
2 Tbsp olive oil
2 Tbsp honey or agave nectar
1 tsp salt
1 cup whole wheat flour
1 ½ cups white bread flour,
  plus up to ¼ cup extra for
  kneading
½ tsp dried oregano
½ tsp dried basil

1. Pour water and yeast into a large bowl and stir until the yeast dissolves.

2. Add the olive oil, honey, and salt and mix until combined.

3. Add the whole wheat and white bread flour, then sprinkle in the oregano and basil. Stir until well mixed—a dough should come together in the middle of the bowl.

4. Turn out onto a lightly floured countertop and knead for 3-5 minutes. You can add some additional flour as you knead, and the dough will still be a little sticky after kneading. Kneading develops the gluten in the dough to give you a nice, stretchy crust. You'll know it's ready when you can take a tiny piece of dough and stretch it thin without it tearing.

5. Scrape out the bowl and lightly oil it. Place the kneaded ball of dough in the bowl, then flip the dough over so the ball is coated in oil on all sides. Cover with a damp, warm towel or plastic wrap, and place in a warm spot to rise.

6. Let rise until doubled in size, about 1 hour.

7. Preheat oven to 450°F and line a large round baking pan with parchment paper, or grease lightly with oil and sprinkle with cornmeal.

8. Punch down the dough. Take it out of the bowl, shape it into a nice round ball, and begin to stretch it into a round, flat shape. If the dough will not stretch all the way into a thin crust, stretch it partway and let it rest for 10 minutes—the dough will be easier to stretch after it relaxes.

9. Place the partially-stretched crust on the pan. Starting in the center, press down and out with the heel of your hand in a spiraling pattern, so that the crust forms from the center out. This method helps create an even thickness, a smooth surface, and a round shape. Keep working until you have a flat crust about ¼ inch thick, leaving a ½ inch thick crust all around the edges.

10. Poke the crust with a fork about 30 times, making tiny holes all over the surface, but leaving the thick crust around the edge un-poked. These holes will help keep the crust flat while allowing the edge of the crust to rise.

11. Let the crust sit for 10 minutes to rise just a little bit.

12. Parbake the crust at 450°F for 8 minutes, until it is light brown on top but still soft. Remove from oven and add your favorite sauce and toppings. Reduce oven to 400°F, return pizza to oven, and bake for 10-15 minutes more, until toppings are done.

NOTE: Many pizza recipes call for high-gluten white flour, which gives the crust a characteristic stretchy and chewy texture, and helps it hold up well when loaded with toppings. High-gluten flour can be expensive and hard to find, but if you can get it, experiment! For a super-stretchy crust, use a high-gluten white flour in place of both the white and whole wheat bread flours. If you don't have bread flour on hand, you can also make the crust with all-purpose flour in a pinch. All-purpose flour has even less gluten than bread flour, so the crust will be a little less stretchy and springy. But, as long as you're not planning to show off by tossing the dough in the air as you shape the crust, all-purpose flour will be fine.

NOTE: If you want to bake off several crusts at a time to use the next day, or to freeze: bake the crust for 10 minutes instead of 8. The crust will be cooked through, and you can let it cool, wrap tightly, and then freeze for up to 1 month.

LAZY BAKER METHOD: My pans are rectangular, so I usually like to make a rectangular crust. This recipe will make enough dough to fill a large rectangular sheet pan. After you punch down the dough, form it into a rectangular shape instead of a circular one, and use that shape as the basis for stretching and shaping your crust.

VEGAN PIZZA

Pizza is one of my comfort foods. It's so tasty, with so many possible flavor combinations. I even like to eat cold leftover pizza right out of the fridge! Here are some suggestions for vegan and vegetarian pizza toppings.

CRUST:

Pizza crust (page 176)
Gluten-free pizza crust (page 180)

SAUCE:

Tomato sauce (page 139)
Pesto (page 140)
Balsamic reduction (page 141) with olive oil

TOPPINGS:

Cashew cheese (page 21)
Certain store-bought vegan cheeses (review note on facing page)
Fresh tomatoes, sliced
Black or green olives, sliced or whole
Kalamata olives, halved or whole
Artichoke hearts, diced or quartered
Banana pepper, cut into rings and tossed in olive oil
Bell pepper, diced or sliced, tossed in olive oil
Mushrooms, sliced and tossed in olive oil
Red onion, cut into rings and tossed in olive oil
Summer squash or zucchini, sliced and tossed in olive oil and salt
Spinach, lightly sautéed
Broccoli, partially steamed, then tossed in olive oil
Garlic, minced or roasted whole
Fennel bulb, sliced, tossed in olive oil and salt, and roasted
Eggplant, sliced, tossed in olive oil and salt, and roasted
Tempeh or tofu, crumbled and sautéed with herbs
Veggie sausage, cut or crumbled and sautéed
Pistachios, roasted and shelled

When I'm making pizza with lots of veggies and a crust that I've pre-baked, I don't put the toppings on raw—they won't have long enough to cook.

But, as a lazy baker, I don't want to pre-cook all the toppings either. A happy medium for many toppings is to simply toss them in olive oil and salt, so they roast quickly on top of the pizza. In most cases, whether to cook the topping beforehand or just toss it in the oil is really a matter of preference: toppings like spinach, broccoli, and garlic will have a different flavor if you sauté, steam, or roast them, so choose what you prefer. Eggplant and soy-based vegan proteins are exceptions: since they take a bit longer to cook, roasting or sautéing them ahead of time will ensure they are cooked through and taste great on your pizza.

A NOTE ON STORE-BOUGHT VEGAN CHEESES:

There are a few hits and misses out there when it comes to vegan cheese. When I make vegan pizza, I usually prefer to leave off the cheese entirely and let the sauce and veggies speak for themselves with their bright tastiness. I find that pizza with too much vegan cheese can become an unpleasant experience. If you do want to add a melty sprinkle of cheese, Daiya cheddar, Follow Your Heart parmesan, and Miyoko's Creamery fresh mozzarella are my favorites. They all melt nicely and add a good flavor.

Gluten-Free Pizza Crust

About five years ago, in search of a good gluten-free pizza crust recipe, I came across Karina Allrich's recipe on her blog, Gluten Free Goddess.[40] *As I continued experimenting, her crust became the base for the recipe that I have adjusted over the years. This gluten-free crust is pleasantly fluffy and chewy, like a pizza crust should be, and pretty fast to make—no kneading required!*

Makes: One 12-inch pizza (serves 3)
Prep time: 15 minutes
Rise time: 30 minutes
Bake time: 10-15 minutes

1 cup wrist temperature water
1 tsp active dry yeast
¼ cup olive oil
2 Tbsp honey or agave nectar
1 ½ Tbsp golden flaxseed meal
½ cup brown rice flour
½ cup sorghum or millet flour
½ cup corn or potato starch
⅓ cup tapioca starch
1 tsp salt
1 tsp guar gum (can substitute xanthan gum)
½ tsp dried oregano
½ tsp dried basil

1. Pour water and yeast into a large bowl, and stir until the yeast dissolves.

2. Add the olive oil, honey, and golden flax meal, and mix until combined.

3. In a small bowl or large measuring cup, whisk together the brown rice flour, sorghum or millet flour, corn or potato starch, tapioca starch, salt, and guar gum until evenly mixed.

4. Add the flour mixture to the yeast mixture and stir until well combined. Add the oregano and basil. Mix well, stirring vigorously until the mixture forms a thick batter. The mixture should be much wetter than bread dough, but if you use a spoon to pull a bit of batter up into a peak, it should hold the peak.

5. Line a large round baking pan with parchment paper, or grease lightly with oil and sprinkle with cornmeal.

6. Use a rubber spatula to scrape the batter into a smooth mound in the center of the bowl, and then scoop it onto the prepared pan. Shape the crust with the spatula or wet hands: spread the batter in a spiraling motion, from the center out, to create a smooth, round shape. If you discover that the shape looks like a blob, just scoop up part of the batter and add it back to the center of the crust, then smooth it out again. When you're done, the crust should be about ½ inch thick. If you like crust on your pizza, be sure to leave an even thicker crust around the edges.

7. Poke the crust with a fork about 30 times, making tiny holes all over the surface, but leaving the thick crust around the edge un-poked. These holes will help keep the crust flat while still allowing the edge of the crust to rise.

8. Preheat oven to 400°F.

9. Let the crust rise, uncovered, for 30 minutes. You may notice it has risen only a little bit, but the yeast is working its magic and will yield a nice light crust.

10. Place in oven and bake for 10-15 minutes. Crust should be golden brown in color, still soft, and cooked through.

11. Remove from oven, add your favorite sauce and toppings, return to oven, and bake for 10-15 minutes more, until toppings are done.

NOTE: Because this crust is gluten-free, the dough will not be stretchy or kneadable like the pizza crusts that you may envision being tossed in the air above a pizza maker's head. The fact that you are creating a pizza crust may not really be apparent from the consistency of the dough until the crust is fully baked. Its texture is achieved through a combination of guar gum and flaxseed meal—which hold the gluten-free flours together—and just the right amount of tapioca starch—which adds a stretchy texture to the crust. For advice about gluten-free baking, review Tips for Gluten-Free and Vegan Baking on page 206.

Tamari-Roasted Almonds

Tamari-roasted almonds are sold in the bulk section of many food cooperatives. I love their salty and savory flavor, and one day I decided to make them at home. The homemade ones are so delicious right out of the oven, and they keep well in a glass jar for several weeks. They make a great travel snack, and I like to keep a little jar of them in the car or in my backpack for snacking. While most soy sauce contains wheat, tamari is a gluten-free soy sauce, so if making this recipe for gluten-free people, make sure you use tamari.

Makes: About 5 cups
Cook time: 20 minutes

4 cups raw whole almonds
5 Tbsp tamari or soy sauce

1. Preheat oven to 375°F.

2. Place almonds on a large sheet pan in a single layer. Toast in the oven for 3 minutes, just to heat them up. Measure out 5 Tbsp soy sauce and place in a small bowl or measuring cup.

3. Take the almonds out of the oven, and use a spoon to sprinkle about half of the soy sauce over them. Use a spatula to toss, coating the almonds evenly with the soy sauce. Return pan to oven and roast for 5 minutes.

4. Repeat step 3, tossing the almonds with the remaining soy sauce, and baking for 5 minutes more.

5. Take the almonds out of the oven and use a spatula to stir them, unsticking them from the pan. They should have darkened in shade and look a little bit damp. Return to oven and roast for 5-7 minutes more, until toasty and dry-looking. Six minutes makes almonds that are pretty brown on the inside, which is how I like them—if you like them less toasted, try a shorter roasting time.

6. Remove from oven, stir, and allow almonds to cool on the pan. They will crackle and snap pleasantly as they cool. Once cool, store in an airtight glass jar for up to 3 weeks.

> NOTE: Once you put away the almonds, you'll be left with a pan that is coated in dried soy sauce. Just soak it in warm water for a few minutes and it will clean up easily with a sponge.

Chapter Six:
DESSERTS

Practicing Freedom
THE KITCHEN AS LIBERATION LAB

"So may every humiliated mouth,
teeth like desecrated headstones,
fill with the angels of bread."
- MARTÍN ESPADA[41]

In the kitchen at the House of Mango, an activist collective house in Durham where I lived from 2005-2008, there was always abundant food, laughter, and freedom dreams—and a sprinkling of drama, too. Posted on the door of one of the kitchen cabinets was a well-worn copy of Martín Espada's poem, "Imagine the Angels of Bread." Every New Year's Day, my community reads this poem as a reminder of what we are fighting for—and the hope and truth that this is the year we make liberation in our lifetimes more possible.

When I was asked to speak at the No Ban, No Wall, No Fear rally in Raleigh a month after Trump's inauguration in 2017, I quoted from that poem: "If the shutdown of extermination camps began as a vision of a landscape without barbed wire or the crematorium, then this is the year."[42] It is crucial for us, no matter the conditions we face, to continue dreaming and envisioning a world beyond what is directly in front of us, and doing so together.

We must practice opening into a space of dreaming and visioning with our full hearts, and then experimenting with what we intuit might work to get us there. When Tim Stallmann and I founded Bread Uprising Bakery, we dove heart-first into creating a future where everyone's needs could be met—beyond wage labor and beyond a market of buying and selling. As a cooperative, Bread Uprising embodied curiosity in action: pairing openness with lots of hard work.

In cooking and community organizing, we can accomplish so much by experimenting in the direction of our longings. Sometimes, when I long for a particular dish, I can almost taste the joy of its textures on my tongue. When developing such a brownie recipe, I tried different proportions of chocolate and cocoa, then different options for eggs. I added a little baking powder, then took out all the baking powder. Then I tried several options for temperature and baking time. After many rounds of experiments, I was satisfied.

Whether we are making brownies or pulling off a community event, it helps to become familiar with our materials—the properties of baking powder, or the logistics of setting up an accessible room. We follow our planned recipe through to the end, or just keep good notes about what we changed along the way; then we debrief, gauging what worked and deciding what to change next time. Once we find a method that works, we can roll with it, riff off of it, and share it.[43]

We probably won't perfect a recipe on the first try—most learning requires mistakes. In community organizing, people's lives and livelihoods may literally be at stake, but in the home kitchen, we are unlikely to poison anyone with our experiments. The kitchen can be a lab not just for recipes, but for building necessary movement skills like creativity, letting go, and celebrating our failures.

At the same time, it's important to understand at whose expense our mistakes come. Food can create a feeling of belonging or it can take that feeling away, allowing some people to feel at home and others, excluded. As a white person catering for multiracial groups, I have had to develop a certain humility and rigor to create food that is nourishing and familiar to those I'm serving.

Once, I cooked for a multiracial retreat that, despite facilitators' best intentions, replicated structures of racism and harmed Black participants. On a particularly intense day, I made a miso soup with sweet potato glass noodles—an ingredient I had never worked with before. I did not realize that these noodles could only survive in soup for a short period of time and have to be cooked quickly, then added just before serving. Instead, I cooked them in the soup pot itself. As the noodles began to fall apart, the entire pot became thick and gelatinous. It was disgusting, and a whole group of participants had to drive into town to buy food. For Black participants who were already marginalized in a white-dominated space, having inedible food on the table magnified that oppression, that lack of being able to find a home at the retreat. In retrospect, I am grateful that participants who needed it had the wisdom and resilience to leave, take a break from the space, and get some comfortable nourishment—and that I was able to somewhat redeem myself with delicious butterscotch brownies that evening. The entire event was a catalyst for the retreat center's cooking team to commit to preparing food in a way that would prioritize comfort for participants with layered experiences of structural oppression.

Experimenting is vital for creating new recipes and a liberated future; we just have to find the right moments and appropriate ways to do it. When we use our time in the kitchen to dream, try new things, and practice doing our work with love while setting aside ego, we can carry what we learn back into our movement work.

Brownies

Once upon a time, I used to make brownies from a mix. Perhaps this is shameful to admit as a baker, but I had given up hope that I could find a from-scratch recipe with which I would be satisfied. There are some mixes out there that are quite tasty, and using them saved me precious time when cooking large, elaborate meals. About ten years ago, I set out to create a brownie recipe that would be chewy, moist, rich, and chocolatey. This recipe is informed by "Cracking the Code to Chewy Brownies," an article and accompanying recipe in Cook's Illustrated *magazine.*[44]

Makes: 12 brownies (one 9x13 inch pan)
Prep time: 20 minutes
Cook time: 30 minutes

3 Tbsp (45 grams) butter
½ cup (110 grams) boiling water
½ cup (75 grams) bittersweet chocolate chips, preferably 70% cacao
¾ cup (70 grams) Dutch-process cocoa powder
½ cup (100 grams) canola oil
1 ½ tsp vanilla extract
2 large eggs
1 ½ cups (330 grams) granulated sugar
1 cup plus 2 Tbsp (165 grams) all-purpose flour
½ tsp salt
1 cup walnut or pecan pieces (optional)

1. Preheat oven to 375°F.

2. Melt the butter by placing it in a small saucepan and heating on medium heat for 3-5 minutes. Alternatively, melt it in a microwave.

3. Boil the water. Place the chocolate chips and cocoa powder in a large bowl. Pour the boiling water over the chocolate and stir until all of the chocolate chips have melted.

4. Add the melted butter, canola oil, and vanilla. Mix well. Add the eggs and stir until the butter mixture is uniform. Mix in sugar.

5. Measure out the flour and salt, and mix them together. Add the flour mixture to the chocolate mixture and stir until just mixed. If using walnut or pecan pieces, add them to the batter and stir gently.

6. Pour batter into a parchment-lined 9x13 inch baking pan. Place in oven and immediately turn oven down to 350°F.

7. Bake for 25-30 minutes. A toothpick inserted in the center of the pan should come out clean after 25 minutes, but I like to give it an extra 5 minutes so the brownies hold together better.

8. Allow to cool before cutting into squares.

LAZY BAKER METHOD: Rather than melting the butter on its own, cut it into small chunks and place in the bowl with the chocolate chips and cocoa. The boiling water will melt it along with the chocolate chips, with just a little extra stirring.

NOTE: The combination of butter and oil, along with both cocoa powder and chocolate chips, gives these brownies a texture that is rich and moist without being too cakey or too fudgy.

Vegan Brownies

These brownies are the product of much experimentation, with the goal of creating a vegan, gluten-free version as rich and decadent as their non-vegan counterparts. I'm happy with the results, and some people even like them better than the conventional recipe! Almond meal and aquafaba give them a lovely, moist texture, while the combination of melted chocolate and cocoa powder is incredibly chocolatey. Because of how long it takes to whip the aquafaba, this recipe works best with a stand mixer.

Makes: 12 brownies (one 9x13 inch pan)
Prep time: 30 minutes
Bake time: 25-30 minutes

1 cup (150 grams) bittersweet chocolate chips, preferably 70% cacao

1 cup aquafaba, chilled (review note on page 189)

½ tsp cream of tartar

1 ⅓ cups (290 grams) granulated sugar

2 ½ (340 grams) packed cups almond meal

½ cup (45 grams) Dutch-process cocoa powder

½ tsp salt

1 tsp vanilla extract

1. Preheat oven to 375°F.

2. In a double boiler, melt the chocolate chips: You can put a little water in a small pot, heat the water to a simmer, and cover the pot with a ceramic or metal bowl that is bigger than the top of the pot. Place chocolate chips in the bowl, and stir frequently until just melted—about 5 minutes. Remove from heat and allow to cool slightly while you prepare the other ingredients.

3. Meanwhile, place the aquafaba and cream of tartar in the bowl of a stand mixer. Using the whisk attachment, beat on high for about 6 minutes, until it has stiff peaks. If you don't have a stand mixer, wait until the chocolate has melted so that you can give this your full attention—then use a handheld electric mixer to whip the aquafaba.

4. Add the sugar to the whipped aquafaba, and whip on medium high about 7 minutes more, until smooth and meringue-like.

5. Measure out the almond meal: If measuring by volume, tap the measuring cup a few times so it settles, then add more almond meal and repeat to make sure you have a full 2 ½ cups. Place in a medium bowl.

6. Add the cocoa powder and salt to the almond meal, and whisk or mix until well blended.

7. Place the almond meal mixture on top of the whipped aquafaba, along with the vanilla. Scrape the melted chocolate on top. The chocolate should still be warm and slightly pourable, but not hot.

8. Use a rubber spatula or wooden spoon to gently fold all ingredients together by hand. You should have a thick batter.

9. Line a 9x13 inch baking pan with parchment paper. Scrape the batter into it, and smooth the top with a spatula.

10. Bake at 375°F for 10 minutes, then turn oven down to 350°F and bake for 15-20 minutes more. The brownies should get a slightly shiny, light-colored crust all over the top. A toothpick inserted in the center should come out clean.

11. Allow to cool before cutting into squares.

Butterscotch Brownies

These brownies are bars of nutty, salty-sweet, fudge-y goodness. I adapted this recipe from one of my favorite non-vegan desserts— the butterscotch brownies recipe in Joy of Cooking.[45] *The vegan version here is made with aquafaba, which requires extensive whipping with an electric mixer. Between all the shenanigans of melting the coconut oil, whipping the aquafaba, and folding everything together, this recipe takes some work. But the resulting vegan treat is so tasty and well worth it!*

Makes: 12 brownies (one 9x13 inch pan)
Prep time: 30 minutes
Cook time: 30 minutes

½ cup (4 ounces) coconut oil
1 ½ packed cups brown sugar
½ cup aquafaba, chilled (review note on page 189)
½ tsp cream of tartar
2 cups all-purpose flour
2 tsp baking powder
1 tsp salt
1 tsp vanilla extract
1 ½ cups raw pecan halves and pieces

1. Preheat oven to 375°F.

2. Place coconut oil in a small pot and heat on low until melted. Add brown sugar and stir until well mixed but still grainy, no more than 2 minutes. Remove from heat and let cool for 10 minutes, until you can touch it comfortably—it will still be warm to the touch.

3. Place cold aquafaba and cream of tartar in the bowl of a stand mixer with the whisk attachment, and beat on high for about 6 minutes until it has stiff peaks.

4. In a small bowl, mix flour, baking powder, and salt with a whisk. Set aside.

5. Add the vanilla extract and the sugar mixture to the whipped aquafaba, and use a rubber spatula or wooden spoon to gently fold it in. You want to completely combine the aquafaba with the sugar mixture, while deflating the aquafaba as little as possible. It will deflate somewhat, but the mixture should still be light, airy, and emulsified.

6. Add the flour mixture to the aquafaba mixture, and fold in until just mixed. Break the pecans into pieces, add them to the bowl, and mix until just combined.

7. The batter will be thick and difficult to pour. Scrape it into a parchment-lined 9x13 inch baking dish, and smooth the batter with a spatula.

8. Place in oven, and immediately turn oven down to 350°F. Bake for 30 minutes, rotating the pan after 15 minutes. The top should be a crusty golden color, and a toothpick inserted in the center should come out clean. Allow to cool completely before cutting into squares.

AQUAFABA!

Aquafaba is a fancy name for a magical vegan substance: the gelatinous water left over after cooking chickpeas. Because of its protein and starch content,[46] it whips up like egg whites and can be used to make vegan meringues, or as an egg substitute in vegan baking. In these brownie recipes, it acts as both a binder and a leavening agent, keeping the brownies from crumbling and adding a lovely lightness to them. To use aquafaba, you can reserve the water from a can of beans, or cook the beans yourself. Any beans will do, and I find that chickpeas and kidney beans work best. The aquafaba will whip up best if you chill it before whipping.

How to make aquafaba: Soak 2 cups chickpeas overnight, drain, and rinse. Place in a pot with 6 cups water. Bring to a boil, then reduce to a low simmer and cook for about 1 ½ hours, with or without adding salt, until chickpeas are very soft. Let chickpeas cool in the water for about 30 minutes, then place a colander over a large bowl to strain. Reserve the beans for another dish—the liquid you're left with is aquafaba! For best results, chill for about 2 hours before using. This will make 1 ½ cups of aquafaba and 5-6 cups chickpeas. If you have extra aquafaba, you can freeze it for later use.

Using aquafaba from canned beans: Gently shake the can of chickpeas or kidney beans. Open and drain it, reserving the beans themselves for a different dish and placing the liquid from the can in a small bowl. For best results, chill the aquafaba before using (you can either chill the whole can of chickpeas, or place the aquafaba in the refrigerator after separating it).

Before measuring the aquafaba for your recipe, whisk it slightly until evenly mixed. Then, measure out how much you need. The liquid can separate slightly, so whisking will ensure that the aquafaba has an even consistency.

Whipping aquafaba: It is in whipping aquafaba that its magic really comes through. Like egg whites, aquafaba whips best with a bit of acid added. Cream of tartar is added while whipping so that the aquafaba will whip into a stiff foam—you can also replace every ½ tsp cream of tartar with 1 tsp lemon juice. If you add sugar and continue to whip, it will form a beautiful, shiny meringue texture. Raw whipped aquafaba is perfectly edible (and whipped with sugar and vanilla, it is quite tasty). Once whipped, it will hold its shape for several hours, depending on humidity and temperature, but will usually begin to break down overnight.

Makes: 15 two-inch cookies
Prep time: 15 minutes
Bake time: 15 minutes

Pecan Sandies

We used to make these cookies all the time at Bread Uprising, and they were also a favorite among my catering clients. The cookie dough itself is buttery and not too sweet, and the cookies are rolled in fluffy powdered sugar for extra sweetness. The recipe was inspired by a recipe in the Joy of Cooking,[47] *though I now forget exactly which one.*

1 cup (100 grams) pecans
1 cup (125 grams)
  all-purpose flour
½ tsp baking powder
½ cup (115 grams) vegan
  butter, such as Earth
  Balance (1 stick)
¼ cup (55 grams)
  granulated sugar
1 tsp vanilla extract
1 cup powdered sugar (to
  coat)

1. Preheat oven to 350°F and place rack in the upper half of the oven.

2. Place pecans in a food processor and pulse about 5 times, until they break into tiny pieces. Add flour and baking powder to food processor, and blend on high for about 2 minutes until pecans turn into a fine meal.

3. In a medium bowl, cream vegan butter and sugar with a spoon until smooth. Mix in vanilla, then add the pecan-flour mixture and mix well. I like to fold the dough a few times with my hands to ensure it is a smooth, even consistency.

4. Roll dough into 1 ½ inch balls, or portion the cookies with a ¾-ounce cookie scoop. Place cookies on a parchment-lined sheet pan, 2 inches apart.

5. Bake for 15 minutes. Cookies should be just golden brown. Remove from oven and use a spatula to carefully transfer the cookies to a rack to cool—they can be a little crumbly at this stage.

6. Once the cookies are cool, sprinkle a thin layer of powdered sugar onto a plate, and place cookies in it. Use a mesh strainer to sprinkle the cookies with more powdered sugar, ensuring they are completely coated, and then transfer cookies to a clean plate to serve.

LAZY BAKER METHOD: After chopping the pecans with the flour and baking powder in the food processor, add the vegan butter, granulated sugar, and vanilla directly to food processor, and blend until a dough forms. Do not overmix.

Peanut Butter Cookies

These cookies are melt-in-your-mouth, sweet, peanut-y goodness and they're vegan and gluten free to boot. They can be a little crumbly, so be careful not to handle them too much right after they come out of the oven. Find chickpea flour, also called garbanzo bean flour or besan, at an Indian grocery or natural foods store.

Makes: About 15 2 ½ inch cookies
Prep time: 15 minutes
Bake time: 12 minutes

2 Tbsp water
2 Tbsp chickpea flour
1 cup creamy peanut butter (preferably salted)
¾ cup + ¼ cup sugar, divided
1 ½ tsp baking powder
½ tsp vanilla extract

1. Preheat oven to 325°F.

2. Whisk water and chickpea flour together in a small bowl, and set aside.

3. In a medium bowl, mix peanut butter, the ¾ cup sugar, baking powder, and vanilla. Add the chickpea mixture and mix well. The dough should hold together nicely.

4. Sprinkle the remaining ¼ cup sugar evenly over the surface of a large plate. Scoop and roll 1 ¼ inch balls of cookie dough, and place in the sugar. Press each ball gently into the sugar with the palm of your hand, so that each cookie is about 2 inches in diameter and 1 centimeter high. Flip each cookie over to coat the other side with sugar. Place cookies on a large, parchment-lined sheet pan, about 2 inches apart.

5. Bake for 12 minutes, rotating halfway through if your oven bakes unevenly. They should be puffy, soft to the touch, and lightly browned—they will deflate and firm up as they cool. Cool on the pan for 5-10 minutes before moving gently with a spatula.

NOTE: If using unsalted peanut butter, add about ¼ tsp salt to the recipe.

LAZY BAKER METHOD: When making these, I always use a ¾ ounce cookie scoop (equal to 1 ½ tablespoons). If you have a cookie scoop, there's no need to roll the dough into neat balls. Just scoop the dough, level it, and release the dome-shaped cookie onto the sugar. Press down to coat with sugar, as described above.

Almond Horns

Almond-y and chewy, I first made these cookies as a Passover treat. They're gluten-free, parve, and delicious year-round. This vegan recipe was inspired by a non-vegan recipe of the same name in the lovely book Inside the Jewish Bakery.[48] *Traditionally, making almond horns requires making almond paste first, but I've created a method here with fewer steps. The dough can be a little tricky to handle, but it's definitely worth the effort!*

Makes: About 12 cookies
Prep time: 20 minutes
Bake time: 13 minutes
Rest time (optional): 1 hour

2 packed cups (275 grams) almond meal (review note)
2 Tbsp (30 grams) water
1 cup (220 grams) granulated sugar
2 Tbsp (34 grams) agave nectar or honey
½ tsp vanilla extract
½ tsp almond extract
½ tsp salt
1 cup (100 grams) slivered almonds, for shaping the cookies

To serve:
½ cup bittersweet chocolate chips (optional)

1. Preheat oven to 350°F. Measure out the almond meal. If measuring by volume, tap the measuring cup a few times so the almond meal settles, then add more almond meal and repeat to make sure you have two full cups. Place in a medium bowl.

2. Place water, sugar, and agave nectar or honey in a small pot. Cook on medium-low heat until the sugar dissolves, about 3-5 minutes. The sugar mixture will be thick, and should just come to a boil before you turn it off. You are doing this just to dissolve the sugar: be sure not to overcook or the sugar will harden in unpleasant ways when it cools.

3. Pour the hot sugar mixture onto the almond meal. Add vanilla extract, almond extract, and salt. Mix well. The dough should hold together in a thick, sticky paste. Use a spatula to scrape it into a ball in the center of the bowl, and let rest for 5 minutes.

4. Sprinkle the slivered almonds onto a countertop or other smooth surface.

5. Using wet hands, take ¼ of the dough and form it into a thick snake. Place the snake on top of the slivered almonds and gently roll it, coating it in almonds and lengthening it until it is about 12 inches long and ¾ inch in diameter. The slivered almonds should coat the snake and prevent it from sticking to the counter and your hands. Pinch the snake into 4 pieces, each about 3 inches long, and shape each into a curved horn shape. Place cookies on a parchment-lined sheet pan 2 inches apart. Repeat this process with the remaining dough.

6. Bake in the upper half of the oven for 13 minutes, until golden brown. To cool, slide the parchment off the baking pan and let cookies rest on the parchment paper on top of a rack or counter. The cookies are delicate at this point, so if you have to leave them on the pan, that is okay—the bottom of the cookies might turn out a bit crunchier. If you're going to leave them on the pan, be sure to remove the cookies promptly from the oven so they remain soft and chewy on the inside.

7. For the chocolate (optional): If you want to dip the ends of the cookies in chocolate, first wait for the cookies to cool. Then melt the chocolate chips in a double boiler: You can put a little water in a small pot, heat the water to a simmer, and cover the pot with a ceramic or metal bowl that is bigger than the top of the pot. Place chocolate chips in the bowl, and stir frequently until just melted—about 5 minutes. Remove from heat. Carefully dip one end of each cookie in the chocolate, allow excess chocolate to drip back into the bowl, and return the cookie to the parchment paper. Allow chocolate-dipped cookies to rest for about an hour, until the chocolate cools and hardens.

8. Store any extra cookies in an airtight container for up to 4 days.

NOTE: You can purchase almond meal or almond flour from many grocery stores—I get mine in a large bag at Costco. You can also grind your own: Weigh out 275 grams of blanched almonds, and pulse in a food processor until finely ground. If you grind your own, you can mix up the whole batch of cookie dough in the food processor to save mixing time. After you've ground the almonds, add the remaining ingredients and pulse until a smooth dough comes together.

VARIATION: This dough also works well for making gluten-free hamantaschen. Make the dough as directed here, but leave out the almond extract. Use a rolling pin to roll the dough out between 2 sheets of plastic wrap to about $^3/_{16}$ inch. While not environmentally friendly, the plastic wrap is necessary because the dough is still a bit sticky, and rolling it in extra gluten-free flour makes it too dry. Cut the dough with a 2 ½ inch round cutter or drinking glass. Fill each circle with about 1 ½ tsp of your favorite filling, shape into triangles, and bake at 350°F for 10-12 minutes. Refer to hamantaschen (page 194) for filling recipes and instructions for how to shape the cookies. This dough recipe will make 3 dozen small hamantaschen.

Hamantaschen
with Poppy Seed and Prune Fillings

Hamantaschen are a delicious Ashkenazi Jewish cookie made in the triangular shape associated with Haman, the villain of the Purim story. When I was a child, my great aunt would always send us hamantaschen, just in time for Purim. She made some with poppy seed and some with prune filling, which are still my favorites. This dough, which I developed as a recipe specifically for vegan hamantaschen, became the basis for Bread Uprising's vegan shortbread cookie dough. The cookies are soft and light; the prune filling has a bit of lemon for a nice kick; and the poppy seed filling combines poppy seeds and almonds for a decadent, nutty flavor. Making the poppy seed filling takes a while and requires a spice/coffee grinder, so make sure to allow enough time. It is definitely worth it—I always have to stop myself from eating the better part of the batch with a spoon before I even get to fill the cookies! The cookies are vegan, which means they're parve for folks who keep kosher. For a gluten-free dough, make a version of the dough for almond horns (page 192).

Cookie Dough

Makes: 3 dozen 2 ½ inch cookies
Prep time: 45 minutes
Chill time: 2 hours or more
Bake time: 14-17 minutes

½ cup (115 grams) vegan butter, such as Earth Balance, softened at room temperature for 30 minutes (1 stick)
¾ cup (165 grams) granulated sugar
1 tsp vanilla extract
¼ cup (55 grams) water
2 ¼ cups (315 grams) all-purpose flour
2 tsp baking powder
¼ tsp salt

1. Place softened vegan butter in a large bowl, and cream with a spoon until smooth. Add the sugar, and cream until smooth and well mixed. Add the vanilla and stir to mix.

2. Add the water little by little, a tablespoon at a time, stirring continuously to emulsify it with the fat. Once all the water is added, beat until well mixed—it should be smooth, fluffy, and light in color.

3. In a small bowl or large measuring cup, mix together the flour, baking power, and salt, and fluff with a whisk or fork. Add half of the flour mixture to the sugar mixture and gently mix until just combined. Add the rest of the flour mixture, and gently mix until just combined. You should have a smooth, soft, evenly mixed dough that can hold together in the middle of the bowl.

4. Wrap dough in a plastic bag or piece of plastic wrap, and chill in the fridge for 2 hours. You can also chill the dough overnight, refrigerating it for up to 3 days before using. If chilling for longer than 2 hours, remove the dough from the fridge 15-20 minutes before rolling out to let it soften slightly. Meanwhile, prepare your fillings.

5. Once the dough has chilled and your fillings are ready, preheat oven to 375°F. Remove dough from plastic wrap and knead about 3 times—this is called breaking the dough, which helps the fats bond together so the dough won't crumble while you work with it.

6. Lightly flour a smooth, flat work surface and roll half of the dough out thin—between ⅛ - ³⁄₁₆ of an inch thick. Use a 2 ½ inch round cutter or drinking glass to cut out the cookies. Maximize your use of the dough by cutting the cookies as close together as possible: the more you work with the dough and the more flour gets added, the tougher it will become.

7. Use a thin spatula to pick up each cookie, placing them on a parchment-lined sheet pan with about 1 inch of space between them.

8. Place about 1 ½ tsp of filling in the center of each cookie, and form the cookie into a triangle around the filling (review illustration). Use 2 index fingers to form the first corner, then the thumb and index finger of one hand to make the other 2 corners so that you have an equilateral triangle and a small opening over the filling in the middle.

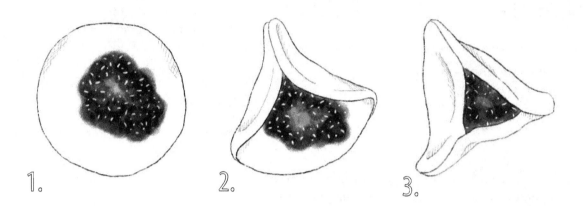

1.   2.   3.

9. Make sure there is at least 1 ½ inches of space between the cookies on the pan, and adjust if necessary.

10. Place pan in oven and immediately turn oven down to 350°F. Bake 14-17 minutes, rotating the pan after 10 minutes. They are done when the tips of each corner have turned a light golden brown.

11. Remove from oven and transfer cookies to a wire rack or a towel to cool. Let cool before eating—if you can wait!

LAZY BAKER METHOD: Using a stand mixer can save you time mixing up the dough. Mixer directions: Place vegan butter and sugar in bowl of mixer and cream on medium speed until lightly whipped, about 1 ½ minutes. With the mixer running, add vanilla, then slowly pour in water, letting these mix for about 2 minutes until well combined and fluffy. Turn off mixer and scrape down bowl. Add half the flour mixture and mix on the lowest speed until mostly combined. With the mixer running, slowly add the rest of the flour. The dough should be well-combined after about 30 seconds—scrape down the bowl and mix again until smooth.

Prune Filling

Makes: About 1 ½ cups, enough for 3 dozen 2 ½ inch cookies
Prep time: 10 minutes
Cook time: 20-25 minutes
Cool time: 20-30 minutes

1 tsp grated lemon peel
3 Tbsp (300 grams) fresh
  lemon juice
1 ½ cups prunes, loosely
  packed
1 cup (220 grams) water
⅛ tsp salt
⅓ packed cup (70 grams)
  brown sugar

1. Zest or grate the lemon peel, using only the yellow parts of the peel. Juice the lemon until you have 3 Tbsp of juice, and remove seeds.

2. Place prunes, water, salt, lemon juice, and grated lemon peel in a small, heavy-bottomed saucepan. Bring to a simmer on medium heat. Immediately reduce heat to the lowest possible simmer and cook, stirring every few minutes or so to prevent sticking.

3. After about 10 minutes, once the prunes begin to get soft, use a wooden spoon to mash them up directly in the pot, and continue cooking. There is no need to create a smooth paste—just break up the large lumps of prune so that it will be easy to fill the cookies. Continue to simmer the mixture on the lowest possible heat for 5-10 more minutes until you have a thick paste.

4. Remove from heat and stir in the brown sugar until it dissolves. Cool for at least 20 minutes before using. The filling doesn't need to be cold—though it can be if you want to make it ahead and store in the fridge until using—it just needs to be comfortable to touch and work with.

Poppy Seed Filling

Makes: About 1 ½ cups, enough for 3 dozen 2 ½ inch cookies
Prep time: 15 minutes
Cook time: 30 minutes
Cool time: 20-30 minutes

½ cup (75 grams) poppy seeds
½ cup (70 grams) almonds or almond meal
1 cup (230 grams) plain unsweetened almond milk
2 tsp tapioca starch or corn starch
1 Tbsp vegan butter, such as Earth Balance
3 Tbsp granulated sugar
2 Tbsp honey (can substitute maple syrup)
1 ½ tsp lemon juice
¼ tsp almond extract
¼ tsp salt
⅛ tsp cinnamon (optional)

1. Grind the poppy seeds and almonds in a spice grinder or a fancy, high-powered blender like a Vitamix (the equipment really matters here—review note). Ground poppy seeds should be darker in color than when they were whole, but still crunchy if you taste a bit of the ground mixture. Almonds can easily be ground in a food processor or spice grinder, or you can use store-bought almond meal. Almonds should be as powdery as possible without turning into a paste.

2. Place ground poppy seeds, ground almonds, and nut milk in a small saucepan. If possible, use a non-stick, heavy-bottomed saucepan. Sprinkle with tapioca or corn starch and stir. Add the vegan butter.

3. On the lowest possible heat, cook the poppy seed mixture for 20 minutes, stirring continuously and scraping the bottom of the pan to prevent sticking. The mixture should turn to a paste thick enough that stiff peaks will hold their shape when a dollop of it is dropped from a spoon.

4. Remove from heat. Stir in sugar, honey, lemon juice, almond extract, salt, and cinnamon (if using). The mixture will become much wetter.

5. Return to heat, still at the lowest possible heat, and cook for 5 minutes more, stirring continuously. It should be the consistency of thick grits—if this means nothing to you, you're missing out on a delicious hot breakfast cereal.

6. Remove from heat and let cool for at least 20 minutes before filling cookies. The filling doesn't need to be cold—though it can be if you want to make it ahead and store it in the fridge until using—it just needs to be comfortable to touch and work with.

NOTE: Poppy seeds are a tiny seed with a very hard outer husk that prevents them from softening while cooking. Many traditional Eastern European recipes that use poppy seeds require soaking them overnight in milk to soften them, but in this recipe, grinding replaces that time-consuming process. By using a spice/coffee grinder or high-powered blender, you can add the entire ½ cup of poppy seeds at once, grind for 20-30 seconds, and voilà: you have ground poppyseeds! Because they are so small, it is not possible to grind them in a food processor, and because they are oily, they break down when crushed in a mortar and pestle. The grinding can be done in a common kitchen blender, but it has to be in 8 tiny batches, 2 tablespoons at a time—very tedious. If you don't have a spice grinder or fancy high-powered blender, I suggest borrowing one from a friend, or just making the prune filling instead. If you use a coffee grinder, your poppy seeds will have a slight coffee flavor even if you clean the grinder out first—which is not necessarily a bad thing.

Chocolate Chip Cookies

When I was a child, baking was a favorite activity, and I was probably no older than ten when I began baking without adult supervision. One friend and I would always bake cookies together, pretending that we ran a bakery called World Class Bakers, Inc. Even before that, I used to love going over to my neighbor's house to bake chocolate chip cookies, because his dad would let us eat the raw cookie dough while we baked. In search of a vegan chocolate chip cookie recipe that would be soft and chewy, I adapted this recipe from one in the Sticky Fingers' Sweets[49] cookbook. Once baked, these are soft on the inside and slightly crunchy on the outside, with a buttery flavor. And, you don't have to worry about eggs in the dough, so eat your fill while baking!

½ cup (115 grams) vegan butter, softened out of the fridge for 30 minutes (1 stick)
½ cup (110 grams) granulated sugar
½ cup (105 grams) brown sugar
2 cups (270 grams) all-purpose flour, sifted before measuring
1 tsp baking powder
½ tsp baking soda
½ tsp salt
¼ cup (60 grams) plain, unsweetened soy or almond milk
2 Tbsp (25 grams) canola oil
½ tsp vanilla extract
⅔ cup (100 grams) bittersweet chocolate chips

Makes: 24 two-inch cookies
Prep time: 20 minutes
Bake time: 10-12 minutes

1. Preheat oven to 350°F.

2. Place vegan butter, granulated sugar, and brown sugar in the bowl of a stand mixer. Using the paddle attachment, whip butter and sugar on medium speed for about 5 minutes until light and fluffy. Scrape down the sides of the bowl.

3. Meanwhile, measure the flour, baking powder, baking soda, and salt into a small bowl, mix until well combined, and set aside.

4. Measure the soy or almond milk, canola oil, and vanilla into a small bowl or measuring cup. Use a fork to whisk these wet ingredients until well combined—they should emulsify almost like a salad dressing.

5. With the mixer running on medium speed, slowly pour in the canola oil mixture in a steady stream. Mix for about 1 minute, until well blended.

6. Turn off mixer and add the flour mixture. Mix on the lowest speed until just combined, about 10 seconds. Scrape down the sides of the bowl.

7. Add chocolate chips and mix until just combined, about 10 seconds.

8. Scoop and roll 1¼ inch balls of cookie dough—a ¾ ounce cookie scoop works well for this, but you can also just use a spoon and your hands. Place on a parchment-lined sheet pan about 2 inches apart. Once you have a full sheet of cookies, gently press each cookie so that it is flat on top, but still about half an inch thick.

9. Bake for 10 minutes. The cookies will have a little crust, but will still be very soft. Immediately remove baked cookies from pan using a thin spatula and cool on a wire rack. Be gentle with them, because they are fairly fragile when warm. They will firm up as they cool.

NOTE: Baking the cookies for 10 minutes will produce a nice, soft interior—my favorite! If you prefer a crunchy cookie, bake for 12 minutes or more.

NOTE: Check ingredients on dark chocolate chips to ensure they're dairy-free: sometimes milkfat is hiding as an ingredient in those chips.

Oatmeal Raisin Cookies

Makes: 24 two-inch cookies
Prep time: 20 minutes
Cook time: 10-12 minutes

At Bread Uprising, we modified my chocolate chip cookie recipe (page 199) to create these oatmeal raisin cookies. They are sweet, nutty, and beloved even by people who don't usually like oatmeal cookies. I often make one batch each of oatmeal raisin and chocolate chip cookies, and serve them on a platter together.

½ cup (115 grams) vegan butter, softened out of the fridge for 30 minutes (1 stick)
⅓ cup (70 grams) granulated sugar
⅔ cup (140 grams) brown sugar
1 ½ cups (200 grams) all-purpose flour, sifted before measuring
1 cup (120 grams) rolled oats
1 tsp baking powder
½ tsp baking soda
½ tsp salt
¼ tsp cinnamon
¼ cup (60 grams) plain unsweetened soy or almond milk
2 Tbsp (25 grams) canola oil
½ tsp vanilla extract
½ cup (60 grams) pecan pieces
½ cup (60 grams) raisins

1. Preheat oven to 350°F.

2. Place vegan butter, granulated sugar, and brown sugar into the bowl of a stand mixer. Using the paddle attachment, whip butter and sugar on medium speed for about 5 minutes until light and fluffy. Scrape down the sides of the bowl.

3. Meanwhile, measure the flour, oats, baking powder, baking soda, salt, and cinnamon into a small bowl, mix until well combined, and set aside.

4. Measure the soy or almond milk, canola oil, and vanilla into a small bowl or measuring cup. Use a fork to whisk these wet ingredients until well combined—they should emulsify almost like a salad dressing.

5. With the mixer running on medium speed, slowly pour in the canola oil mixture in a steady stream. Mix for about 1 minute, until well blended.

6. Turn off mixer and add the flour mixture. Mix on the lowest speed until just combined, about 10 seconds. Scrape down the sides of the bowl.

7. Add pecans and raisins and mix until just combined, about 10 seconds.

8. Scoop and roll 1¼ inch balls of cookie dough—a ¾ ounce cookie scoop works well for this, but you can also just use a spoon and your hands. Place on a parchment-lined sheet pan about 2 inches apart. Once you have a full sheet of cookies, gently press each cookie so that it is flat on top, but still about half an inch thick.

9. Bake for 10 minutes. The cookies will have a little crust, but will still be soft inside. Immediately remove baked cookies from pan using a thin spatula, and cool on a wire rack. Be gentle with them because they are fairly fragile when warm. They will firm up as they cool.

NOTE: Both the chocolate chip and oatmeal raisin cookie doughs freeze well. Wrap tightly in plastic wrap or a freezer-safe bag, and freeze for up to a month. Allow dough to come to room temperature before scooping and rolling the cookies.

NOTE: Using a stand mixer yields cookies with a particularly excellent texture, but you can easily mix them up by hand, too. Cream the vegan butter and sugar together with a spoon. Then add the canola oil mixture a little at a time, mixing after each addition so that it combines well with the sugar mixture.

Chocolate Cake with Strawberry Frosting

This was one of our classic Bread Uprising recipes. I can't quite remember how we started making it, because it feels like I've been making it forever—the recipe may be adapted from a chocolate cake recipe given to me by a friend when I first went vegan in 1999. The cake is rich and chocolatey, and especially delightful with the strawberry frosting.

Makes: One double-layer 8-inch cake or 1 dozen cupcakes
Prep time: 20 minutes
Bake time: 25 minutes

Dry ingredients:
1 ½ cups (220 grams) all-purpose flour
½ cup (45 grams) Dutch-process cocoa powder
1 tsp baking powder
1 tsp baking soda
¼ tsp salt

Wet ingredients:
1 ½ cups (330 grams) water
1 cup (220 grams) granulated sugar
½ cup (100 grams) canola oil
2 tsp apple cider vinegar
1 ½ tsp vanilla extract

Strawberry frosting, 1 batch (facing page)

1. Preheat oven to 375°F. Oil and flour two 8-inch baking pans.

2. Combine all dry ingredients in a large bowl, and whisk to combine.

3. Combine all wet ingredients in a large bowl, and whisk until emulsified.

4. Add wet ingredients to dry, and mix until just combined. Quickly divide batter between the 2 pans. The cake rises from the reaction between the baking powder, baking soda, and vinegar, so you'll want to get it into the oven as quickly as possible after combining the wet and dry ingredients.

5. Place pans in upper half of the oven and bake for 25 minutes, or until a toothpick inserted in the center of the cake comes out clean.

6. Let cool for 15 minutes in the pan, then carefully remove cake from pans and continue to cool on a rack. Cool completely before frosting. You can speed up cooling time by placing the cake in the refrigerator.

VARIATION: To make as cupcakes, line a muffin pan with paper liners. Fill liners ¾ of the way with batter. Bake for 20 minutes at 375°F, or until a toothpick inserted in one of the middle cupcakes comes out clean. Cool completely before frosting.

STRAWBERRY FROSTING

At Bread Uprising, we used to freeze fresh local strawberries every spring, then thaw and purée them throughout the year whenever we needed to make strawberry frosting. Bright and tasty, this frosting holds its shape quite firmly, so it works well for decorating. Just make sure to purée the strawberries well to prevent bits of strawberry from clogging the tip of your piping bag.

Makes: Enough for one 8-inch cake or 1 dozen cupcakes
Prep time: 10 minutes

¼ cup fresh strawberry purée (55 grams, about 2-3 large strawberries)
1 cup plus 1 Tbsp vegetable shortening, such as refined palm shortening (180 grams)
⅛ tsp salt
½ tsp vanilla extract
½ tsp almond extract
3 ¾ cups powdered sugar (1 pound)
1 Tbsp lemon juice

1. Ensure that all ingredients are at room temperature.

2. Wash and de-stem strawberries and cut into quarters. Place in a blender and purée until very smooth, then measure to make sure you have ¼ cup of purée.

3. Place palm shortening in the bowl of a stand mixer fitted with the mixer's whisk attachment. Run the mixer on medium speed and slowly add the strawberry purée, 1 tablespoon at a time. Allow to mix until well combined after each addition. The shortening and purée should emulsify nicely.

4. Add salt, vanilla, and almond extract, and mix until combined. Scrape down the bowl.

5. Measure out the powdered sugar. Add half the sugar to the mixer bowl and stir, then mix on medium speed until thoroughly combined. Add the remaining sugar and stir, then mix on medium high until well combined. Scrape down the bowl.

6. With the mixer running on medium high, slowly add the lemon juice, a half-teaspoon at a time. Continue to mix for about 1 minute, or until light and fluffy.

7. Frost cake within 2 hours of making the frosting, or refrigerate frosting until you are ready to use it. Frosting will keep in the fridge for several weeks. For easy spreading, bring it to room temperature before using.

NOTE: The shortening used for this frosting needs to be one that is thick and solid at room temperature. Spectrum makes a refined, non-hydrogenated palm shortening that comes in a large tub—sold at natural foods stores and some supermarkets, this is my go-to for frostings. If you can't find or don't want to use palm shortening, this recipe can be made with Crisco or other vegetable shortening, which will probably be hydrogenated. Don't try to substitute vegan butter or coconut oil, or you'll end up with a frosting too soft to hold its shape on top of a cupcake.

Gluten-Free Chocolate Cupcakes with Chocolate Frosting

This is a Bread Uprising favorite—dark chocolatey and with a really nice crumb to it. Fellow bakers Tim Stallmann, Javiera Caballero, and I developed this recipe, and kept adapting it to make it simpler. I have adjusted and converted it here for easy home baking if you don't have a kitchen scale. You can also use this recipe to make a double-layer 8-inch round cake.

Dry ingredients:
1 cup tapioca starch (105 grams) (also called tapioca flour)
1 Tbsp chickpea flour (7 grams) (also called garbanzo bean flour or besan)
⅓ cup white rice flour or sorghum flour (40 grams)
½ cup brown rice flour (75 grams)
⅔ cup Dutch-process cocoa powder (60 grams)
1 ¼ cups granulated sugar (275 grams)
1 tsp baking powder
1 tsp baking soda
½ tsp salt
1 ½ tsp guar gum

Wet ingredients:
1 ¼ cups water (275 grams)
½ cup canola oil (100 grams)
1 ½ tsp apple cider vinegar
1 ½ tsp vanilla extract

Chocolate frosting, 1 batch (facing page)

Makes: 1 dozen cupcakes
Prep time: 20 minutes
Cook time: 25 minutes

1. Preheat oven to 375°F. Line a muffin pan with paper liners.

2. Place all dry ingredients in a large bowl, and mix well with a whisk.

3. In a separate bowl or measuring cup, thoroughly mix all wet ingredients.

4. Add wet ingredients to dry, then mix vigorously with a whisk or spoon until the batter thickens: guar gum, a thickener that holds gluten-free baked goods together, is activated by mixing.

5. Portion the batter into the muffin pans. To avoid lots of drips, ladle batter into a large measuring cup with a spout, then use the measuring cup to pour it into the pans. Keep refilling the measuring cup as needed. The liners should be close to full of batter. If you prefer smaller cupcakes, you can make more than 12 dozen cupcakes.

6. Place pan in upper half of the oven and bake at 375°F for 10 minutes. Do not open the oven at this point, but turn the oven down to 350°F and bake for another 10-15 minutes. If your oven bakes unevenly, rotate the pan once the cupcakes look solid and dome-shaped on top. Bake for 20-25 minutes total, or until a toothpick inserted into one of the middle cupcakes comes out clean.

7. Allow to cool completely before frosting with your favorite vegan frosting recipe. Unfrosted cupcakes can be kept out of the fridge, but once frosted, store in the refrigerator.

> VARIATION: To convert 1 dozen cupcakes to a cake, use two 8-inch-round cake pans. Add 10-15 minutes to the baking time, baking for 35-40 minutes total. Check that a toothpick or butter knife inserted in the center of each layer comes out clean. This recipe will make a tall, double-layer cake.

CHOCOLATE FROSTING

This is modified from Bread Uprising's rich and chocolatey frosting recipe, which is great on chocolate cupcakes, or pretty much any cake! It's thick enough to pipe into nice swirls on a cupcake, or to use for decorating the top of a cake. This recipe is easiest with a stand mixer, and can also be made with a hand-held electric mixer. If you don't have any type of electric mixer, use a fork to mix it up, though it will be a bit lumpy and not as fluffy.

Makes: Enough for 1 dozen cupcakes or one 8-inch cake
Prep time: 10 minutes

¼ cup (55 grams) vegan butter such as Earth Balance
½ cup (85 grams) vegetable shortening, such as refined palm shortening
1 ½ tsp (6 grams) vanilla extract
⅛ tsp salt
½ cup (45 grams) Dutch-process cocoa powder
3 ¾ cups (1 pound) powdered sugar
⅓ cup (70 grams) tap water

1. Ensure that all ingredients are at room temperature.

2. Place vegan butter and shortening in the bowl of a stand mixer. Mix on medium speed for about 2 minutes until well mixed and fluffy. Add vanilla, salt, and cocoa powder, and mix on medium speed until well combined.

3. Measure out the powdered sugar in one container and the water in another. Add half the sugar to the mixer bowl and stir to combine, then mix on medium speed. With the mixer running, slowly add half the water by the teaspoonful, letting each addition absorb completely before adding the next. Pause mixing and scrape down the sides of the bowl.

4. Repeat this process with the second half of the sugar: Add it to the mixer, stir, then mix on medium speed. Slowly add the rest of the water. Once well combined, scrape down the bowl and continue to mix for about 1 minute until light and fluffy.

5. Frost cupcakes immediately, or refrigerate frosting until using. It will keep in the fridge for several weeks. Bring to room temperature before frosting cupcakes.

NOTE: Temperature is crucial for most vegan frosting recipes. To make light, fluffy frosting, you need to create a smooth emulsion between the fat and water, which works best when both are at room temperature. If either the fat or liquid is much colder than the other, the frosting is liable to break, which means it can break apart into little pieces of fat and liquid, and won't be completely smooth. Adding the water slowly also helps to ensure that it emulsifies. If your frosting does break, chill it in the fridge, then bring back to room temperature and beat it vigorously for several minutes to revive it.

TIPS FOR GLUTEN-FREE AND VEGAN BAKING

Vegan and gluten-free baking can be tasty, both for people with these food needs and for everyone else. These baking methods can also be very intimidating, and the results quite dry, tough, and unsatisfying when misses occur. Here are my favorite tips for delicious, successful baking.

Vegan Baking Tips:

Both vegan and gluten-free baked goods tend to be a little more crumbly than their egg- and wheat-filled counterparts. Lining your baking pans with parchment paper or coating them with oil and then flour before pouring in the batter will help ensure that pieces don't break off when removing them from the pan. Allowing your cookies, brownies, or breads to cool completely before moving them around will also help ensure they hold their shape.

To achieve muffins or cupcakes with a nice large muffin top, use a cooking oil spray to lightly grease the entire top of the muffin pan. This will ensure the muffin tops don't stick to the pan when you remove the muffins. You can also lightly oil the muffin paper liners, which will help them peel off easily—this is especially important for muffin recipes that are low-fat, where the batter tends to stick to the liners. Then, when filling the liners with batter, fill them up so the batter is within ¼ inch of the top of the liners—really!

Remember that elementary school science project where a baking soda and vinegar volcano erupted out of a mound of sand? Baking soda and baking powder help baked goods rise through a reaction between acidic and alkaline ingredients. In non-vegan recipes, eggs help baked goods rise; this acidic-alkaline reaction is the only way many vegan baked goods get a lift. Baking soda is an alkaline compound, so for it to work in a recipe, there has to be a corresponding acidic ingredient to react with it. Baking powder is a mixture of baking soda, cream of tartar (an acidic agent), and a starch filler (usually corn starch). The cream of tartar reacts with the baking soda as soon as it comes into contact with the moisture in the batter, which means that it can work its leavening magic without adding an additional acidic ingredient.

This acidic-alkaline reaction begins as soon as you mix the wet and dry ingredients. In order to take advantage of it for fluffy baked goods, get your cake, muffins, or brownies in the oven as soon as possible. Make sure your oven is pre-heated, and don't dilly-dally and start another project before getting that cake into the oven.

Do not overmix. This is important for baked goods made with any type of wheat flour. The gluten in wheat flour can become tough if mixed extensively, giving you an unpleasantly chewy rather than fluffy cake.

If converting recipes from dairy/egg to vegan, the type of egg substitute you'll need depends on the role the egg is playing in the recipe. Read more about egg substitutes on page 8.

Gluten-Free Baking Tips:

Because gluten is what allows wheat-filled baked goods to hold their shape, most gluten-free baked treats require additional ingredients to thicken and bind them together: xanthan gum, guar gum, or a gooey seed like psyllium seed husk, flaxseed, or chia seed. You can experiment to figure out what you prefer. Guar gum is extracted from a bean, so it is relatively natural, doesn't add an unpleasant taste, and works very well. It is hard to find in most grocery stores, but can be ordered online from Bob's Red Mill. Xanthan gum is the easiest ingredient to substitute if you can't find guar gum, since it is sold at most supermarkets with a gluten-free baking section. Xanthan gum is produced by bacteria in a lab, which is a little gross, and some folks have negative reactions to it, so guar gum is my preferred binding ingredient.

When using guar gum, be sure to mix the batter a lot—this activates the guar gum and thickens the batter. Since there's no gluten in the batter, you never have to worry about over-mixing.

Most gluten-free recipes combine several different types of gluten-free flours in order to replicate the structure of gluten. This combination is important! At Bread Uprising, we used to make a mix of brown rice, millet, sorghum, and chickpea flours along with tapioca, corn, and potato starches. We'd mix up big batches of this 7-flour mix, then use it for baking our gluten-free breads, cakes, and other goods. To make your life easier, I've tested these recipes using a mix of less than 7 flours, but in most cases there are still at least 4. Making substitutions is possible, but you can't just substitute any gluten-free flour for another one—this is a science. Different flours absorb liquid differently and impart different textures. There are some high-quality gluten-free mixes available in many grocery stores but in our test kitchens, we found that substituting a variety of these mixes was hit or miss. You can use the recommended blend of flours for each recipe, or prepare to do your own experimenting with available mixes.

If making a recipe with pea or garbanzo bean flour, use just a little bit. These flours help add crucial structure to baked goods, but can give the finished product a bitter flavor if included in excessive quantity.

If substituting almond or coconut flour in a recipe, you may want to reduce the amount of oil, as these flours naturally contain fats and can yield to an overly oily baked good.

Vegan Tres Leches Cake

Pastel de tres leches, or "three milks cake," is so named because this vanilla cake is soaked overnight in a mixture of 3 milks: evaporated milk, whole milk, and sweetened condensed milk. It's then topped with whipped cream. Needless to say, this is a very non-vegan situation, though a delicious one, and for years I wanted to craft a vegan version of this tasty treat. While there aren't exactly 3 milks in the cake, the flavors and textures mirror a tres leches cake: here is a vanilla cake soaked in coconut milk with a sweetened condensed nut milk filling and a coconut cream topping. The cake recipe here is adapted from Bread Uprising's vanilla cake recipe.

Makes: One double-layer 8-inch cake or 1 dozen cupcakes
Prep time: 40 minutes
Bake time: 25 minutes
Soak time: 4 hours or overnight
Chill time: 30 minutes

For the cake:
1 ¾ cups (230 grams) all-purpose flour
1 tsp baking powder
½ tsp baking soda
¼ tsp salt
1 ⅓ cups (315 grams) plain unsweetened soy or almond milk
½ cup (100 grams) canola oil
¾ cup (165 grams) granulated sugar
1 tsp apple cider vinegar
1 ½ tsp vanilla extract

For soaking & topping the cake:
2 13.5-ounce cans full-fat coconut milk, chilled overnight in the fridge (review note)
2 Tbsp granulated sugar
2 Tbsp maple syrup
⅛ tsp vanilla
pinch salt
1 recipe sweetened condensed nut milk (page 210)
1 cup fresh berries

First, make sure you've chilled the cans of coconut milk overnight in the refrigerator.

Make the cake:

1. Preheat oven to 375°F. Oil and flour two 8-inch baking pans.

2. Combine the flour, baking powder, baking soda, and salt in a large bowl, and whisk to combine.

3. Combine the vegan milk, canola oil, sugar, vinegar, and vanilla in a large bowl, and whisk until well combined.

4. Add wet ingredients to dry and mix until just combined, with no large lumps remaining. Quickly divide batter between the 2 pans. The cake rises from the reaction between the baking powder, baking soda, and vinegar, so you'll want to get it into the oven as quickly as possible after combining the wet and dry ingredients.

5. Place in upper half of the oven and bake for 25 minutes, or until a toothpick inserted in the center of the cake comes out clean.

6. Let cool for 15 minutes in the pan, then carefully remove from pan and continue to cool on a rack.

Soak the cake:

1. Open one of the chilled cans of coconut milk. There should be a fairly solid white mass of coconut cream on top, separate from a foggy water below it. Scrape the cream out into a bowl and set aside to use later. Pour the foggy, watery substance into a small bowl or large measuring cup. Add the 2 Tbsp of granulated sugar to this liquid and mix until dissolved. You'll pour this mixture over the cake to make it extra moist and creamy.

2. Once the cake has cooled, use a bread knife to slice a very thin ⅛ inch sliver off the rounded top of each cake layer, so that the top of each cake layer is flat. This will expose the lovely air bubbles throughout the cake so that the liquid can soak into these pockets.

3. You are going to place each cake layer back into its pan to soak. But first, place a piece of parchment or wax paper on the bottom of each cake pan—this will help you to easily remove the moist cake from the pan later. Place cake layers in pans.

4. Spoon the sweetened coconut water over the cake layers a little at a time, allowing each addition to soak into the cake before adding the next. Make sure to go all the way to the edge!

5. Cover layers with plastic wrap or a plate and place in the refrigerator for 4 hours, or overnight.

Prepare the fillings and assemble the cake:

1. Prepare sweetened condensed nut milk (following page) and allow to cool.

2. Make the coconut cream topping: Get out the bowl with the reserved coconut cream. Open the second can of coconut milk and add its cream to the bowl. Add the maple syrup, ⅛ tsp vanilla, and pinch of salt, and mix well with a spoon—or, whip with an electric mixer until fluffy. Place in the fridge to chill until you need it. Reserve the cloudy liquid from this second can for another use.

3. Wash berries and allow to dry on a towel.

4. Place one layer of the soaked cake on a serving plate. The cake will be very moist and difficult to move around, so it's best to go ahead and set it up on its serving plate now. Top with a generous layer of the sweetened condensed nut milk. If you like, arrange half the berries on top.

5. Place the second cake layer on top. Spread with a thin layer of sweetened condensed nut milk.

6. Place cake in the fridge to chill for 30 minutes. Meanwhile, remove coconut cream topping from fridge and stir. If the topping seems soft and spreadable, return it to the fridge. If it is stiff and hard to spread, allow it to rest at room temperature.

7. Remove cake from fridge. Use a spatula or butter knife to spread the coconut cream topping over the top and sides of the cake. Decorate with remaining berries.

8. Serve immediately, or store in the refrigerator until ready to serve.

A NOTE ABOUT COCONUT MILK: The quality of your coconut cream topping depends a lot on the quality of your can of coconut milk. It's important to choose one that is not sweetened and that has a fat content of at least 14 grams per ⅓ cup (check the nutrition facts for this information). Some brands are better than others, and there are too many to list here, so you may have to experiment a bit. The Minimalist Baker blog has a great list ranking different brands, which you can visit at: https://minimalistbaker.com/how-to-make-coconut-whipped-cream.

SWEETENED CONDENSED NUT MILK

Use this as a filling in tres leches cake, as a spread on toast, or as a sweet dip for fruit.

Makes: About ½ cup
Soak time: 30 minutes
Prep time: 10 minutes
Cook time: 30-35 minutes

- ½ cup roasted macadamia nuts or raw almonds
- 1 cup hot water
- ½ cup sugar
- ¼ tsp vanilla extract
- Pinch salt

1. Place nuts in a medium bowl. Cover with hot water and allow to soak for 30 minutes.

2. Place soaked nuts and soaking water in a blender, and blend on high for 3 minutes. You should have a smooth, white, creamy liquid.

3. Strain the nut milk. It is important to remove as much nut fiber as possible, so you'll need to strain it through a fine mesh. Several layers of cheesecloth works well for this, or a thin kitchen towel. To use a towel, dampen it first, then squeeze it out: this will help the milk pass through more easily. Place a large strainer or colander over a bowl, and line the strainer with the cloth. Pour the milk into it, and use a spatula to move the pulp around in the cloth, scraping the sides of the cloth-lined strainer to allow the milk to drain through. When most of the liquid has drained out, form the cloth into a pouch around the remaining pulp and squeeze out as much liquid as possible. Discard the pulp, or save to use in oatmeal or smoothies.

4. Place the strained nut milk in a small saucepan with the sugar. Heat on medium heat, stirring until the sugar dissolves. Allow the mixture to come to a boil, then immediately reduce heat to the lowest possible simmer.

5. Continue cooking, uncovered, stirring every 5-10 minutes, until the milk has reduced by half, about 30 minutes. When stirring, make sure to scrape the bottom and sides of the pot—a silicone spatula works well for this. After about 20 minutes, the color will change from milky white to a shiny, semi-transparent sauce—if using unbleached sugar, it will be a light reddish-brown color.

6. Once the mixture has reduced by half and is about the consistency of honey or molasses when dropped from a spoon, remove from heat. Add vanilla and salt and stir. Allow to cool. The sweetened condensed nut milk will continue to thicken as it cools.

NOTE ON NUT MILKS: For this recipe to work right, you have to use homemade nut milk. Most packaged nut milks have additives that will change the texture of the milk as it cooks, thickening it in weird, goopy ways. Straining the milk is also a necessary step, as the presence of nut pulp will impact the texture of the condensed milk as it cooks. Macadamia nuts are my preferred nut for this recipe, yielding a condensed milk with a deliciously creamy flavor. Almonds work fine too, giving you a condensed milk with a milder flavor.

Fresh Fruit Cheesecake

Rich and decadent, this cake is a bit denser than most cheesecakes. The recipe was developed in conversation with many people and the land. I first had version of this dish at a potluck—an apple tart prepared by friend Christy Tronnier. I was cooking at The Stone House at the time, where there were bountiful fig trees. Over the years, I started making a cheesy tart-cake as a delicious celebration of fig season, and people eating it on retreats would refer to it as "the fig cheesecake." Here, I've added several options for fruit, though I still think that using fresh figs is best when they are in season.

NOTE: Before you begin, cut a piece of parchment paper the width of the pan and a few inches longer (about 7½ x 12 inches). Place in the bottom of the pan with the edges hanging over the sides like wings. Spread the crust in the bottom of the pan, then the filling and topping. After the tart is baked, you'll be able to slide a knife around the edges of the pan, then use the wings to pull the whole tart out of the pan to cut easily or serve from a serving dish.

Makes: One 8x8 inch pan
   (serves 9)
Total time: 30 minutes
Cook time: 45 minutes
Cool time: 1 hour

For the crust:
½ cup butter, softened out of the fridge for 30 minutes
½ cup brown sugar
½ tsp vanilla extract
1 ¼ cups all-purpose flour
pinch salt

For the filling:
2 8-ounce packages cream cheese
1 cup granulated sugar
½ tsp vanilla extract
¼ tsp salt
2 eggs

For the topping:
2 cups sliced fresh fruit (about 10 fresh figs)
¼ tsp ground cardamom
several dashes ground nutmeg

1. Make the crust: In a medium bowl, cream the butter, brown sugar, and vanilla until smooth. Add flour and salt, and mix until well combined. Ingredients should come together into a crumbly dough. Press into an 8x8 inch baking pan so that the bottom of the pan is evenly covered in a thin layer of crust.

2. Make the filling: Reusing the same bowl, blend the cream cheese, sugar, vanilla, and salt together with a wooden spoon, or use an electric mixer. Add the eggs one at a time. If you are mixing by hand, be sure to mix the first egg evenly into the cream cheese until no lumps remain, before adding the next egg.

3. Pour the filling on top of the crust, spreading it with a spatula so it is evenly distributed and the top is smooth.

4. Preheat oven to 350°F. Prepare the fruit. If using fresh figs, slice the figs into thin rounds. Arrange the figs on top of the filling, pressing them in gently. I like to create a pattern of circles, rows, or a spiral. Keep in mind that the pieces of fruit will shrink while cooking, so it's good to overlap them slightly. Carefully sprinkle the cardamom and nutmeg over the figs.

5. Bake for about 45 minutes, or until cake is set in the center and light brown around the edges.

6. Place on a wire rack and cool for at least 1 hour before serving.

VARIATIONS: Sliced pears, mango, strawberry, guava, and apples are all tasty here. I like to use a combination of mango slices and whole blackberries. Whatever combination you choose, measure out 2 cups of fruit in all.

Carrot Cake with Vegan Cream Cheese Frosting

I love carrot cake! I created this recipe to eat at home, and it became the basis for both the carrot cake and carrot muffins recipes at Bread Uprising. This cake can easily be made gluten-free (refer to note for details); and to make it as muffin, review note for a few small modifications.

Makes: One double 9-inch cake or 1 dozen large cupcakes
Prep time: 25 minutes
Bake time: 35 minutes

Dry ingredients:
2 ½ cups (355 grams) all-purpose flour, or review note for gluten-free options
2 tsp baking powder
1 tsp baking soda
½ tsp salt
1 tsp ground cinnamon
½ tsp ground ginger
¼ tsp ground nutmeg

Wet ingredients:
¾ cup (80 grams) pecan or walnut pieces
⅔ cup (150 grams) plain unsweetened soy or almond milk
1 Tbsp (13 grams) apple cider vinegar
2 packed cups (285 grams) grated carrots (about 4 medium carrots)
1¼ cups (270 grams) granulated sugar
½ cup (100 grams) canola oil
1 tsp vanilla extract

Vegan cream cheese frosting, 1 batch (facing page)

1. Preheat oven to 375°F. Spread pecan or walnut pieces out on a sheet pan and toast in the oven for about 5 minutes, until they just begin to brown. Remove from oven.

2. Place all dry ingredients in a large bowl and mix with a whisk until well combined and airy.

3. Place soy or almond milk in a large bowl with the vinegar, and stir to mix. Set aside to curdle while you grate the carrots.

4. Wash and peel carrots, and grate. Add grated carrots to the vinegar mixture. Add sugar, canola oil, and vanilla to the vinegar mixture, and mix well. Add toasted nuts and mix.

5. Oil, then flour two 9-inch cake pans.

6. Add dry ingredients to wet, and mix. If using all-purpose flour, mix until just combined, being careful not to overmix. If using gluten-free flour, mix vigorously until the batter thickens, which is necessary to activate the guar gum.

7. Divide batter evenly between the 2 pans.

8. Place pans in upper half of the oven and bake at 375°F for 20 minutes. Turn oven down to 350°F and bake for 15 minutes more, or until a toothpick inserted in the center of the cake comes out clean.

9. Remove cake from oven. Let cool for 15 minutes in the pan, then carefully remove cake from pans and continue to cool on a rack. Cool completely before frosting.

VARIATION: CARROT MUFFINS

To make muffins, reduce the sugar from 1 ¼ to ¾ cup, and add ¾ cup raisins to the wet ingredients. Line a muffin pan with papers, then spray the top surface of the muffin pan with cooking oil spray. Fill the muffin pans with at least ⅓ cup batter each —they should be very full, which ensures you end up with a nice muffin top. Bake for 25 minutes at 375°F, or until a toothpick comes out clean.

VARIATION: GLUTEN-FREE CARROT CAKE

You can make this recipe gluten-free by replacing the all-purpose flour with your favorite cup-for-cup gluten-free mix. Make sure that guar or xanthan gum is included in the mix as a thickener, and mix the batter well to activate it. Or, make your own mix—here is a combination of gluten-free flours that works great for this cake, based on our Bread Uprising recipe:

- 1 cup (110 grams) tapioca starch
- ½ cup (75 grams) white rice flour
- ½ cup (75 grams) brown rice flour
- ¼ cup (30 grams) sorghum or millet flour
- ¼ cup (28 grams) corn or potato starch
- 1 Tbsp (10 grams) chickpea flour
- 1 ½ tsp guar gum (can substitute xanthan gum)

VEGAN CREAM CHEESE FROSTING

Making a vegan cream cheese frosting thick enough to hold its shape is a science, and this one does a good job. It will hold its shape well at room temperature—but not any warmer than that! If you plan to transport your cake, I recommend storing the frosted cake in the refrigerator overnight first to ensure that the frosting holds up well when traveling.

Makes: Enough for 1 dozen cupcakes or one 9-inch cake
Prep time: 10 minutes
Chill time: 30 minutes

- 5 ounces (½ cup plus 2 Tbsp) vegan cream cheese
- ½ cup (85 grams or 3 ounces) vegetable shortening, such as refined palm shortening
- 1 ½ tsp vanilla extract
- ⅛ tsp salt
- 3 ¾ cups (1 pound) powdered sugar
- 1 ½ tsp lemon juice

1. Place vegan cream cheese and shortening in the bowl of a stand mixer. Mix on medium speed for about 15 seconds until well combined. Add vanilla and salt, and mix on medium until well combined.

2. Measure out the sugar. Add half the sugar to the mixer bowl and stir, then mix on medium speed until thoroughly combined. Add the remaining sugar and stir, then mix on medium high until well combined. Scrape down the bowl.

3. With the mixer running on medium high, slowly add the lemon juice, a half-teaspoon at a time. Continue to mix for about 1 minute, or until light and fluffy.

4. Chill frosting in fridge for 30 minutes before using. If storing frosting overnight before using, allow it to come to room temperature before frosting cupcakes. It will keep in the fridge for several weeks.

NOTE: As with all vegan cheeses, some vegan cream cheese brands are better than others. This recipe is tastiest with Trader Joe's brand vegan cream cheese; Tofutti brand also works well.

Pumpkin Pie

This pie is lightly spiced, with a hint of maple and a great custardy texture. The recipe is modified from Bread Uprising's vegan pumpkin pie recipe—in the fall, we used to bake 50 of these tasty pies at once. To get ready for this extravaganza, we would prepare mass quantities of fresh pumpkin, taking hours to roast dozens of pumpkins and freeze the pulp for pie-baking—and for muffins year-round. These days, I love to make it using pumpkin from my garden, though canned pumpkin will also do just fine. To make gluten-free, use your favorite gluten-free pie crust.

Makes: One 9-inch pie
Roast time for pumpkin:
  1-2 hours (optional)
Prep time: 10 minutes
Cook time: 45 minutes
Chill time: 1-2 hours

- 1 9-inch pie crust (page 174)
- 1 ¾ cups roasted, puréed pumpkin (instructions below, or use one 14-ounce can)
- ¾ cup (190 grams) full-fat canned coconut milk
- ½ cup (105 grams) brown sugar
- 2 Tbsp (35 grams) maple syrup
- 2 tsp (10 grams) vanilla extract
- 2 Tbsp (15 grams) corn starch
- 2 Tbsp (15 grams) tapioca starch
- ½ tsp salt
- 1 tsp ground cinnamon
- ½ tsp ground ginger
- 2 pinches ground nutmeg
- 2 pinches ground cloves

1. If using a home-baked pumpkin, cut pumpkin in half or quarters, remove the seeds, and roast it at 375°F until the flesh is soft. This will take 1-2 hours, depending on pumpkin size and variety. Cool, peel off and discard the skin, and purée the pumpkin flesh. Measure out 1 ¾ cups of the purée, making sure it's packed into the measuring cup.

2. Prepare a 9-inch pie crust; make sure the crust has chilled before using it.

3. Preheat oven to 400°F.

4. Place puréed pumpkin and all remaining ingredients in a blender and purée for about 1 minute, until smooth. Scrape down sides and purée again.

5. Pour filling into pie crust.

6. Place pie in oven and bake at 400°F for 30 minutes. Turn oven down to 350°F and bake for 15 minutes more. It is done when the filling is very bubbly and liquidy, with a film over the center of the pie. It should jiggle if you gently shake the pie from side to side, but will firm up as it cools. Remove from oven and allow to cool. After about 10 minutes, the filling shouldn't jiggle when you gently shake the pie.

7. Chill in the refrigerator until the custard is firm, about 1-2 hours.

8. Serve cold or at room temperature, with your favorite vegan ice cream.

> **NOTE:** The custardy texture in this pie comes from the combination of corn starch and tapioca starch. By itself, tapioca starch will make the filling a bit gooey, while cornstarch by itself gives it a slightly chalky flavor. When their powers are combined, they yield a great texture that holds together lightly while still being sliceable.

> **LAZY BAKER METHOD:** After roasting your pumpkin, remove the skin, then weigh out 14 ounces of the roasted pumpkin in large chunks and add it directly to the blender with the other pie filling ingredients—no need to purée it ahead of making the pie.

Strawberry Shortcake

This is one of my favorite desserts in the springtime, and sometimes I enjoy it as a special breakfast treat.

> 1 recipe vegan biscuits (page 172),
>   made with modifications below
> 1 13.5-ounce can full-fat coconut milk
> 4 cups fresh strawberries
> up to ½ cup granulated sugar
> 2 Tbsp maple syrup
> ⅛ tsp vanilla extract
> pinch salt

1. Chill a 13.5-ounce can of full-fat coconut milk or coconut cream in the refrigerator overnight.

2. Make 1 recipe vegan biscuits (page 172), adding ¼ cup granulated sugar to the flour mixture and following the rest of the recipe as written. Allow biscuits to cool completely.

3. Wash and dry 4 cups of whole fresh strawberries, then slice them. In a small bowl, gently toss sliced berries with ¼ to ½ cup granulated sugar until just mixed, and set aside for 15 minutes. The sugar will begin to draw the juices out of the berries, creating a nice sauce.

4. Make a coconut cream topping: Pull the chilled can of coconut milk out of the fridge and open it. There should be a fairly solid white mass of coconut cream on top, separate from a foggy water below it. Scrape the cream out into a bowl. Add 2 Tbsp maple syrup, ⅛ tsp vanilla, and a pinch of salt to the coconut cream, and mix well with a spoon, or whip with an electric mixer until fluffy. Place in the fridge to chill until you're ready to use it.

5. When ready to serve, assemble the shortcakes: Slice biscuits in half. Spoon berries onto the bottom half of the biscuit, allowing juices to soak in. Add a generous dollop of coconut cream, then add the biscuit top like a little hat. Eat it like a sandwich! Or, if you prefer, make open-faced sandwiches; either way, these can be deliciously messy, so it helps to serve them with plates and napkins.

Avocado Chocolate Mousse

This mousse is rich and chocolatey. Serve it in cups with fresh fruit, or as a mousse pie with a graham cracker crust (recipe follows). Avocados are a secret ingredient here, virtually undetectable in flavor but lending the mousse its rich and velvety texture.

Makes: About 2 cups mousse or one 9-inch pie
Prep time: 15 minutes
Chill time: 2 hours

For the mousse:
1 pound ripe avocados (2 large or 3 small)
½ cup bittersweet chocolate chips, melted
¼ cup plain unsweetened soy or almond milk
⅓ cup agave nectar or maple syrup
½ cup Dutch-process cocoa powder
1 tsp vanilla extract
¼ tsp almond extract
⅛ tsp salt

To serve:
1 cup fresh blueberries, blackberries, or sliced strawberries

1. Slice the avocados open, remove the pits, and scoop the avocado flesh into a food processor.

2. Microwave the chocolate chips in a ceramic bowl until melted, about 2 minutes, pausing every 30 seconds to stir. Or melt them in a double boiler: You can put a little water in a small pot, heat the water to a simmer, and cover the pot with a ceramic or metal bowl that is bigger than the top of the pot. Place chocolate chips in the bowl, and stir frequently until just melted—about 5 minutes.

3. Add melted chocolate and all remaining mousse ingredients to food processor with the avocados, and blend on high about 3 minutes until smooth and uniform. You may want to pause and scrape down the sides of the food processor partway through.

4. Eat immediately with fresh fruit or scrape into a medium bowl and refrigerate for 2 hours. Once chilled, the mousse will hold its shape well. For a beautiful and delicious dessert, after refrigerating, spoon or pipe swirls of the mousse into small cups or bowls, garnish with fresh fruit, and serve.

VARIATION: To make a chocolate mousse pie, fill a graham cracker crust (recipe follows) with fresh mousse that has not been chilled. Smooth the surface with a flat metal or rubber spatula. Cover and refrigerate for at least 2 hours, garnish with fruit, and serve. Chilling the pie will make it sliceable!

GRAHAM CRACKER CRUST

Makes: One 9-inch pie crust

> 1 ¾ cups graham cracker crumbs
> (1 sleeve of graham crackers in
> most boxes)
> 6 Tbsp vegan butter, such as Earth
> Balance, melted
> 1 Tbsp powdered sugar

To make the graham cracker crumbs, place graham crackers in a heavy, sealable bag, close, and roll over the bag several times with a rolling pin; or place crackers in a food processor and pulse until crumbly. Place crumbs in a bowl, add the melted butter and powdered sugar, and mix well. Press the crust into a pie pan, using your fingers to spread it evenly and pack it in tightly to form the crust. This recipe makes a nice, thick crust. Bake at 350°F for 10 minutes, until the edges are golden brown. Handle gently when hot, so that the crust doesn't get any cracks. Cool before filling.

To make ahead of time, place the baked, completely cooled crust in a plastic bag and close tightly. Store in a cool, dry pantry, where it will keep for up to a month.

Apple Crisp

I developed this recipe while cooking in The Stone House kitchen. Apple trees on the land gave us an abundance of fruit in the fall, and I wanted to make a dessert that featured them. I like apple crisp with enough topping to really dig into, so this recipe has a hefty helping of it. This is the recipe that prompted one retreat attendee to complement my "unorthodox use of cloves." Make sure to choose a tart variety of apples, such as Granny Smith, Stayman, or Arkansas Black.

Makes: One 9x13 inch pan (serves 8)
Prep time: 30 minutes
Bake time: 40 minutes

For the filling:
1 ½ pounds tart apples
1 tsp lemon juice
2 Tbsp all-purpose flour
2 Tbsp granulated sugar
¼ tsp ground ginger
¼ tsp ground cloves

For the topping:
1 ½ cups all-purpose flour
1 ½ cups rolled oats
¾ cup granulated sugar
½ tsp baking powder
½ tsp salt
1 tsp ground cinnamon
½ tsp ground ginger
¼ tsp ground cloves
¼ tsp ground cardamom
½ cup canola oil

1. Preheat oven to 375°F.

2. Wash, core, and thinly slice the apples, leaving skins on. The apples should measure about 6 cups when sliced. Place apples in a 9x13 inch baking dish. Sprinkle with lemon juice, then with flour, sugar, ginger, and cloves. Mix well.

3. In a large bowl, mix together all the topping ingredients except the canola oil. Pour the canola oil into the mixture, and stir until well mixed. It should be crumbly, but not dry.

4. Spread the topping evenly over the apple mixture, making sure you spread it all the way to the edges of the pan.

5. Place pan in upper half of the oven and bake for about 40 minutes. The top should be a light golden brown, and the apples soft when poked with a fork.

6. Serve plain, or with ice cream.

VARIATIONS: You can also make this crisp with peaches, pears, strawberries, blackberries, or a combination of these—I like to use what's in season! Frozen fruit works well, too, and you can even freeze your own sliced peaches or apples in season to use in a crisp later in the year. Omit the cinnamon if making it with peaches or berries.

Chapter Seven:
BEVERAGES

Land, Cycles, and Seasons
THE HERB GARDEN

"The mountain slid and shifted under the heavy autumn rainfall, the garden left untended grew lush and tangled overnight and it was never the same place for long. How can you own something that changes under your hands, that is so fully alive? Ecology undermines ownership."
-AURORA LEVINS MORALES[50]

Just outside the kitchen at The Stone House, a retreat center in Mebane, North Carolina—the land of the Occaneechi Band of the Saponi Nation—was a big, beautiful herb garden.[51] Lavender, sage, spearmint, basil, rosemary, and lemon balm greeted me every day, and I welcomed their pungent aromas as familiar friends. I first tasted anise hyssop, lemongrass, and lemon verbena because of this garden. Some plants grew abundant year-round, and many of them ebbed with the cycles of the seasons. As kitchen manager and cook, I started making iced herbal teas for guests on the land, harvesting whichever fragrant herb was most abundant and serving it up.

The farming team, led by land steward Tahz Walker, planted and tended the herb garden.[52] One morning I looked up from washing dishes at the kitchen sink to see Tahz pause, passing by on his way to another task. Hands moving through the basil patch fast as a honeybee between flowers, he plucked the budding flower heads off the plants so the basil could keep growing. The scent of fresh herbs wafted through the window.

Working in that kitchen, I witnessed and felt the land's abundance every day, along with the hard work that went into tending its gifts. When our connection to the source of our food is made visible, cooking can be a reminder that the land is alive, that we depend on it and are interdependent with it. The biblical Hebrew word for human, adam, comes from the same root as the word for soil (adamah) and the word for the color red (adom). We are adam, earthlings of red earth, able to live only here. We honor this interdependence through our relationship with food.

Honoring the land means honoring the earth's cycles, and understanding ourselves as part of them. In the kitchen, we can think about and feel for what will nourish ourselves and other people in this season: Do we need food that is cooling or warming? Fresh or cooked? What is growing in abundance? Cucumber water is a summer treat, born from the garden's abundance of fresh cucumbers and mint, and our bodies' need to be refreshed after time in the hot sun.

Working with the land's produce reminds me that the land has its own story, much older than me. Honoring the land means listening to and honoring the story of the land, not superimposing another story on top of it.[53] Scholars Eve Tuck and K. Wayne Yang write, "Indigenous peoples are those who have creation stories, not colonization stories, about how we/they came to be in a particular place—indeed how we/they came to be a place."[54] As someone who is not Indigenous and whose origin story is not of this land on which I reside, I strive to listen to and honor the full story of the land and the people of it in all of my work. As someone who is diasporic, without homeland, I seek only a resting place like the biblical figure Ruth, a plot in which to bury my dead like the biblical figure Abraham.[55]

When I was a child, a huge rue plant grew in the herb garden that my mother tended. When swallowtail butterfly caterpillars, with their bright orange horns that came out when we gently squeezed their sides, climbed up our precious parsley plants, we would move them over to the bountiful rue plant to continue feasting into their chrysalis stage. This is care like the farming practiced by Baba Bernard Obie of Abanitu Organics in Roxboro, NC.[56] When I visited his family farm as part of the Ubuntu Grows gardening collective over a decade ago, Baba Obie told us about how he plants extra crops for the creatures that he expects will come to eat: because we are not separate from them, and they love the taste of sweet corn as much as we do.[57] This generosity towards all life is a knowing that we, too, need to eat to grow, and our lives are not separate from this whole living world.

I am writing this in springtime, held by tall, shaggy oaks and blue-tailed skinks scampering through leaves. On the back porch just outside the kitchen, wasps are humming as they build their nests, apple mint and sweet peas growing taller every morning, and lemon verbena has miraculously come back after a cold winter. A hummingbird comes to visit and I breathe deeper.

May we honor the land that feeds us by working towards full Indigenous sovereignty and rematriation.[58] May we honor this land by ending the climate catastrophe brought on by capitalism, colonialism, and greed. May we honor the land by growing food in partnership, listening, and giving back with practices of regeneration: compost, letting the land rest, and sharing food in community.

Cucumber Water with Lime and Mint

This is a staple in my summer kitchen: fresh herbs and the magic of cucumber combine to make extra-refreshing drinking water for a hot day. Use spearmint, apple mint, peppermint, or any type of mint you have available. Lemon balm is nice too!

Makes: ½ gallon, 4-6 glasses
Prep time: 5 minutes
Chill time: 1 hour (optional)

8 cups water
½ medium cucumber
½ small lime
2 large sprigs fresh mint
4 cups ice (about 12 ice cubes)

1. Place the water in a large pitcher.

2. Wash and peel half of a cucumber. Cut diagonally into slices, and add the slices to the pitcher.

3. Cut the lime into thin round slices and add these to the pitcher, squeezing them very lightly.

4. Wash the spearmint well. Rub the leaves gently with your fingers to release their flavor, then add to pitcher. Stir to mix.

5. Add ice and serve immediately. Or chill for an hour or overnight. The cucumber and lime flavors show up immediately, and the mint flavor will get stronger the longer it sits.

Agua de Jamaica

This tangy, sweet drink is made from dried hibiscus flowers. Also called flor de Jamaica, these flowers are rich in vitamin C. The beverage is served across the world under many names: Sorrel in Jamaica and parts of the Caribbean; agua de Jamaica (pronounced hah-my-kuh) in Mexico and much of Central America; bissap in parts of West Africa; and karkadé in Egypt. I have been making it for many years and have received advice about how to prepare it from friends and strangers. Once, a man behind me in the checkout line at Compare Foods, a Latin American supermarket in Durham, saw that I was buying the dried flowers and excitedly advised me to include nutmeg, which I've done ever since. While this recipe has a lot of sugar, some people like it even sweeter, so you can try out different amounts of sugar, to taste.

Makes: ½ gallon, 4-6 glasses
Cook time: 30 minutes
Prep time: 10 minutes

1-inch piece fresh ginger root
4 cups water
2 cups dried hibiscus flowers
  (flor de Jamaica)
2 whole cloves
2 pinches ground nutmeg
¾ to 1 cup granulated sugar,
  to taste
4 cups ice (about 12 ice cubes),
  plus more for serving
2 cups cold tap water

1. Wash and thinly slice the ginger. You don't need to peel it, but you can if you like. Place it in a large pot with the 4 of cups water and hibiscus flowers. Cover, and bring to a boil.

2. Add the cloves and nutmeg, and stir to combine. Reduce heat to low and simmer, covered, for 10 minutes. Turn off heat and let sit for 15 minutes. Add ¾ cup of the sugar and stir until it dissolves. Add additional sugar if desired.

3. Strain the agua: Place the ice in another pot or a large pitcher (plastic or metal, not glass). Place a large mesh strainer over this vessel, and strain the hot liquid through it. To pour without spilling, use a large 2-cup measuring cup to scoop the hot liquid and pour it through the strainer. Once you've scooped out about ⅔ of the liquid, it should be easy to pour the rest directly from the pot.

4. With the hibiscus flowers still in the strainer, slowly pour the 2 cups of cold water over them, then squeeze the flowers to extract the last bits of juice.

5. Serve cold over ice.

NOTE: You won't find flor de Jamaica at most chain supermarkets, but it should be readily available in the bulk section of any large Latin American grocery, or alongside spices and teas at most international markets.

LAZY BAKER METHOD:

If you have more time on your hands and don't want to use so much ice, don't add any ice when straining the agua in step 3. Instead, add a total of 4 cups cold water in step 4. Place the agua in a large pitcher and chill until ready to use; it will take about 3 hours to chill completely. If you're short on fridge space, you can also store it in the fridge without the 4 cups cold water, and just add extra water when serving.

NOTE: This bright red liquid can stain, so look out for splattering and promptly clean up any spills.

HERBAL TEAS

Iced herbal teas are a staple in my kitchen, just lightly sweetened. When possible, I especially love to make tea from fresh, in-season herbs. Here's a guide to working with some of my favorites.

Delicious Tea Combinations:

Rooibos with rose petals, rose water, or cinnamon sticks, sweetened with honey
Lavender and sage, sweetened with agave
Mint with green tea, sweet or unsweet
Tulsi (holy basil) with lemon balm or mint, sweet or unsweet
Lemon balm with a touch of lemon verbena and rosemary, sweet or unsweet

To Make a Half-Gallon of Tea:

8 cups water
about 1 cup fresh herbs, washed and lightly chopped, or ½ cup dried
sweetener to taste (honey, agave nectar, or sugar)
1 tsp lemon juice or 2 slices fresh lemon
4 cups ice (about 12 ice cubes)

Boil the water. Place herbs in an empty pot. Pour water over herbs—or add herbs to water and mix vigorously with a wooden spoon—and steep for the desired amount of time for the herb you are using (review instructions below). Strain through a fine sieve, or through a clean, damp towel placed over a colander. Pour an additional 1 cup of tap water over the leaves while they are draining to get all the flavor from the leaves. If adding sweetener, add it while the tea is hot. Then chill tea in the refrigerator for at least 3 hours. Add lemon and ice just before serving.

Steeping Herbs for Tea:

If making tea from a combination of ingredients that require different steeping times, place the herbs in 2 separate small pots and pour a portion of hot water into each one. After straining, combine the teas into one container and mix gently with a spoon.

For green tea, sage, lavender, and rosemary: Heat water until it steams a lot, but does not yet boil—it should be about 180°F. Pour water over the herbs, steep for just 5 minutes, then strain. When steeped too long, these teas can become bitter.

For rooibos, rose, mint, tulsi, lemon balm, and lemon verbena: Heat water to between 180°F and boiling. You can also boil the water, then let it cool for 5 minutes before pouring it over the herbs. Steep for 5-15 minutes, then strain. When steeped too long, these teas change flavor and taste.

For cinnamon and ginger: Heat water to boiling. Pour over herbs and steep at least 10 minutes, or up to 30 minutes if desired. Strain.

Tips for Working with Herbs:

A good way to cut up any leafy fresh herb is to snip it into pieces with a pair of clean, sharp scissors. You can include both the leaf and stem. If using dried herbs, make sure they are whole or cut, not ground, so they strain easily. If ordering dried herbs online, Mountain Rose Herbs and Frontier Co-op both have good products. If ordering dried rose petals or lavender flowers, make sure to order food grade flowers, as they are also sold for use in potpourri and crafts.

•••

Ginger root is particularly tasty when it is in season, but fresh ginger from the store at any time of year will work just fine.

•••

Green tea contains some caffeine, and combines well with many of the herbs here. I buy it dried in the bulk section of the local co-op.

•••

Lavender flowers are tasty fresh or dried. Don't include the stems, as these have a bitter flavor when steeped.

•••

Lemon balm is delicious fresh, and does not retain its flavor well when dried. I only use it when it's in season.

•••

Lemon verbena has a potent lemony flavor, so use it sparingly. It is good fresh or dried.

•••

Mint is delicious fresh or dried. I'd venture that any variety of mint—and there are hundreds—would be tasty in tea; steeping time may vary slightly depending on the variety.

•••

Rooibos, meaning "red bush" in Afrikaans, is an herbal tea that is only grown in South Africa. I buy it dried in the bulk section of the local co-op.

•••

Rose petals can be used fresh, but I usually order dried petals online. Alternatively, a tiny bit of rose water can be added to a tea after it cools for a pungent floral scent and flavor.

•••

Sage will work well fresh or dried, but finding whole dried leaves can be difficult, so it's often easier to just use fresh leaves. Avoid rubbed sage, as it will be hard to strain out of the brewed tea. You can dry whole leaves at home, or purchase dried leaves online.

•••

Tulsi, or holy basil, has been used in India for centuries as a calming medicinal, and is a sacred plant in Hinduism. It's tasty fresh or dried; grow it at home, or purchase online.

NOTE: Left unsweetened, a touch of brewed herbal tea can add a light, refreshing flavoring to cold water or lemonade.

Lemonade
with Fresh Herbs

The extra freshness that herbs add to lemonade is so tasty. Basil is my favorite, but when lemon balm is in season in my garden, I love to use it instead for a floral undertone. Rosemary adds a pungent, earthy flavor. Choose one herb per batch, and experiment!

Makes: ½ gallon, 4-6 glasses
Prep time: 15 minutes
Chill time: 2 hours

3 large sprigs fresh lemon balm or basil or
  2 small sprigs fresh rosemary
¾ cup granulated sugar
1 cup bottled lemon juice
8 cups water
½ of a large lemon
ice (for serving)

1. Rinse the herbs well. Place whole sprigs in a large pitcher, cover with sugar, and let rest 10 minutes.

2. Add lemon juice and water to the pitcher and stir until sugar dissolves. Use the spoon to agitate the herbs a bit.

3. Place in refrigerator for two hours to chill and to allow the flavors from the herbs to infuse into the lemonade.

4. Just before serving, slice the lemon into rounds. If the herbs look wilted from steeping in the lemonade, strain them out and add a fresh sprig of whichever herb you used as a garnish. Then add the lemon slices and serve over ice.

NOTE: To make this recipe with fresh lemons: squeeze the lemons, strain out any seeds, and use the fresh juice in place of the bottled juice. It will require about 4 large lemons.

AFTERWORD

A Note About Bread Uprising

"Creo que el mundo es bello
que la poesía es como el pan, de todos.

I believe the world is beautiful
and that poetry, like bread, is for everyone."
-ROQUE DALTON[59]

Panadería Bread Uprising/Bread Uprising Bakery was a liberation-oriented bakery cooperative that ran out of my home on Yancey Street in Durham from 2009-2014. An incredibly transformative project for many of us, it was the air I breathed, my dreams at night, the source of my sweat, and the bread that filled by belly for five long years.

Begun as a collective with two bakers and twenty-five member households, we baked bread in the cozy, light-filled kitchen of my one-bedroom duplex, and shared it in homes across Durham and beyond. In the world of cooperatives and solidarity economies, this structure is called a multi-stakeholder cooperative, consisting of both worker-owners and consumer-owners.[60] We went beyond this framework to envision a way of being and sharing food outside of wage labor and consumptive capitalism, in the now. Each season, households had the opportunity to sign up for any bread and baked goods they needed and desired, and pledged to contribute whatever they were able to the bakery. As bakers, we created a list of what was needed to sustain both the baking and the bakers, to guide members' pledges. We understood the pledge process as a way of meeting each other's needs collectively, rather than buying bread on a sliding scale and getting paid some type of wage.

The bakery was a project with a radical vision and a very material impact. One afternoon in the first year, I ran into a friend who told me, "What y'all have done is created a standard for our movements—that when our work is as idealistic and ambitious as freeing our time beyond capitalism, it can also have an impact as concrete as bread on the table each week." We did both of these things in such fullness, and the transformation this made possible within us is part of why the bakery was so precious to those of us who were part of it. Members talked about how being part of the bakery changed their relationship to food, to sharing, to time, and to each other.

It was an organizing experiment of how to build a multiracial food justice project that included and also de-centered white people, in a rapidly gentrifying city where local-food-as-commodity was increasingly a tool of gentrification. We were, collectively, incredibly thoughtful about how to approach membership in this context: implementing membership policies to center people who needed bread the most; trying different outreach strategies to reach neighbors, youth, and friends; creating a multilingual bakery; constantly balancing the contradictions of being simultaneously within and beyond capitalism; and simply being caring people who strove to treat each other with dignity and respect.

Bread Uprising was a profound experiment in building community. We were constantly pushing each other to root our work even deeper in relationships. We would drive around Eastern North Carolina, filling a car to the brim with bulk flour, pecans, and jugs of canola oil directly from farmers and processors. We made the bread with so much love that you could taste it.

It was a resource-sharing experiment to find out whether our community had the resources to sustain the community bakers. After several years of abundant generosity and creativity, we found that we needed additional inputs of money for the project to be sustainable. We experimented with wholesale baking on top of continuing the membership program, and after much openness and hard work, the community eventually made a decision to close the project with dignity because we were not able to sustain it while continuing to operate on such an intimate scale.

Many of the breads and sweets in this book were impacted by Bread Uprising in some way. Some were recipes that I shared with the bakery, which then changed and adapted as we began to make them together; some were created collectively by our baker team and made their way into my catering repertoire from there. The recipes that I've chosen to include here are some of my favorites, recipes I continued to make after the bakery closed. I include them with permission from the baker team. I hope I have been able to adequately name and give credit to the specific people involved in creating those recipes that originated in the collective.

As a collective project, Bread Uprising was shaped by so many people. It was shaped by my fellow bakers Tim Stallmann, Javiera Caballero, and Mya Hunter. And it was sustained by the many members who served on the Bread Team and "muffin" working groups; grew ingredients for the bread in their own gardens; came to clean the kitchen and deliver bread to fellow members every week; translated English-Spanish materials and did childcare at assemblies and wrote stories about their ancestral bread traditions to share with everyone; brought the bakers flowers when we were tired; stayed in the visioning conversations when it was hard—and by those who were too exhausted to give much, and stayed in community anyway. I have infinite gratitude for all those who made the bakery possible, and give special thanks to member and resident elder Bro Ray Eurquhart (z"l) for his history lessons, belief in cooperatives, and constant encouragement.

Bread Uprising's work, including the usually fun and often informative zines that we created every week alongside the bread, is archived at www.breaduprising.org.

Bread Uprising's Vision Statement

We believe that every person has a right to food that is appropriate to that person and their culture. By food, we mean delicious food, nutritious food, comfort food, food of ritual, and food of celebration. By the right to food we mean not just immediate access to food on the table, but the resources and time to choose, grow, store, preserve, prepare and share food.

We believe in an economy based on love and solidarity, where people can be daily bread for each other, and provide for our communal well-being.

We believe in a food system which is ecologically just, healing and sustaining.

We understand that people's access to food is limited by oppression in all forms, including the exploitative and dehumanizing relationships structured by the capitalist system, the global dominance of a destructive and profit-driven industrial food system, sexism, racism, heterosexism, transphobia, ableism and classism.

And so, we:
Knead relationships of dignity, respect and appreciation centered around food.
Leaven the growing struggle for food sovereignty in North Carolina.
Form a community institution rooted in queer, people-of-color and working class communities.
Bake and eat delicious bread.

Gratitudes

"Kol haneshama tehallel Yah
Every soul, each with our whole being,
praises the Holy"
-PSALM 150[61]

How do we thank the entire sacred web of existence that makes us possible? We only have our ceremony, our lives, and our work to give as praise. This book is an offering back into the fabric of life on this beautiful planet. Deep gratitude for life is woven throughout these recipes and stories, and this is a place to name some specific beings.

First, the land. I am child of diaspora, and this book is possible because of the living land on which I wrote these words and shared this food. The land speaks to us when we listen, makes all food possible, holds our ceremony, holds our dead. In this place presently called the United States of America, these recipes and words came into being specifically on lands that are the homelands of the Occaneechi Band of the Saponi Nation, the Catawba Nation, the Cherokee people, and the Lenape people.[62] I seek to be a respectful guest here, and I am committed to building connection with the land and Indigenous sovereignty. Ken yehi ratzon (may it be so).

This book is possible because of the many ancestors who, named and unnamed, travel through kitchens with me, and through the pages of this book. This is true of my blood-lineage and my chosen and movement lineages. As a white-privileged trans and queer person, my survival is possible because of generations of liberation work led by Black queer people, women, and femmes. We all owe that back and forward to fight for Black queer liberation and feminism. Audre Lorde wrote, "if we lose / some day women's blood will congeal / upon a dead planet / if we win / there is no telling." [63] Let's win.

These recipes are possible because of the farmers whose produce has been such amazing and delicious material to work with over the years: Baba Obie and Abanitu Organics; Mr. Stanley Hughes and Pine Knot Farm; Will Cramer and EverLaughter farm; Tahz Walker, Cristina Rivera Chapman, and Tierra Negra Farms; George O'Neil and Lil Farm. Your work in connection and collaboration with the land and the season's cycles inspires me so much. Infinite gratitude to all the farmworkers without whom none of us would eat, to Student Action with Farmworkers and the NC farmworker justice movement for their tireless work for justice and dignity for those who work in the fields. Gratitude to all who work for reparations and justice in relationship to land—especially Indigenous peoples, and Black land-loss struggles like the Federation of Southern Co-operatives and the Land Loss Prevention Project.[64]

Gratitude to all the kitchens where I have cooked, and everyone in them. The Stone House, especially those I worked with in the kitchen: Lizzie, Miriam, Jes, Kifu, Leslie, Marcella; Bread Uprising co-bakers Tim, Javiera, and Mya and the community who created and sustained the bakery; the Curryblossom crew especially my favorite band, The Night Crew; Mama Vimala for your irreplaceable mentorship, generosity, and faith over the years; everyone at Ninth Street Bakery, La Gemma Fine Italian Pastries, and Bread and Butter Bakery; and the inspiring lovelies I have shared kitchen space with over the years: Alex, Justin, Melanie, Vivette, Santos, Sijal, Faith, Manju, José; and my housemates, for constant culinary inspiration and shared meals as I developed and finalized these recipes over the years: Jilly, Tony, Denise, Kriti, Laurin, Colin, YM, Tav, and Devin.

Gratitude to everyone at the Center for Documentary Studies at Duke University, especially April, Rahi, Mark, Dione, Courtney, Alexa, and Shea. After years of cooking there and being invited to sit in on sessions and be part of the learning community, the documentary itch has rubbed off on me! This cookbook is my documentary project, and I'm grateful for all of the inspiration from the thoughtful folks with whom I have shared food, space, and conversation.

Special thanks to the Sharma family for years of hospitality and your bright, gorgeous kitchen made for feeding community, to Tema for sharing that little hideaway by the ocean which provided such a necessary writing retreat, and to my parents for a last-minute writing retreat (mostly in their hammock) that got the book through its final push. And to the other home kitchens in my life: the House of Mango, Fairchild Co-op, my first home in Lockridge community, the ancestral home at Blue Hills Terrace. I can see now how the light falls through each of these windows onto a floury countertop or steaming pot of soup, and feel how the many hands that have prepared food there move through these recipes.

It was a joy to hear beautiful stories about what happened when these recipes were tested in community—one of my favorites was a potluck where attendees arrived to find that almost every dish was a recipe from this book, because everyone attending happened to be testing recipes. I'm grateful for the work of many amazing recipe testers who made and shared these dishes after I scaled them down for the purposes of this book. Thanks to: Alexis Pauline Gumbs and Sangodare Wallace, Allison Swaim, Amos Kfir, Andreina Malki, Becca Munro, Beth Bruch, Bex Kolins, Bridgette Burge, Catherine Berman, Charla Hodges, Christy Tronnier, Clara Hazlett-Norman, Colin Maxwell, Courtney Woods, Danny Blose, Dhruv Arora, Elyse Crystall, Emerson Goldstein, Erin Hazlett-Norman, Esther Mack, Gabriel Baldasare, James Wilson, Jazmynne Williams, Jecca Namakkal and Eli Meyerhoff, Jes Kelley, Kavanah Anderson, Kristen Cox, Laurin Penland, Leah Erlbaum, Loan Tran, Marc Maximov, Marcella Galvez Wagner, Marian Abernathy, Melinda Wiggins and Dave DeVito, Mendal Polish, Mikel Barton, Miriam Brodersen, Rachael Grossman, Rahi Hasan, Rebecca Mendelson, Russell Herman, Sandra Korn, Sandra Rodriguez, Sarah Cross, Sarah Rubin, Sarryn Shapero with Ella, Suzi Pietroluongo, Tema Okun, Tim Stallmann with Zoilo, Samari, and Gabriel Cobarrubias-Casas, and Tony Macias. Special thanks to Leah Erlbaum and Esther Mack for being cookbook cheerleaders all along the way. So many people have helped to move this book from a dream to reality.

I'm especially grateful to Assata Goff for sharing her creative magic here on these pages, bringing the recipes to life; Assata, thanks for sharing your genius with this project and with the world. Zelda Lockhart's generous wisdom about publishing and writing tips made all the difference in making this book a reality; Zelda, you make so much possible! Thanks to Lara Haft for creative help coming up with the title, and to Kriti Sharma for shared writing partnership at a crucial point in the process. Thanks to Sandra Korn for such incredibly generous editing support and publishing advice. Thanks to Queer Black Editing for such grounded and thoughtful work on the whole manuscript. Thanks to Tema Okun and Tim Stallmann for helpful writing feedback, and to Beth Bruch for her librarian citation brilliance. Tony Macias provided social media support for which I'm very grateful. And Saif Wideman's design skills are what makes this book both beautiful and functional for use in the kitchen—thanks for being such a thoughtful collaborator in so many ways.

To the communities whose joy about these recipes inspired me to carry this project to completion: thank you. It is impossible to name everyone who has made this project possible. I really made this book for everyone I've ever cooked for, so if that's you, thank you for being an inspiration. I hope making these recipes brings you as much joy as it's brought me.

And to the people who I am blessed to call family, in all of its queer complications: including Mom, Dad, Danny, Jay, Fresh, Nikita, Paola, Allan, Suriyana, Mayu, Tony, Anna, Lulú, Alma Ramona, Tim, Zach, Beth, Tema, Aiden, and Zeny. Sometimes it's the big things like planning our lives, or knowing I can always come home to you; and it's also the little things like when you told me dinner was "not quite as terrible," or let me borrow your knife-sharpener for years. I am grateful every day to share this life with y'all.

Lastly and importantly, I want to thank the food itself. This project has been about doing honor to the food, to the way these recipes have moved in me and in us over the past decade and a half. Letting them move through me and tell their stories has been humbling, grounding, and inspiring.

Gratitudes   231

Endnotes

1   Audre Lorde, "A Litany for Survival," in *The Collected Poems of Audre Lorde* (New York: W. W. Norton, 1997), 225.

2   Alexis Pauline Gumbs, "Register Now for the Juneteenth Freedom Academy for Facilitators: Nov 1-2 in Durham, NC," *brokenbeautiful press*, September 29, 2014. https://brokenbeautiful.wordpress.com/2014/09/29/register-now-for-the-juneteenth-freedom-academy-for-facilitators-nov-1-2-in-durham-nc/.

3   Deuteronomy 8:10.

4   I have heard this from many people over the years, and cannot find a source. If you know the origins of this statement, please contact us.

5   Demilitarize! Durham2Palestine: http://www.durham2palestine.org. Accessed October 4, 2020.

6   Activist, organizer and trainer Betsy Raasch-Gilman, quoted on artist Ricardo Levins Morales' 2007 poster "Recipes," which hung in my kitchen at Bread Uprising and the Center for Documentary Studies. The poster can be found at http://www.rlmartstudio.com/product/recipes.

7   Ella Shohat, "Arab Jews, Diasporas, and Multicultural Feminism (A Conversation Conducted by Evelyn Alsultany)," in *On the Arab-Jew, Palestine, and Other Displacements: Selected Writings of Ella Shohat* (London: Pluto Press, 2017), 375.

8   Thanks to my friend Paola Guerrero for introducing me to the framework of being part of a "we" as a way to understand ourselves and our identity; and thanks to my grandpa, Louis Rubin (z"l), with whom I often experienced this.

9   Charlie Cascio, *Esalen Cookbook: Healthy and Organic Recipes from Big Sur* (Salt Lake City: Gibbs Smith, 2006). Thanks to my colleague Lizze Jacobs for introducing me to this book.

10   Devra Dedeaux, *The Sugar Reef Caribbean Cookbook* (New York: Dell, 1991).

11   Sarah Kramer, *La Dolce Vegan! Vegan Livin' Made Easy* (Vancouver, BC: Arsenal Pulp Press, 2005).

12   Elise Bauer, "Spanish Rice," Simply Recipes, Dotdash, accessed October 4, 2020. https://www.simplyrecipes.com/recipes/spanish_rice.

13   More info about "When We Free," a film created by Sangodare Wallace and produced by Alexis Pauline Gumbs and Angel Harris, can be found at http://whenwefree.jroxmedia.com/current-projects/when-we-free-the-film/. Accessed October 4, 2020.

14   Blue Nile was run by Friesh Dabei, who went on to run Queen of Sheba restaurant in Chapel Hill for

years. Queen of Sheba closed in 2017.

15   Vanessa Johnson and Ryan Splint, *Hot Damn & Hell Yeah / The Dirty South Cookbook* (Portland: Microcosm Publishing, 2005)
.

16   Mollie Katzen, *The Moosewood Cookbook: Recipes from Moosewood Restaurant, Ithaca, New York* (New York: Ten Speed Press, 1977).

17   Neomonde Mediterranian: https://www.neomonde.com. Accessed October 4, 2020.

18   Lucille Clifton, "i am not done yet," in *The Collected Poems of Lucille Clifton 1965-2010,* ed. Kevin Young and Michael S. Glaser (Rochester: BOA Editions, 2012), 165.

19   Vimala's Curryblossom Cafe: https://curryblossom.com/. Accessed October 4, 2020.

20   I am grateful for the work of disability justice organizers and thinkers, whose work illuminates the connections between ableism, capitalism, patriarchy, and white supremacy. One great resource on these topics is Leah Lakshmi Piepzna-Samarasinha, *Care Work: Dreaming Disability Justice* (Vancouver, BC: Arsenal Pulp Press, 2019).

21   The Fight for $15 is an example of powerful organizing among food service workers: https://fightfor15.org. Accessed October 4, 2020.

22   I learned a lot about Southern Black women's labor and how it shaped both Black women's own lives and Southern food as a student in Dr. Pamela Brooks' African American Women's History course at Oberlin College in 2003. I remember learning, for example, about pan-toting—Black women who worked as domestic workers for white households in the post-slavery South, secretly carrying leftovers that they had cooked home to their own families: both resistance and survival.

23   Food historian Michael Twitty writes about the complex history of collards on his blog, *Afroculinaria*, and particularly their importance to Black Southerners. He writes that "the green craze in the South is supported by tastes for spring greens among Celtic and Germanic Southerners but was really spearheaded by people of African descent. In tropical West Africa, greens were available year round in gardens and markets and figured prominently in regular meals." Michael Twitty, "A Letter to the Newgrorati: Of Collards and Amnesia," *Afroculinaria* (blog), January 16, 2016. https://afroculinaria.com/2016/01/16/a-letter-to-the-newgrorati-of-collards-and-amnesia.

24   Audre Lorde, "Uses of the Erotic: The Erotic As Power," in *Sister Outsider: Essays and Speeches* (Trumansburg, NY: Crossing Press, 1984), 55.

25   JFREJ Jews of Color Caucus, "Juneteenth Seder Haggadah," Jews For Racial & Economic Justice (JFREJ), 2018. https://www.jfrej.org/assets/uploads/JFREJ-Juneteenth-Haggadah_Color_HiRes_v6.pdf. Thanks to my friend Kendra Watkins for bringing this tradition to our community in NC.

26   Adrienne Rich, "At the Jewish New Year," in *Collected Poems: 1950-2012,* ed. Pablo Conrad (New York: W.W. Norton and Company, 2016), 160.

27   "Sancocho de Gallina," *Horizonte,* August 22-28, 2012. Page 12.

28   Thanks to recipe tester Esther Mack for this suggestion.

29   Baking soda is technically Kosher for Passover because it is a chemical leavening, not a yeast-based one, but some people have the custom not to eat it during the holiday. Joan Nathan, "It's Passover, Lighten Up," *New York Times* (New York, NY), Apr. 5 2006. https://www.nytimes.com/2006/04/05/dining/05leav.html. Flaxseed is considered kitniyot, which are off limits during Passover for some Ashkenazi Jews.

30   Student Action with Farmworkers: https://saf-unite.org/. Accessed October 4, 2020.

31   Marge Piercy, "Amidah: On our feet we speak to you," in *The Art of Blessing the Day* (New York, Knopf, 1999), 136.

32   We used *The Children's Jewish Holiday Kitchen* by Joan Nathan (New York: Schocken Books, 1987), a fun cookbook whose recipe instructions specify which parts of the recipe are good for kids to lead and which parts require the help of an adult.

33   Started in 2007, Historic Thousands on Jones Street, or HKonJ, is a coalition of over 200 movement organizations, led by the NC NAACP: https://naacpnc.org/hkonj-peoples-assembly-coalition. Accessed October 4, 2020.

34   This is, of course, also a both/and where many people have the lived experience of being on both sides of this consumption/consumed dynamic.

35   Thanks to recipe testers Zoilo, Samari, and Gabriel Cobarrubias-Casas, with Tim Stallmann, for this suggestion.

36   Thanks to Tim Stallmann for teaching me about this, and for helping to write this tip.

37   Edward Espe Brown, *The Tassajara Bread Book: 25th Anniversary Edition* (Boston: Shambhala Publications, 1995), 16.

38   Thanks to recipe tester Marc Maximov for this suggestion.

39   Mollie Katzen, "Calzone," in *The Moosewood Cookbook: Recipes from Moosewood Restaurant, Ithaca, New York* (New York: Ten Speed Press, 1977), 159.

40   Karri Allrich, "The Best Gluten-Free Pizza Crust, Goddess Style," *Gluten-Free Goddess Recipes*, February 1, 2011. https://www.glutenfreegoddessrecipes.com/all/the-best-gluten-free-pizza-crust-goddess-style

41   Martín Espada, "Imagine the Angels of Bread," in *Imagine the Angels of Bread* (New York: W.W. Norton, 1996).

42   Ibid.

43   Thanks to friend, housemate, and visionary biologist Kriti Sharma for drawing the parallel between my recipe-testing notes and the lab notes from her experiments.

44 Andrea Geary, "Cracking the Code to Chewy Brownies," *Cooks' Illustrated* no. 105 (March-April 2010): 21-22.

45 Irma Rombauer and Marion Rombauer Becker, "Butterscotch Brownies," in *Joy of Cooking* (New York: Bobbs-Merrill Company, 1975), 702.

46 Grace Henderson, "Aquafaba—is it really the new egg white?" Nutrition Press, April 19, 2018. http://web.archive.org/web/20180817062331/http://thenutritionpress.com/aquafaba-is-it-really-the-new-egg-white/

47 Irma Rombauer and Marion Rombauer Becker, *Joy of Cooking* (New York: Bobbs-Merrill Company, 1975).

48 Stanley Ginsberg and Norman Berg, "Almond Horns," in *Inside the Jewish Bakery: Recipes and Memories from the Golden Age of Jewish Baking* (Philadelphia: Camino Books, 2011), 232.

49 Doron Petersan, "Chocolate Chip Cookies," in *Sticky Fingers' Sweets: 100 Super-Secret Vegan Recipes* (Garden City, NY: Avery, 2012), 123.

50 Aurora Levins Morales, "Nadie la Tiene," in *Medicine Stories: History, Culture and the Politics of Integrity* (Cambridge: South End Press, 1998), 100.

51 The Occaneechi Band of the Saponi Nation's ancestral land includes the area that is currently known as Mebane and Hillsborough, NC. Their website is: https://obsn.org.

52 Learn more about Tahz Walker's work as visionary farmer and co-founder of Tierra Negra Farms and Earthseed Land Cooperative at https://earthseedlandcoop.org/about/.

53 Thanks to my friend Leah Erlbaum for this insight, drawn from her work with Indigenous communities in Bolivia.

54 Eve Tuck and K. Wayne Yang, "Decolonization is not a metaphor," in *Decolonization: Indigeneity, Education & Society*, 1, no. 1 (2012): 6. Adrienne Keene and Matika Wilbur also talk about this concept on their podcast, *All My Relations*, https://www.allmyrelationspodcast.com.

55 Naomi seeks a "resting-place" for her chosen family daughter Ruth in Ruth 3:1. Abraham seeks a burial plot for his late wife Sarah in Genesis 23:4.

56 Abanitu Organics: http://www.abanituorganics.com/. Accessed October 4, 2020.

57 Ubuntu Grows was a community projects of Ubuntu, a women of color and survivor-led coalition organizing to end sexual violence, based in Durham, NC. Ubuntu's archived blog can be found at https://iambecauseweare.wordpress.com/.

58 An example of organizing for rematriation led by Indigenous women is the Sogorea Te' Land Trust on Ohlone land: https://sogoreate-landtrust.org. Accessed October 4, 2020.

59 Roque Dalton, "Como Tú/Like You," trans. Jack Hirschman, *Poetry Like Bread: Poets of the Political Imagina-*

tion, ed. Martín Espada (Curbstone Press, 2000).

60 Learn more about multi-stakeholder cooperatives from the US Federation of Worker Cooperatives' Democracy at Work Institute: https://institute.coop/audiences/multi-stakeholder-coops. Accessed October 4, 2020.

61 Psalm 150, part of traditional Jewish morning liturgy. Translation by the author.

62 If you live on Turtle Island and don't know whose land you are on, you can begin to learn by using the map at https://native-land.ca. The Nations named here can be found at: https://obsn.org. (Occaneechi Band of the Saponi Nation), https://www.catawbaindian.net (Catawba Indian Nation), https://ebci.com (Eastern Band of Cherokee Indians), and https://nlltribe.com (Nanticoke Lenni-Lenape Tribal Nation). Accessed October 4, 2020.

63 Audre Lorde, "Outlines," in *The Collected Poems of Audre Lorde* (New York: W. W. Norton, 1997), 361-366.

64 The Federation of Southern Cooperatives/Land Assistance Fund: https://www.federation.coop. Land Loss Prevention Project: https://www.landloss.org. Accessed October 4, 2020.

Index

CPSIA information can be obtained
at www.ICGtesting.com
Printed in the USA
BVHW061442250421
605672BV00002BA/3